MOVIES
WORD SEARCH
& CROSSWORD
PUZZLES

Thunder Bay Press
An imprint of Printers Row Publishing Group
9717 Pacific Heights Blvd, San Diego, CA 92121
www.thunderbaybooks.com • mail@thunderbaybooks.com

Correspondence regarding the content of this book should be sent to Thunder Bay Press, Editorial Department, at the above address. Author and rights inquiries should be addressed to Pyramid, an imprint of Octopus Publishing Group Ltd., Carmelite House, 50 Victoria Embankment, London, EC4Y 0DZ
www.octopusbooks.co.uk

Thunder Bay Press
Publisher: Peter Norton • Associate Publisher: Ana Parker
Editor: Dan Mansfield
Acquisitions Editor: Kathryn Chipinka Dalby

Produced by Pyramid
Publisher: Lucy Pessell
Editor: Sarah Kennedy • Designer: Hannah Coughlin
Editorial Assistant: Emily Martin

ISBN: 978-1-64517-912-2

Printed in China

25 24 23 22 21   1 2 3 4 5

MOVIES
WORD SEARCH
& CROSSWORD
PUZZLES

THUNDER BAY
P·R·E·S·S

San Diego, California

INTRODUCTION

What is this phenomenon called "movies"? For many of the younger generation, it's nearly unimaginable that when movies first appeared on the big screen, they were not only in black and white (gasp!) but also silent (that's right, you read that correctly), with absolutely no noise, or if you were lucky, you might be treated to some music that mirrored the scene.

Movies, of course, have come a long, long way since the birth of "talkies"—when suddenly actors' voices could actually be heard. And although the "big screen" is still out there, movies can now be viewed in so many ways—on your smartphone, laptop, computer, or smart TV. And in a myriad of formats—wide screen, 3D, HD, digital, made for TV—the list is almost endless.

But movies also offer us a choice of how we want to be entertained, and many are instantly on demand. Whether you like to snuggle up on a Sunday afternoon to a romcom such as *Pretty Woman* or hide behind the sofa while watching the horror movie *It* through your fingers, the choice is yours. Perhaps you just want to laugh out loud to the silliness of *Dumb and Dumber*, immerse yourself in the marvel and sheer scale of *Avatar*, or wonder at the brilliantly innovative one-take camerawork of *1917*. Or maybe just release your inner child with a Disney classic—the movies have so much to offer.

My personal top ten countdown (which changes by the minute) is:

10. *Kind Hearts and Coronets* (1949)
9. *Lawrence of Arabia* (1962)
8. *Silver Linings Playbook* (2012)
7. *A Star Is Born* (2018)
6. *Monty Python and the Holy Grail* (1975)
5. *The Shining* (1980)
4. *Dead Poets Society* (1989)
3. *One Flew Over the Cuckoo's Nest* (1975)
2. *The Godfather* (1972)
1. *True Romance* (1993)

Compiling this puzzle book was not a simple task. First, we had to take into account the different genres: action, comedy, cartoon, drama, fantasy, horror, mystery, romance, and thriller. Then we had the actors to consider—are you enthralled by Leonardo DiCaprio, Brad Pitt, Saoirse Ronan, or Jennifer Lawrence? Or do the stalwarts like Harrison Ford, Jack Nicholson, Marilyn Monroe, or Bette Davis get you itching for the movie to start? Others follow a particular director, so maybe the work of James Cameron, Kathryn Bigelow, or Akira Kurosawa floats your boat?

Whatever your personal choice, I think we can all agree that movies are here to stay. Sure, they will, through technology, progress to points beyond our imagination. Perhaps in the not-too-distant future you will be able to star in your own personalized movie!

This book, with its comprehensive lists of ten of the most popular answers in each puzzle, is split into two parts—crosswords and word searches (which follow the same themes as the crosswords)—with all of the answers at the back of the book (only to be used in an emergency!). Like all crosswords, they are only easy if you know the answers, but some are worth a guess or even a Google. Have fun!

MOVIES
CROSSWORD
PUZZLES

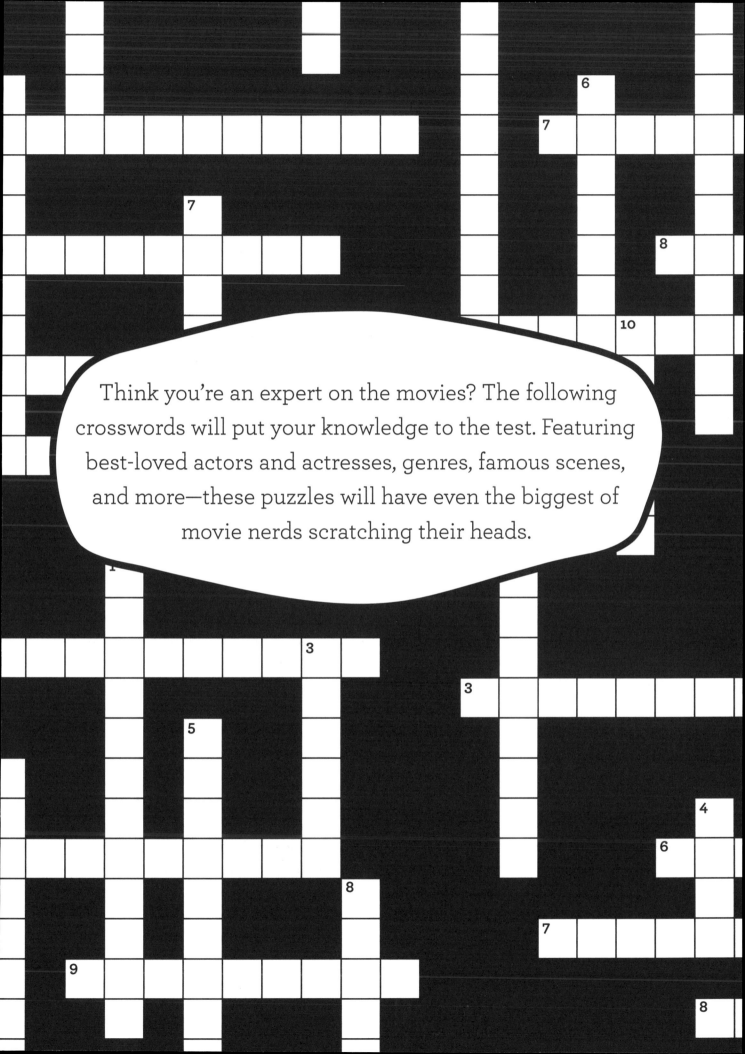

Think you're an expert on the movies? The following crosswords will put your knowledge to the test. Featuring best-loved actors and actresses, genres, famous scenes, and more—these puzzles will have even the biggest of movie nerds scratching their heads.

1. ANTIHEROES

The definition shifts as we redefine our ideas of heroism, but the antihero is always a figure at odds with the values of their society. They're seldom malicious and might inadvertently do good as they plow their narcissistic furrow throughout the movie plot.

ACROSS

2. *The Man* ____ __ ____. Clint Eastwood's iconic gunslinger plays both sides of a feuding village in Sergio Leone's *Dollars* trilogy.

4. After accepting a bet to haul a truckload of illicit beer from Texas to Georgia, Bo Darville, "___ _____," and his partner "Snowman" (Jerry Reed) encounter a screwball sheriff obsessed with stopping them.

8. Sentenced to a Florida chain gang for a trivial crime, ____ _____ refuses to accept the authority of corrupt guards and is determined to escape.

9. The archetypal antihero, _____ Plisskin is a former bank robber, gunfighter, smuggler, and all-around degenerate reprobate.

DOWN

1. On release, *The Wild One* kicked up a storm for glamorizing delinquents. With hindsight, we can see it's a potent allegory about the chasm between the attitudes of _____'s generation and that which came before.

3. The enfant terrible of antiheroes, _____ _____ (a.k.a. The Sausage King of Chicago) skips school for the day and still ends up the good guy.

4. Clearly losing his grip on reality, _____ _____ is a former U.S. Marine who takes a job as a graveyard shift cab driver in New York City.

5. _____ takes succinctness to the extreme in what seems to be *Taxi Driver* for a new generation.

6. *Oldboy* is a stylized tale of an unlikable businessman, __ ___-__, trying to learn why he was imprisoned and then released without explanation.

7. Fresh out of prison, cockney Charlie _____ organizes a robbery of gold bullion in Turin by British gangsters driving red, white, and blue Minis.

2. MANIC PIXIE DREAM GIRLS

Manic Pixie Dream Girls (M.P.D.G.s) are identifiable by their likability, exuberant personality, and girlish femininity. Their role in cinema is to show the male lead that life is pretty good, which risks them seeming one-dimensional when not played as well as those mentioned below.

ACROSS

3.   Beautiful singer ____ _____ becomes the object of affection for two cross-dressing saxophone players on the run from the mob after witnessing the Valentine's Day Massacre.

8.   In *Jules and Jim* (1962), the capricious _____ seduces two friends and has a lasting effect on both their lives.

9.   In *Eternal Sunshine of the Spotless Mind*, Joel and _____ discover they have been in a relationship before, but had their memories erased.

10.   Unlucky in love, grocer Allen Bauer (Tom Hanks) falls in love with _____, a mermaid who twice saves his life.

DOWN

1.   Acerbic extrovert _____ _____ hijacks level-headed paleontologist Dr. David Huxley's life in a series of farcical escapades in *Bringing Up Baby*.

2.   ___, an eccentric pathological liar, shakes Andrew (Zach Braff) back to life when he returns to his hometown for his mother's funeral.

4.   The ethereal Audrey Hepburn's signature role as Holly _____ allows her unique blend of vulnerability and confidence to shine.

5.   The highbrow M.P.D.G. comes in the form of _____ ____, outwardly confident, but actually suffering as many insecurities as lover Alvy Singer.

6.   Straight-laced dentist Dr. Julian Winston (Walter Matthau) and his free-spirited neighbor ____ _____ are common factors in various love lives.

7.   Dunst excels as flight attendant Claire _____, the character that inspired film critic Nathan Rabin to coin the term "Manic Pixie Dream Girl."

3. SPORTING MOMENTS

Sport is one of the most indispensable tools at the moviemaker's disposal. The inherent conflict makes it an excellent dramatic device—it works perfectly as allegory and can manipulate emotion. The following great sporting movie moments touch on several ways in which the movies have used sport to make us cry, cheer, or think.

ACROSS

2. Offered one last big fight as a favor, underdog Jim Braddock surprises everyone by winning and becoming the _____ champ.

3. "__ ___ _____ __, he will come!" Farmer Ray Kinsella places his faith in a disembodied voice that commands him to build a baseball diamond.

5. Going the _____. What makes the final bout in *Rocky* so interesting is that we aren't inspired by how the winner wins, but by how the loser loses.

10. The "_____" _____. If you need an actor to deliver a stirring motivational speech, you can do worse than Al Pacino.

DOWN

1. A member of the Bushwood Country Club challenges a caddy to a match, with wagers soon flying around. The result is settled when a lunatic groundskeeper provides an _____ golf course.

4. Playing ___ _____ ____. In a clash between upstart Fast Eddie and the elder statesman Minnesota Fats, the younger man sprints into an early lead before realizing he's competing in a marathon, not the 100 meters.

6. The improbable story of the Jamaican bobsled team's 1988 Winter Olympics was a big hit in 1993, largely thanks to the rousing finale, which saw them _____ the finish line.

7. Mighty Steel Leg Sing's soccer squad reach the finals of a Hong Kong tournament where they must face _____ _____, a steroid-enhanced team of cheating malevolence.

8. Daniel _____ (Ralph Macchio) is routinely bullied by students of the Cobra Kai karate dojo. One of them injures Daniel with an illegal move in a tournament, meaning he is initially ruled out.

9. Harold _____ sacrifices much training for the 1924 Olympics. After being beaten in the 200 meters, he triumphs in the 100 meters.

4. QUESTS

A quest can provide the perfect narrative structure for a movie. It keeps things moving; enables characters to encounter almost anything or anyone; can be manipulated to create easy suspense, pathos, or humor; and allows for a neatly tied-up conclusion.

ACROSS

3. Dorothy's attempt to find a ___ ____ from Oz has inspired many movies. But this early color classic is categorically the perfect specimen.

6. After escaping from a chain gang with two other convicts, McGill leads a wild goose chase, supposedly to recover _____ before its hiding place is flooded.

9. *Jason and the Argonauts* is arguably the definitive classical mythology adventure movie as they search for the _____ _____.

10. In ___ ____, the Stalker guides clients through the physics-defying world of the Zone to a hidden room somewhere within.

DOWN

1. In the quest to destroy the ring, Elijah Wood is exceptional as Frodo, the reluctant hero, as he attempts to return the One Ring to _____.

2. Their community threatened with demolition, a bunch of kids set out on a journey to find long hidden _____ _____. On the way they encounter a criminal family, local bullies, and are threatened by ancient booby traps.

4. The big screen outing for Sacha Baron Cohen's Kazakh journalist, Borat, is filmed in the style of a documentary. But Borat becomes more interested in marrying _____ _____.

5. In *2001: A Space Odyssey*, a beacon is found on the Moon which emits a signal to _____. It turns out to be something quite important.

7. Klaus Kinski's performance as Aguirre is an electrifying descent through obsession into madness as he searches for the lost city of __ _____.

8. In Indy's first expedition, with the Nazis also on the hunt for the Ark of the _____, perhaps leaving it where it was might not have been a bad idea.

5. CARS

Potentially the most charismatic of all noncognizant movie characters, cars have been central to cinema's history and culture since their near simultaneous rise to popularity. To avoid half the puzzle being Lotuses and Aston Martins, we've excluded James Bond from this puzzle.

ACROSS

6. Of all the cars to feature on the big screen, the _____, this fish-tailing, overly sculpted boat on wheels has to be the best.

8. The Ecto-1 _____ was converted from a dilapidated dual-purpose hearse/ambulance into the striking vehicle we know from *Ghostbusters*.

10. Kowalski must deliver the Dodge _____ to its rightful owner on the other side of the country.

DOWN

1. One of the biggest selling cars in history was originally designed and manufactured by Ferdinand Porsche. However, _____'s sporty credentials probably don't match up to those of its illustrious creator.

2. Perhaps "The General Lee" is the better known _____, but Dominic Toretto's is apparently indestructible in the *Fast and Furious* movies.

3. Bulletproof and equipped with a homing robot bird, rotary saws, tire shields, and all sorts of other gadgets, the _____ _____ is designed to compete in futuristic combative races.

4. Most people of a certain age picture an enormous cowboy hat behind the wheel when they see a black _____ Trans Am. The movie that made Burt Reynolds a megastar did at least as much for this iconic muscle car.

5. The _____ Continental MKIII is the undoubted star of the movie in which it appears, although Satanic influences don't fully explain how it works without a driver.

7. This _____ 1974 sedan was chosen by car nut Dan Aykroyd for its reputation as the fastest vehicle in the Illinois police fleet of the 1970s.

9. The story of John _____'s doomed attempt to revolutionize the sports car industry is worthy of its own movie. Until then, it will remain best known as the time machine in which Marty McFly travels back to 1955.

6. HAUNTED HOUSES

The haunted house has been a movie staple around the world since cinema's inception. Cheap to produce, universal in appeal, endlessly variable, potentially scary, funny, dramatic, or gruesome . . . it's no surprise so many haunted house movies have been produced.

ACROSS

4.   *The* _____, the first in the series of movies based on real-life paranormal investigators the Warrens, is a throwback to the 1960s and 1970s heyday.

5.   *The* _____, set in a remote Spanish orphanage, is the setting for this genuinely scary tale of a family who may have lost their son to some sort of evil spirit.

6.   An inventive premise that sees the protagonist's children rendered allergic to light does wonders for the creepy atmosphere of this psychological horror, ____ _____.

7.   According to Martin Scorsese, *The* _____ (1963) is the most terrifying movie ever made.

8.   Tobe Hooper and Steven Spielberg collaborate in _____, a chilling tale of a haunted house built on an Indian burial ground.

9.   Cyrus Zorba can't believe his luck when he inherits a rundown mansion. After moving his family in, they start to experience strange goings-on in this tale of *13* _____.

DOWN

1.   A standout in Japanese horror movies, ____ _____ is formed from a series of vignettes revolving around a family home.

2.   The beautiful _____ _____ is haunted by its former owner, Captain Daniel Gregg (Rex Harrison). The arrival of recently widowed Lucy (Gene Tierney) does nothing to encourage his departure.

3.   Miss Giddens, governess to two orphaned children living at Bly, begins to suspect the spirits of a pair of former employees are inhabiting the children in *The* _____.

7.   Skeptical physicist Professor Lionel Barrett leads the search for evidence of life after death at _____ _____, the most haunted house in the world.

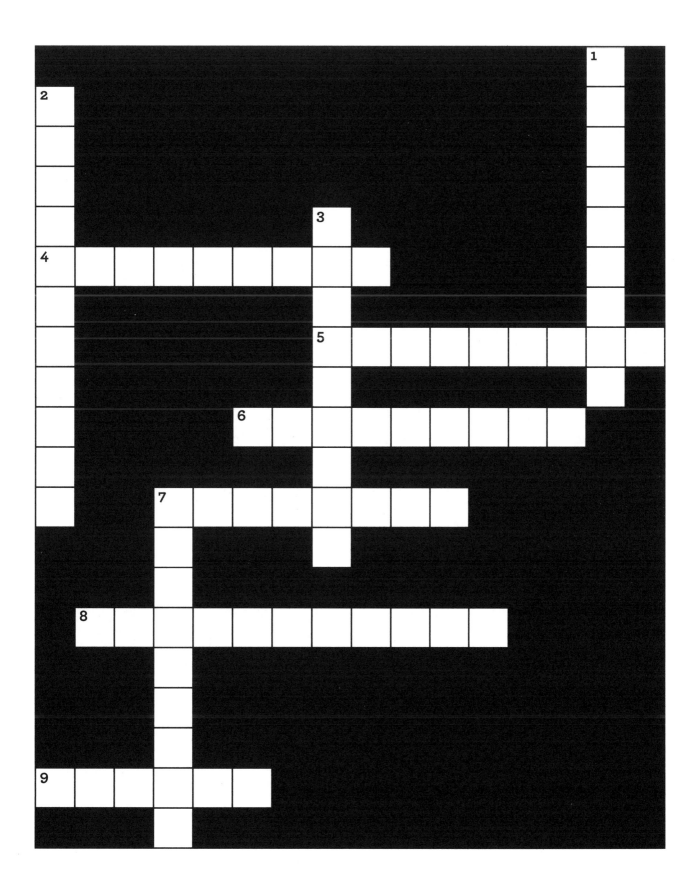

7. HIGH SCHOOL MOVIES

The peculiarly American high school movie genre has long been an effective means of tracking the shifting social concerns and trends of the nation. As an allegory for the wider United States, the high school is unbeatable, regardless of whether you're saying something serious or silly.

ACROSS

1. A high school in-crowd meets its match in _____, when school bad boy J.D. (Christian Slater) decides they've done enough harm.

3. A disillusioned teacher, Jim McAllister, becomes obsessed with preventing a precocious student from winning by backing a rival candidate in _____.

4. Five students, each conforming to one traditional stereotype or another, report for school detention on a sunny Saturday morning in a Chicago suburb in The _____ ____.

7. _____. Jane Austen's novel *Emma* is the unlikely source material for this look at superficial rich girls finding their places in life.

9. Max Fischer, a far-from-gifted student at the _____ Academy private school, forms a friendship with industrialist Herman Blume, and both fall in love with teacher Mrs. Cross.

10. ____ _____ is a teen comedy that parodies the perilous world of the modern school clique (the Plastics) in this sharp comedy adapted by *Saturday Night Live*'s Tina Fey.

DOWN

2. _____ ____ is a burgeoning sex comedy following a group of teen boys as they try every trick in the book to lose their virginity before graduation.

5. In The _____ *Jungle*, a new teacher encounters obnoxious students in a 1950s high school.

6. Convoluted love lives at Padua High School are the subject of ____ _____ *I Hate About You*, based on Shakespeare's *The Taming of the Shrew*.

8. In _____, the senior term at Rydell High School starts as Danny recounts the story of his summer romance with Sandy.

8. MONSTERS

Since at least 1915's *Der Golem*, monsters have been integral to the movie landscape. With so many to choose from (many of which are rather obvious), some rules have been introduced in the creation of this puzzle to exclude common standards, such as ghosts, zombies, vampires, and aliens.

ACROSS

5. Part comedy, part western, and part horror movie, *Tremors* features gigantic, wormlike _____, who terrorize a small Nevada settlement.

7. Students investigating bear killings in rural Norway stumble upon Hans, a hunter employed by the government to track down several _____ _____.

10. The _____ ____. In a remote Swiss resort a strange force concealed in a radioactive cloud decapitates or possesses various hardy types.

DOWN

1. Billy Peltzer (Zach Galligan) soon makes a hash of caring for his Mogwai. First, he gets it wet, causing it to multiply. Then he feeds the resulting _____ after midnight, which turns them into little monsters.

2. ____ _____ stems from Norse mythology, but in the movie exists in a world governed by the Greek gods.

3. _____ brings to mind a Japanese stuntman in a comedy rubber suit. But in the original, *Gojira,* it's a lizard mutated into a huge raging monster by radioactive fallout, following mankind's pursuit of nuclear power.

4. Willis O'Brien's stop-motion giant ape _____ is legendary, inspiring an endless stream of budding makeup artists, animators, and model makers.

6. The _____ (named after a British racing driver) must be one of the most alarming and execrable creatures in the movies—the result of the genetic melding of man and insect.

8. ____ _____. The most important movie of Universal's 1930s and 1940s horror cycle still stands out as one of the best creature features ever made.

9. _____ a.k.a. LSA. An unusual "found footage" approach lends *Cloverfield* some unique qualities. We see the beast only fleetingly and never learn what it wants or where it came from.

9. FAMILIES

The traditional cinematic stereotype of the family unit might leave some of us feeling our own is imperfect. But as cinema has evolved, so has its depiction of the family, and we might be reassured to see more defective tribes than we used to on screen.

ACROSS

4. The _____. Director Wes Anderson hit the big time with this brilliantly stylish movie about a dysfunctional family of high achievers.

5. *The* _____. The first family of television have so far only made one big-screen outing, but that's enough to qualify for a top-ten list.

7. _____ __ _____ showcases the everyday challenges of an unidentified working-class North London family in this beautifully subtle film from acclaimed director Mike Leigh.

9. The _____ are certainly a diverse bunch who embark on a road trip to take youngest child Olive to the Little Miss Sunshine beauty pageant.

10. Determined to make the long drive to Wally World in order to enjoy a family vacation, the _____ must overcome an endless slew of unreasonable challenges, which leads to a series of sequels of distinctly variable quality.

DOWN

1. The _____. It's hard to say whether this is a family you'd want to be involved with or not. On one hand, they clearly have a strong bond; on the other, most of them are murderous gangsters.

2. *The* _____ *Family* became a hit TV show and cartoon serial before finally landing in movie theaters.

3. The _____ are an interesting family. Teddy thinks he's Theodore Roosevelt, Jonathan is an escaped convict, and elderly aunts Abby and Martha poison anyone they feel sorry for and bury them in the basement.

6. The _____. This tribe of cannibalistic abattoir workers would be more interested in carving up the host than the turkey at Christmas.

8. The _____. Harassed parents (Spencer Tracy and Joan Bennett) of Kay (Elizabeth Taylor) deal with the trials of organizing her expensive nuptials.

10. AVENGERS

Similar to a quest or road movie, revenge movies come with a ready-made plot structure, should anybody fancy having a go at making one. For a long time the preserve of westerns, then exploitation cinema, revenge movies are mainstream fare these days.

ACROSS

3. Although this John Wayne western is an undoubted classic, the remake is even better. But Kim Darby's portrayal of teenage tomboy _____ ____ in the 1969 version is just a little more engaging.

5. Master Huo Yuanjia has been murdered by members of a Japanese dojo. Star pupil ____ ____ discovers the conspiracy and repeatedly raises the stakes in a bloody war.

6. Betrayed by Bill (David Carradine), ___ _____ is left comatose in a hospital bed. Upon waking, there is just one thing on her mind.

8. _____ _____ takes a house in rural Connecticut to finish her latest manuscript but is attacked and sexually assaulted by a group of local hicks.

9. With her sister's life ruined and best friend crippled by drug dealers, a surprisingly tough nurse, _____ (Pam Grier), goes on the rampage.

10. Framed and jailed for the murder of a child, ____-__ ___ gains early release and is determined to do two things: find her daughter, and kill anyone involved in the original crime.

DOWN

1. After years of captivity in a Vietnamese P.O.W. camp, Major _____ ____ sees his family murdered by petty thieves and vows vengeance.

2. When the wife of pacifist architect Paul _____ is murdered and his daughter raped, he decides to clean up the streets of his native New York.

4. By favoring the popular General _____ over his own psychopathic son Commodus, Emperor Marcus Aurelius unwittingly signs his own death warrant and that of his protégé's family.

7. After his wealthy parents are killed in a botched mugging, young heir _____ _____ grows up to fight crime on the streets of his native Gotham.

11. HEISTS

Audiences clearly derive satisfaction from watching charming men form and execute complicated plans, to the extent that we don't really care that they're inherently unlawful. If anything, we tend not to want them to get caught.

ACROSS

1. In _____, very cool men plan and carry out a very cool diamond heist. This exceptionally classy French masterpiece has the (silent) burglary at its center, one of the tensest scenes in cinema.

3. _____ ___. Spike Lee utilizes one of the most original escape plans imaginable to keep Russell one step ahead of both police and audience.

8. ____ __ _____. This brilliantly played British take on the heist movie is a uniquely civilized and low-key affair. The crook is impeccably polite and the bank manager unquestioningly cooperative.

10. *The* _____ _____ *Mob*. Charged with supervising gold bullion deliveries, Henry Holland seems to be an unambitious bank clerk; in reality he has spent 20 years developing the perfect cover and planning the perfect crime.

DOWN

2. *The* _____ ___ sees a band of professional thieves brought together by a charismatic crime boss to conduct a near-impossible robbery right under the noses of the Italian mafia.

4. Although the diamond heist sequence in _____ is just there to set up later plot points, Guy Ritchie still executes it with a stylish explosion of energy.

5. Based on a true story, ___ ___ *Afternoon* portrays the robbery of a Brooklyn bank in order to pay for surgery for one of the participants' girlfriends.

6. _____ _____. Not content with robbing one Las Vegas casino, Danny and his cohorts plan to rob three at the same time.

7. ___ _____ ___. Lola must find money for her low-level gangster boyfriend or he will be killed by his boss.

9. Stanley Kubrick's breakout film ___ _____ is both a tightly plotted thriller and an examination of how human weakness and simple bad luck can scupper even the most perfectly conceived plan.

12. PERFORMANCES AGAINST TYPE

In the days of the studio system, it was common for stars to play just one character type. Although that's less the case nowadays, a tendency to typecast actors persists, and their inevitable attempts to escape those pigeonholes can result in fascinating performances.

ACROSS

4. Usually: a seeker of truth. Here: a ruthless gunslinger. Sergio Leone challenges audiences when he has Frank (_____ _____) kill children in cold blood within the first few minutes of the movie.

5. Usually: the guy who brings the funny. Here: a killer psychopath. _____ Williams plays a photo lab worker obsessed with a local family.

6. Usually: a loving mother. But in *Mother*: a sociopathic mother. Although unknown in the west, ___-__ ___ is renowned in her native South Korea.

8. Usually: a cuddly neurotic. But in *Drive*: a brutal criminal kingpin. _____ Brooks has as much fun playing this evil crime boss as the audience has watching him.

10. Usually: a Hollywood princess. Here: a prostitute. If there was surprise when _____ _____ won the role of dowdy serial killer Aileen Wuornos, it soon evaporated when she won the plaudits.

DOWN

1. Usually: a prim and proper English rose. But in *From Here to Eternity*: a beach-romping adulteress, _____ ____, which caused quite a stir.

2. Usually: a ditzy love interest. But in *Horrible Bosses*: a nymphomaniac bully. Director Seth Gordon cast _____ against type in this black comedy.

3. Usually: a cooler-than-cool ladies' man. But here: a child pornographer. _____ _____ is superb as hideous hypocrite Jim Cunningham.

7. Usually: everyone's favorite aunt. Here: the mother from hell. Given _____'s later TV career playing top sleuth Jessica Fletcher, her playing pure evil in *The Manchurian Candidate* is even more striking.

9. Usually: a man of honor. Here: a corrupt cop. _____ Washington seems to exude moral responsibility, so it was a shock to see him in this role.

13. FILM NOIR

Essentially, "film noir" describes American films of the 1940s and 1950s that marry a stark, expressionistic visual style to the themes, plots, and characters of hard-boiled crime fiction. Although the genre moved beyond post–WWII Hollywood, there's no doubting that is its home.

ACROSS

2. The plot is secondary to Bacall's smoldering performance and the chemistry she shares with Bogart's private eye Philip Marlowe in *The* ___ _____.

3. *The* _____ _____. This Marilyn Monroe movie tells the story of the fallout from a major jewelry heist, which threatens to swallow up all concerned as double crosses and bad luck scupper a perfect plan.

6. _____ _____. Insurance agent Walter is convinced by unhappily married Phyllis to murder her husband as part of a life insurance scam.

9. Less well known than many of its contemporaries, *The* ___ _____ sees successful magazine editor George (Ray Milland) framed for murder.

10. Dana Andrews investigating the murder of a beautiful woman, _____, gradually falls in love with her while interviewing people she knew.

DOWN

1. Nick Garcos returns home from war a hero only to find his father has been crippled by a corrupt market dealer in _____ _____.

4. In the Coen brothers' debut feature, _____ _____, rich Texas club owner Julian Marty hires private detective Loren Visser to kill his wife Abby.

5. Small-time crook Johnny Farrell becomes the right-hand man of crime boss Ballin Mundson, who has a beautiful girlfriend, _____ (Rita Hayworth).

7. Needing to raise funds for the Irish Nationalist group, Johnny (James Mason) takes too many risks and the holdup is a disaster in ___ ___ ___.

8. Drifter Frank is working at a roadside burger bar when he falls in love with Cora, the wife of friendly proprietor Nick. Together they hatch a plan to bump off Nick and live happily ever after, but paranoia and guilt start to compromise the perfect crime in *The* _____ *Always Rings Twice*.

14. DOCUMENTARIES ABOUT CINEMA

Passion for the subject is essential for a documentary maker dealing with art and entertainment. It follows that if you're passionate enough to want to make movies, you'll be passionate about movies, and that shows in the plethora of exceptional documentaries on the subject.

ACROSS

1.   A quarter of a century on _____ of Light is still indispensable for anyone interested in the visual aesthetic of film.

5.   *Hearts of Darkness: A Filmmaker's* _____. It's a common opinion that this documentary, filmed on the set of Francis Ford Coppola's *Apocalypse Now*, is a better film than its subject.

8.   *The* _____ *Closet* (1995). Based on Vito Russo's book of the same name, this film examines how cinema has represented members of the L.G.B.T. community.

10. *Man with a* _____ _____. Although ostensibly a documentary on urban life, this 1929 movie becomes an analysis of filmmaking itself.

DOWN

2.   *The* _____ *of* ____ (2011). This staggering 15-hour monument to cinema is a fantastic achievement by Cousins.

3.   __ ____ _____. Herzog's wry reminiscence on his explosive relationship with actor Klaus Kinski makes for a compelling watch.

4.   *A Personal Journey with Martin* _____ *Through American Movies* (1995). Martin could lay claim to producing the most important body of work of any American filmmaker.

6.   _._. (1985). Chris Marker, the French writer, photographer, and documentarian, was fascinated by Japanese culture, so it's no surprise he should have chosen to make a film about Akira Kurosawa.

7.   *The* _____'_ _____ *to Cinema* (2006). Celebrated Russian philosopher and cultural critic Slavoj Zizek examines a series of films from a psychoanalytical perspective.

9.   *Lost in* __ _____ (2002). The calamitous shoot for Terry Gilliam's aborted *Don Quixote* adaptation is documented in harrowing detail.

15. ANDROIDS

Androids have been grabbing our imagination at least since the 1886 novel *The Future Eve*. And, as they become a reality, our fascination isn't letting up. The term "android" is here used very loosely to define any vaguely anthropomorphic android, cyborg, or robot that appears in the movies.

ACROSS

6. In *Westworld,* Yul Brynner's dead-eyed, unstoppable killer, the _____, was a key inspiration for the Terminator character made famous by Arnold Schwarzenegger.

8. Over seven seasons of TV and four movies, _____'s desire to become more human and his effort to understand our idiosyncrasies have exposed the nature of humanity to an extent non-fans might find surprising.

9. Possibly the last masterpiece of American animation not to be dominated by C.G.I., *The _____ _____* is a sadly under-appreciated throwback to 1950s sci-fi.

DOWN

1. Although intended for *Forbidden Planet* only, _____ ___ _____'s popularity was such that he developed a healthier career than many of his co-stars.

2. Mamoru Oshii's movie presents a future in which androids are commonplace. _____, an operative for Public Security Section 9, is charged with capturing a hacker known as the Puppet Master.

3. Beating inside Pixar's eponymous caretaker, _____-_, is a unique heart. He doesn't look like an android, but it's arguably all human characteristics, including personality, that distinguish an android from a robot.

4. The caterpillar-tracked _____ _____ started life as a military robot before gaining a self-aware human intelligence when struck by lightning.

5. Jude Law is well cast as a lovebot called _____ ____, a robot designed to pleasure women, in Spielberg's *Pinocchio*-themed sci-fi drama.

7. A future society has split in two. The wealthy live among the clouds, the rest toil underground to keep the lights on upstairs. Freder, the son of Metropolis's ruler, falls in love with _____, a lowly worker.

10. The genius that brings _____ (as he's known to his friends) to life was Anthony Daniels's decision to play him as a priggishly fussy English butler.

16. SIDEKICKS

Whether sounding board, tail-gunner, whipping boy, or hero in waiting, there have been some great sidekicks in the movies over the years. This puzzle highlights some of the most memorable.

ACROSS

4. There could be no more faithful sidekick than _____ _____, gardener and best friend to ring bearer Frodo Baggins.

6. Put upon ___ _____ Jr. plays wingman to Will Ferrell's Ricky, a star NASCAR driver in *Talladega Nights: The Ballad of Ricky Bobby*.

7. With *Saturday Night Live* skits stretching back to 1988, affable Wayne (Mike Myers) and nervous sidekick _____ _____ have been part of the cultural furniture for a long time.

9. It's never explained how orphaned taxicab driver _____ _____ came to be in the service of Indiana Jones. But he is instrumental in saving both Indy and the child slaves of Mola Ram.

10. Karl Malden spent much of his career being Marlon Brando's sidekick. In *Streetcar* he plays _____, best friend and apologist to Brando's vile Stanley.

DOWN

1. Thrown together when the two men move into shared rooms together, __. _____ soon becomes personally, if not professionally, essential to Holmes.

2. Drunken former sheriff's deputy _____ is penniless and desperate when old friend John Chance finds him on the floor of a saloon.

3. Loudmouth truck driver Jack Burton and his restaurant-owning buddy _____ ___ become embroiled in an ancient Chinese curse when his girlfriend is kidnapped by a sorcerer.

5. Near-mute Mexican exchange student _____ _____ bonds with local crackpot Napoleon Dynamite, largely because nobody else wants to be friends with either.

8. Dracula's brainwashed, bug-eating vassal, _____, is brought to life with a deranged intensity by Waits in Francis Ford Coppola's epic adaptation.

17. PARTIES

The movies have presented us with many an extravagant and excessive festivity, but interesting on-screen parties come in many forms. Whether the sort of in-crowd blowout we'd love to be invited to, or the cultist rituals we'd rather avoid, they're all covered here.

ACROSS

5. In *Masque of the* ___ _____, evil Prince Prospero hosts a lengthy ball as a means of keeping himself and his guests safe from the plague.

6. In *Eyes* ____ ____, Bill and Alice Harford (Cruise and Kidman) each lap up the attention of sophisticated admirers amid the luxurious decor.

7. The Delta Tau Chi fraternity is facing exclusion after one prank too many in *National Lampoon's* _____ _____, and there's only one thing that can be done about it: Toga! Toga! Toga!

9. Outside, the apocalypse rages and the worthy ascend to heaven. Inside, Hollywood's comedy elite have barricaded the doors and decided to keep the party going in ____ __ ___ ___.

10. The bizarre black comedy _____ sees Bill return home to find his parents hosting a party for friends. All seems well until everyone starts eating a young kidnap victim. Bill doesn't fancy staying.

DOWN

1. Two teenage boys create their dream woman from a computer program. She decides to organize a party to make them popular in _____ _____.

2. In this Blake Edwards movie, *The* _____, things are kept simple as Peter Sellers performs a string of hilarious set pieces.

3. Leave it to Fellini to use a party to examine the issues of his protagonists. The cool Marcello leads the debauched mayhem in *La* _____ ____.

4. The infamous party at the Playboy Mansion in _____ _____ features the most stylish and refined of cinematic techniques.

8. ___ _____. Central to this comedy is a fraternity house party as excessive as any on film. It effectively made Will Ferrell's big-screen career with his performance as Frank "the Tank" becoming an instant classic.

18. TOUGH GIRLS

This is not a list of female characters who can deal with adversity or have the tenacity to achieve the impossible (hence no Ripley from *Alien*). This is a list of female characters who are born to kick serious ass, and in some cases do nothing but that throughout the movie.

ACROSS

1. In *The House of Flying Daggers*, rebel groups have sprung up across the region. One of them is _____ ___, an exceptional martial artist.

5. Based on the computer games that follow an evil corporation that has created a zombifying virus, the central figure in *Resident Evil* mythology is _____.

9. Former member of the Deadly Viper Assassination Squad, and one of few practitioners of the Five Point Exploding Heart Technique. You don't mess with ___ _____.

10. Based on the exploits of the Marvel comic heroine, ___ _____ is a sword-wielding avenger who can give Arnold Schwarzenegger a run for his money.

DOWN

2. _____ _____ is a promising boxer who rises to the top of her profession only to have success cruelly snatched away.

3. With the popularity of martial arts movies in the 1980s, a number of Western performers picked up the baton from the Asian film industries. Although few were women, Rothrock was the best of them, with _____ _'_____.

4. Grace Jones's ___ ___ is the bodyguard of industrialist Max Zorin. She shows superhuman strength and martial arts skills during her spats with James Bond.

6. Having spent years becoming the perfect fighting machine, _____ _____ is as ready as she can be for *Judgment Day*.

7. _____. Any 10-foot-tall, bright blue alien can be intimidating. When defending their home from aggressors, they can be outright terrifying.

8. _____ is a vampire, descended from an ancient race of warriors who have done battle through the ages with the Lycans, a fierce species of werewolf.

19. SEQUELS AS GOOD AS THE ORIGINALS

Often assumed to be a hasty rehash designed to cash in on success, the sequel doesn't have a great image. But the best of them develop characters and ideas that were already strong.

ACROSS

4. Danny Boyle's original *28 Days Later* was a breath of fresh air when it hit screens in 2002. The sequel *28 _____ Later* captures all the same qualities.

7. Having flirted with social commentary in *Night of the Living Dead*, Romero ramps up the allegory in this sequel _____ ___ ___ _____.

8. While the first film toyed with the idea of a shattered society terrorized by feral gangs, the sequel, ___ ___ 2, throws itself wholeheartedly into an apocalyptic nightmare.

9. Critics were pleasantly surprised by *The Bourne Identity*. Many were convinced that the sequel wouldn't match up, so imagine the surprise when *The Bourne _____* became one of the best action thrillers of the era.

10. Originally planned as a budget, straight-to-video release, ___ _____ *II* arguably had a more profound effect on moviegoers (not to mention Pixar, the studio behind it) than the original.

DOWN

1. The inevitable sequel to *Jean de Florette*, _____ ___ _____ details the attempts of Manon (Emmanuelle Béart) to avenge the death of her father.

2. _____ _____ *II* (2003). This prequel to the great Hong Kong thriller that inspired Martin Scorsese's *The Departed* focuses on the early careers of the first film's protagonists, Yue and Chen.

3. With *Frankenstein*, James Whale kicked off a craze for Gothic horror that would bankroll Universal for years. But in _____ __ *Frankenstein,* Whale surpasses the near perfection of that first film.

5. More martial arts antics for Jet Li's heroic kung fu legend Wong Fei Hung in *Once Upon a Time in _____ II*.

6. _____ *II: The Golden Army*. Having established the characters and relationships in the first film, del Toro sits back and lets them do their thing.

20. FICTIONAL MOVIE PLACES IT WOULD BE GREAT TO VISIT

While few of us would want to visit Sin City, and less still Mordor or the Death Star, the movies have given us a plethora of fanciful locations it would be interesting to look in on. Some are impossibly quaint, some are incredibly good fun, while others a little bit unsettling; sadly, all are fictional.

ACROSS

2. Just when we think we've seen everything the bizarre alternative universe of Roger Rabbit has to offer, we're taken to _____. In this cartoon world everything is alive, with cars, trees, and even buildings given a personality.

5. The only town in Britain to be inhabited solely by magical folk, _____ sits adjacent to Hogwarts School of Witchcraft and Wizardry.

7. You would need to carefully time your visit to _____, the magical realm located behind a wardrobe. Avoid the period ruled over by Jadis, the White Witch, and instead head for the Golden Age that followed her downfall.

8. A bit like a pepped-up Shangri-La, The _____ is located through a rift in space-time and has the power to provide anything the heart desires.

9. _____. A town so perfect it can't be real, and, sure enough, it isn't in *The Truman Show*.

10. In the totalitarian world of the *Hunger Games* movies, the Capitol is the base of power from which _____ is ruled.

DOWN

1. Who wouldn't like to stroll through _____ ____ ____, perhaps visiting the bridge for a game of Pooh Sticks with Piglet?

3. The plane of a British diplomat and his party crash-lands in a remote part of the Himalayas. They are rescued and taken to _____-__, a mythical nirvana that doesn't conform to any of Earth's natural laws.

4. Populated by mermaids, fairies, and pirates, as well as ageless children, _____ is the enchanted world created by J. M. Barrie for his *Peter Pan*.

6. Perhaps a little menacing for some travelers of the imagination, the surreal world of _____ must nevertheless be among the most desirable of hallucinatory vacation hot spots with its Mad Hatter and Cheshire Cat.

21. MISGUIDED BELIEVERS

Although no legitimate devotee would consider religious affiliation (or lack of it) a reason to victimize others or a means to exploit or control, the movies have given us numerous less worthy, misguided, deranged, or plain phony believers.

ACROSS

6. Apparently inspired by the infamous Fred Phelps of the Westboro Baptist Church, _____ _____ is a snake-like figure of pure evil in *Red State*.

8. Believing he is doing God's work, this self-appointed preacher roams America marrying and killing women for their money. Pure evil has seldom been better personified than in the Reverend _____ _____.

9. In love with local priest Urban Grandier, the head of a 17th-century convent, _____ _____ slips into madness when she realizes he has secretly wed.

10. Christopher Lee gives one of his finest performances as Lord _____, the patriarch of a Hebridean island community. He and his pagan followers lure Police Sergeant Howie from the mainland in order to sacrifice him.

DOWN

1. Thuggee high priest _____ ___ is responsible for enslaving hundreds of children, and can rip the beating heart from his victims with his bare hands.

2. Jimmy Lee _____, the TV evangelist, isn't the most dishonest character in the movie, but he comes pretty close.

3. _____ the Holy Man, after taking a vow of silence, spends 18 years sitting in a hole, until Brian turns up and stands on his foot.

4. Occasional cannibal and full-time evil mastermind _____ _____ and his corrupt family pulls the strings in Basin City. He has the prostitute Goldie murdered, which kick-starts the movie's central plot.

5. Joaquin Phoenix's _____ _____ is a war veteran struggling to find meaning in his life when he's taken in by Lancaster Dodd, the charismatic leader of "The Cause."

7. _____, a white, British fundamentalist Muslim, is an aspiring suicide bomber in this hilarious satire from the comedy genius Chris Morris.

22. HEROES

Even though it's arguably cinema's defining character archetype, what makes a hero is extremely subjective. For this puzzle, it's been kept very simple: a hero is the kind of person who will sacrifice everything for what's right, and for those who need help.

ACROSS

2. Residents of a small town suffer abnormally high rates of cancer, until struggling mother turned legal assistant Erin _____ vows to help.

4. Voted the greatest hero of the 20th century by the A.F.I., _____ _____ is a respected lawyer tasked with defending an African American accused of rape in 1930s Alabama.

8. 1939 was a time when politicians could be presented as heroes and the audience would go along with it. Naïve young Senator _____ Smith arrives in Washington and resolves to tackle the corruption.

9. When cinema owner _____ Dreyfuss is forced to host a premiere attended by the Nazi party, she resolves to burn the cinema to the ground, even though it means certain death.

10. The brother of a powerful rancher is arrested for murder in a Texas town. The sheriff, _____ _____, and his allies hole up in the jailhouse and hold off a gang of hired guns.

DOWN

1. There has been much discussion as to whether _____ ____ was a real figure, robbing the rich to give to the poor.

3. The second film in the series (*Temple of Doom*) sees _____ _____ spurn safe passage home and risk his life to free hundreds of child slaves.

5. Surely the definition of a hero, Thracian gladiator _____ leads an uprising against the Roman Republic in the first century B.C.

6. In *Winter's Bone*, teenager ___ _____ is the soul carer for her younger siblings and mentally ill mother in an impoverished Ozark community.

7. The marshal of a New Mexico town receives word that a murderer is returning on the noon train. In spite of the locals urging him to run and refusing to help, ____ ____ knows what he must do.

23. BUDDY MOVIES

The Hollywood studio system apparently failed to identify the potential of the buddy movie dynamic. Although there were examples of a sort, it wasn't really until the American new wave that the archetype was established, and from there it's never looked back.

ACROSS

5. In *Butch Cassidy and the* _____ ___, the chemistry between Paul Newman and Robert Redford made them the perfect choice to play these celebrated outlaws.

8. Jackie Chan's _____ __ _____ is pleasingly slick and accessible, making it a good place to start for anyone wanting to dip their toes in the water of classic kung fu cinema.

9. Catching De Niro between serious method roles and the generic comedy roles that would later make his fortune, _____ ___ has the best of both worlds. Endlessly quotable, rewatchable, satisfying fun.

10. Failing writer Skip and equally unsuccessful actor Harry are framed for a bank robbery and sentenced to 125 years in prison in _____ _____.

DOWN

1. Cheech and Chong's debut feature, __ __ _____, is by far their best, assuming you enjoy this sort of thing.

2. On the face of it _____ *Cowboy* is a depressing movie about seedy people. But if there is anything uplifting to be found, it's the strength of the friendship between Ratso and Joe.

3. _____ _____ throws Riggs and Murtaugh—with diametrically opposed personalities—together, then injects stress.

4. *The* _____ ____. After escaping from a crashed prison truck, two convicts (crucially one white and one black), chained together and full of mutual hatred, must learn to work together.

6. ____ *and* _____. Lloyd and Harry have nothing in the world but each other, and you feel they're quite happy about it.

7. Psychotics need buddies too. _____ *Creatures*, about murderous teens, completely changed the way we perceived the director Peter Jackson.

24. MEDICAL DOCTORS

Doctors are among the most prolific characters in the movies, perhaps because drama, pathos, and even comedy are inherent at the point where life and death meet. However, it's unfortunate to note how few women have had the chance to play memorable doctors, and, as such, none make this puzzle.

ACROSS

1. Decades after an encephalitis epidemic consigns a number of patients to comas, Dr. _____ _____ develops an experimental treatment that produces astounding results in *Awakenings*.

3. Amidst the Russian revolution and World War I, the romantically inclined doctor ____ _____ falls helplessly in love with Lara, a beautiful nurse.

6. J.J. McClure and Victor Prinzim field a souped-up ambulance in order to avoid police attention. They need a doctor to add authenticity, but can only find ___ _____.

7. In *Planet Terror*, Dr. _____ could be Van Helsing's son in some terrifying parallel universe.

9. The crazed modern-day Frankenstein of Lindsay Anderson's acerbic satire *Britannia Hospital*, Professor _____ is as vivid and enjoyable a character as any to appear in the films of the great director.

10. The Charles Darwin–inspired Dr. _____ _____ acts as conscience, sounding board, and physician to Captain Jack Aubrey in *Master and Commander*, the first of Patrick O'Brian's series of novels to be screened.

DOWN

2. *Marathon Man* sees history student Babe embroiled in a plot by former Nazi Dr. _____ _____ to acquire a fortune in stolen diamonds.

4. Upon graduating medical school in his native Scotland, _____ _____ travels to Uganda to work in a missionary clinic. After a chance encounter with Idi Amin, he becomes the dictator's personal doctor and advisor.

5. The gloomy Dr. _____ has a small but unforgettable part in *Waterloo Road*, a quiet movie about a World War II deserter attempting to save his marriage.

8. Dr. _____ Pierce's caustic wit and self-deprecating sense of humor have endeared him to more than one generation. Played brilliantly by Donald Sutherland in the movie, and on TV by Alan Alda.

25. UNDERRATED MASTERPIECES

An underrated masterpiece is usually relatively well known. It's not about being an undiscovered gem or obscure arthouse classic; it's about being misinterpreted or misunderstood, perhaps because it wasn't what the audiences were expecting or was ahead of its time.

ACROSS

1. ____ ____ deals with how men cope living in the shadow of a legend, and how they react when those legends prove to be fraudulent.

5. Although well-respected, _____ is seldom compared favorably with Kurosawa's better known earlier masterpieces.

8. _____ the Vampyre (1979). This atmospheric remake of the 1922 original is frequently overlooked in the discussion on vampire cinema. Centered around an unsettling lead performance from Klaus Kinski.

9. ____ _____—the last installment of Park's Vengeance trilogy—suffered from following on the heels of his hugely successful breakout hit Oldboy.

10. After the success of Se7en, Fincher continued to mine the darker reaches of the human psyche in his highly original thriller ___ ____.

DOWN

2. The heroic Autobots defend their world from the evil Decepticons. Based on the TV series, The _____: The Movie is a master class in screenplay construction.

3. ____ ____ ____ was widely regarded as a disappointment on release, despite starring Tom Cruise and Nicole Kidman. But Kubrick's swan song is impressive and rewarding.

4. Saturday ____ ____. Can one of the most popular movies of all time be underrated? If it's seen as some sort of kitsch time capsule and not as an examination of the travails facing teenage America, yes, it can.

6. ____ ____ has a peculiar relationship with both cinemagoers and fans of author William S. Burroughs. Some revel in the surreal mash-up of Burroughs's (real) life, while others struggle with the onslaught of crazy.

7. Starring Jim Carrey, directed by Ben Stiller, and produced by Judd Apatow, ____ ___ would surely be a smash if released today.

26. 1980s ACTION MOVIES

Some say the 1980s saw the high mark for big, dumb, and shiny action movies. Others believe the popular subgenre was reduced to generic flag-waving spectacles that eschewed traditional acting talent in favor of muscle-bound grunters. But what's wrong with that?

ACROSS

2. *The* _____ ___. In the future, ordinary people obsess over a TV reality game show and vie to become contestants. However, the system is corrupt and only the executives can really win.

4. The second of four installments (so far) in the _____ franchise sees our hero returning to Vietnam to rescue American P.O.W.s abandoned by their country, which wants to wash its hands of the war.

5. *The* _____ is arguably Chuck Norris's signature movie. With support from Lee Marvin, Chuck's Major McCoy must overcome the Lebanese hijackers of a New York–bound jet.

6. Pure 1980s hokum, _____ sees a super-tough bouncer move to a small town in the middle of nowhere and start working at a particularly rough trucker bar.

8. ___ ____. It's hard to believe now, but Bruce Willis wasn't offered the role that would define him until a succession of unlikely candidates had turned it down.

9. Based on the experiences of martial artist Frank Dux, _____ marks the first significant role for action legend Jean-Claude van Damme.

DOWN

1. Deciding it was folly to try and outdo the tense scares of the first movie, director James Cameron took the sequel, _____, in a different direction.

2. In Director Paul Verhoeven's _____, near-future Detroit society is crumbling and a disillusioned police force is effectively privatized.

3. _____ _____'s mix of blistering action, cartoon villains, and acerbic one-liners lifts much from James Bond.

7. Suggesting Rocky would one day have to fight an alien if the sequels kept coming, _____ tells the tale of commandos hunted by a deadly foe.

27. INSPIRATIONAL MOVIES

Movies can clearly be very effective at tapping into our deepest emotions, so it's no surprise they can be very inspiring. Told well, a simple story of humanity triumphing over harsh indifference will speak to all of us, and maybe even make a difference in our lives.

ACROSS

3. When the Joad clan lose the family ranch during the Great Depression, they head west in search of work. The injustices young Tom (Henry Fonda) witnesses on the journey encourage him to fight for social reform in *The* _____ __ _____.

6. *To Kill a* _____. In 1930s Alabama, a community must deal with the fallout when a white woman accuses a black man of rape.

9. *The* _____. A Polish Jew is forced into the Warsaw Ghetto when the Nazis invade Poland. His talent and determination to survive help him endure the aftermath of the Treblinka concentration camp.

10. The story of a free-spirited teacher galvanizing schoolchildren into passionate enthusiasm is not unique to *The* _____ *of* ____.

DOWN

1. Wrongly jailed for the murder of his wife, Andy Dufresne (Tim Robbins) spends decades in a brutal prison while hatching a daring plan to escape in *The* _____ *Redemption*.

2. Encouraged by their English teacher to seize the day, two shy and awkward students start to come out of their shells in ____ _____ *Society*.

4. *It's a* _____ delves into a kind of magical realism to show suicidal family man George Bailey (James Stewart) just how much better off his community is thanks to his kindness.

5. In a tough Northern England mining community, 11-year-old _____ _____ discovers a love for ballet.

7. Guido Orefice, his wife, and their child are consigned to a World War II concentration camp where he makes a game of their incarceration in *Life Is* _____.

8. The very definition of charm, _____ (Audrey Tautou) is a waitress to various eccentric customers at a Montmartre café.

28. AMBIGUOUS ENDINGS

In one way an ambiguous ending is incompatible with a traditional narrative. As an audience we tend to find closure important—it's a key return on our emotional investment. But handled carefully, it's a way of keeping the movie alive even after the credits roll.

ACROSS

2. Several viewings are required to even begin to understand the dream within a dream within a dream structure of _____.

4. ____ ____. Stranded on an uninhabited island for four years, time-obsessed FedEx worker Chuck Noland (Tom Hanks) finally returns home.

7. ____ ____ _____ (1970). A troubled former piano prodigy leads a simple life working the California oil fields. After taking his gauche girlfriend to meet his family, their difficult relationship worsens.

8. Gunslinger _____ (Alan Ladd) wades into a dispute between an evil cattle baron and a hard-toiling homesteader. After a saloon gunfight, he inadvertently reveals he has been badly wounded and may die.

10. Jailed for kidnapping his TV host hero, struggling comedian Rupert Pupkin (Robert De Niro) seems to achieve fame for his crime and is released into the media spotlight he so craves in *The King of* _____.

DOWN

1. In Franco-era Spain, Ofelia moves in with her brutal stepfather, soon retreating into what seems to be a fantasy world in ___'_ _____.

3. The patriarch of an Ohio family dreams of a terrible yellow storm and is compelled to ____ _____. When the storm doesn't come, it seems he's suffering from mental illness.

5. _____ *of a Murder*. This superb courtroom drama presents us with a conundrum. A husband kills a man who his wife claims raped her. But was she really raped?

6. A shape-shifting alien, ___ _____, invades an American Antarctic research station, picking off the scientists one by one.

9. ____, _____ *and Two Smoking Barrels*. After a series of cons, bluffs, and misfortunes, a pair of shotguns are all that's left at the end.

29. FEMALE VILLAINS

This is not a puzzle for murderous monsters. There are no serial killers or child abductors. This puzzle features the sort of nasty, vindictive, and manipulative types that enjoy making people miserable or would step over their own mother to get ahead.

ACROSS

2. After joining the army, Judy Benjamin (Goldie Hawn) finds herself under the thumb of _____ _____, a miserable, bullying old battle-axe with a vendetta against perky Judy.

4. The softly spoken stepmother to Cinderella, ____ _____ conceals a loathsome nature behind her demure demeanor.

6. Bette Davis dishes out rather than takes the abuse. She plays a former child star, ____ ____, slowly losing her mind while tormenting her disabled sister Blanche (Joan Crawford).

9. Ambitious acting ingenue Eve _____ ingratiates herself into the inner circle of established star Margo (Bette Davis).

10. Louise Fletcher won an Academy Award for her portrayal of the sadistic nurse _____, who dominates the vulnerable patients of a mental institution.

DOWN

1. The spiteful leader of high school in-crowd "the Plastics," _____ _____ gets a taste of her own medicine when Cady Heron becomes Queen Bee.

3. After stealing her secretary Tess McGill's (Melanie Griffith) plan for a client to diversify, _____ is forced off work after a skiing accident.

5. Mother to the titular telekinetic teen, _____ _____ is a twisted religious fanatic who seems intent on battering the character out of her troubled daughter, until it all becomes too much for Carrie.

7. The ultimate teenage Queen Bee persecutor must be Heather _____, the leader of the dominant clique (made up entirely of girls named Heather).

8. With an otherworldly calm and air of superiority that could intimidate the child of a Russian oligarch, the po-faced housekeeper of Manderley, _____, sets about destroying the confidence of her employer's new wife.

30. BIOPICS

Playing a real person generally recognized by the audience is considered to be among the greatest challenges an actor can take on. It's little wonder such roles have a reputation for attracting career-boosting acclaim, not to mention awards.

ACROSS

2. _____ _____ at first appears to be something of a departure for Mike Leigh. But although the brash performances appear out of character for the director, they neatly reflect Gilbert and Sullivan's style of opera.

6. *The* _____ *Man* is the bleak tale of Joseph (a.k.a. John) Merrick, a severely deformed Victorian era sideshow curiosity who escaped a cycle of exploitation to live his final years in relative peace at the London Hospital.

7. __ ___ __ _____ tells the extraordinary life of Édith Piaf, the Little Sparrow, as she was known, who inherited her mother's passion for singing and began plying her trade on the streets of Paris.

8. _____. Spielberg's account of the 16th president of the United States features a bravura performance from Daniel Day-Lewis.

10. Spike Lee's heartfelt chronicle of the human rights activist and Muslim minister, _____ _ attracted controversy both before and after its release.

DOWN

1. *The* _____ _____. On the face of it, computer geeks setting up a website isn't the most intriguing of subjects. But Zuckerberg's performance ensures some of the oldest dramatic tropes are present and correct.

3. In _____'_ *List*, altruism knows no bounds as the protagonist works to save Jews from the Nazi concentration camps of World War II.

4. _____ is the life story of a girl growing up in Iran after the defeat of the Shah in 1979. Her unwillingness to conform to the now strictly Islamic culture leads to many challenges.

5. James Cagney is cast against type but excels as the vaudeville legend George M. Cohan in _____ _____ *Dandy*.

9. The highly charged music scene in Manchester, England, in the 1980s is documented in *24 Hour* _____ *People*.

31. FAMILY MOVIES

Usually the term "family movie" is a euphemism for "kids' movie," but not here. Unless they're a devout cynic, each entry in this puzzle should be just as entertaining for parents as it is for kids.

ACROSS

2. Channeling *Alice in Wonderland*, Miyazaki's remarkable anime, _____ ____, is a striking example of a great imagination let off the leash.

5. _._. Little boy finds alien in his shed, movie history is made.

6. The most watched movie in history, *The* _____ __ __ is a curious mix of political allegory and musical fantasy. Literally something for all ages.

7. The first adaptation of Roald Dahl's book, _____ _____ *& the Chocolate Factory* has the charm and personality so lacking in the 2005 version.

8. Arguably the highlight of Aardman Animation's popular *Wallace & Gromit* series. *The* _____ _____ sees the unlikely inventor and his faithful hound foiling a diamond robbery.

9. Pixar's debut movie, ___ _____ is also the first fully C.G.I. feature, the first animated movie to be nominated for a best screenplay Academy Award, and the first to receive one for Special Achievement.

10. *The* _____ ____, based on Rudyard Kipling's 1894 book of the same name, must be among the most universally loved of all Disney movies.

DOWN

1. *Where the* ____ _____ ___. It's hard to imagine how such a slight book could be adapted into a full-length movie, but it was and works so wonderfully well.

3. Starting life as a bedtime story, *The* _____ _____ is a throwback to the sort of wholesome fantasies of yesteryear. With heroes, giants, villains, and princesses, it's comparable to a classic animated Disney.

4. *My Neighbor* _____. A simple tale of two sisters who discover a forest spirit living near their new home. The "Japanese Disney" Hayao Miyazaki found unprecedented success (eventually) with this gentle masterpiece.

32. ANTI-ESTABLISHMENT MOVIES

Most creative mediums provide an outlet for artists compelled to criticize or highlight flaws in the world's pervasive authority systems. Cinema perhaps offers the most literal and universal opportunity, and as a result there are many movies that challenge the establishment in one way or another.

ACROSS

2. The British class system is denounced for its inequities in this portrayal of life at an English boarding school. After building to a crescendo of violence, the audience is left exhausted by a first-class intellectual workout in __.

7. *One Flew Over the _____'_ ____*. R. P. McMurphy, either mentally ill or feigning madness to avoid a prison sentence, fails to adapt to the authority of an unsympathetic and unyielding mental health institution.

8. *The Ninth _____*. Set in an insane asylum for military personnel, what starts as a surreal farce soon becomes something far more.

9. ____ _____ is a searing strike at the values of an indifferent government and the corruption of the American dream.

10. One of the most prescient movies of the 1970s, _____ is a satirical swipe at TV's quest for ratings.

DOWN

1. In an alternate 1970, President Nixon decrees a state of emergency and sentences thousands of students, feminists, and civil rights activists to _____ *Park*.

3. ____. An American journalist is caught up in the 1917 Russian Communist revolution and attempts to introduce some of its spirit to American shores.

4. The establishment can be the bigoted elders of a small town just as much as a dictatorial government. Kevin Bacon's Ren McCormack challenges the oppressive patriarchs of his small town in _____.

5. _____ _____. An allegorical tale of an advertising firm that accidentally places its only African American board member in charge, eventually attracting the attention of the government.

6. *The Loneliness of the ____ _____ Runner* focuses on a "Borstal" boy who starts to question the system.

33. VILLAINS

A character paradigm that has led to some of the most memorable performances in movies. Free from any responsibility to traditional behavioral codes, their free will can be as intoxicating as their profligacy is disturbing.

ACROSS

5. One sensation shared by almost everyone who saw *Chitty Chitty Bang Bang* as children is an almighty terror of the _____ _____.

6. With so many great Bond villains over the years, it's hard to single out just one. There may be more celebrated examples, but _____ (Javier Bardem) wins out through being so unique and enigmatic.

8. _____ ____. This brutal and utterly reprehensible matriarch of a Melbourne crime family has no compunction over doing what's necessary. Even killing her grandson doesn't require a second thought.

9. In *The Lion King*, ____'s betrayal of his family and attempt to seize control of their kingdom is Shakespearean in its malevolent skullduggery.

10. _____ _____ maintains an iron grip on Bedford Falls. He exploits honest workers, intimidates anyone who challenges him, and brings about the near suicide of his thoroughly decent rival.

DOWN

1. It was a stroke of genius to cast legendary director John Huston as the villain ____ _____ in this dark tale of greed and power.

2. Anyone with a phobia of dentistry will remember Dr. _____, the former Nazi, master criminal, double agent, and torture enthusiast.

3. The superbly extravagant performance from Montalban as ____ is the most fun aspect to this popular entry in the *Star Trek* movie series.

4. Fassbender's portrayal of slave owner _____ ____, who believes he has a biblical right to beat, rape, and murder who he chooses chills to the bone.

7. Flitting between friendly conversationist and brutal executioner, Nazi "Jew hunter" ____ _____ is possibly the most memorable and certainly the most execrable of Quentin Tarantino's numerous villains.

34. SCENE-STEALING PERFORMANCES

Whether the actor has a single line or plays an important second-string character doesn't matter. They can appear as someone integral to the plot or an irrelevant diversion. The only criteria for this puzzle are that the part is not a lead, and that the actor does something remarkable with it.

ACROSS

2. _____ became a mainstream icon in *Titanic,* but four years earlier he gave an exceptional performance as a young boy with special needs.

3. Even prior to his tragic death just a few months before the movie came out, _____ _____'s portrayal of Batman's nutty nemesis was tipped as something special.

6. _____ _____ and director Stanley Kubrick's first partnership produced one of the definitive scene-stealing performances in *Lolita.*

10. Pixar's *Up* risks being hijacked by pathos at times. That it never quite happens is largely thanks to Dug, voiced by Bob _____.

DOWN

1. As the conflicted mother of a (possibly) sexually abused son in *Doubt,* _____ _____ has nothing but talent to rely on, and doesn't come up short.

4. The part of the irrepressibly mercurial medium who inadvertently causes havoc for a middle-class couple in *Blythe Spirit* could have been written for Margaret _____.

5. In *Glengarry Glen Ross,* ____ _____ steals the show. If there's a single standout role it has to be Blake, the sharp-suited motivational speaker sent to shake things up among the sales team.

7. In this crass but undeniably funny portrayal of high school boys looking for love, about the only thing everyone seems to agree on is that _____ ____ is hilarious as Jim's lovably awkward dad.

8. _____ ____'s iconic performance in *Withnail and I* as the drug dealer to our eponymous heroes is unforgettable.

9. With only eight minutes of screen time, ____ _____ was a controversial winner of the Best Supporting Actress Oscar for her performance in *Shakespeare in Love.*

35. WAR MOVIES WITH A DIFFERENT PERSPECTIVE

With such an abundance of prominent war movies, it seems a good idea to perform a flanking maneuver on the genre. By limiting the puzzle to movies showing war from a perspective different to the norm, it might highlight both some original choices and contrasting viewpoints.

ACROSS

2. As World War II breaks out, a group of Dutch friends pick sides in Paul Verhoeven's _____ of _____. Some are only too willing to fall in line with the Nazi ideology, while others become fighters with the resistance.

4. *The Battle of* _____ (in which British forces crushed the Jacobite uprising) is restaged in this faux documentary seen from both sides.

6. Uniquely shot as two separate productions (one in the United States and the other in Japan), ____! ____! ____! attempts to be the last word on the attack on Pearl Harbor.

8. In _____ *and* ____, based on the true story of Le Ly Hayslip, an ordinary villager struggles to survive the Vietnam War.

9. _____ __ ____ is a fairly straightforward World War II movie, only told from the "other" side. We learn that class warfare and petty rivalries were as much of an issue for the Nazis as any other army.

10. _____ *at the* _____. During the Battle of Stalingrad, an expanded game of cat and mouse is played out between two expert snipers.

DOWN

1. Often cited as the first German movie to portray Hitler, _____ is a study of the dictator's last weeks, holed up in his Berlin bunker.

3. *Letters from* ___ ____. Eastwood's brace of epic war films (the other being *Flags of Our Fathers*) shows the battle from both sides. Here the action is seen from the Japanese viewpoint.

5. ____ ___ ___. After stumbling on a rifle, a young and idealistic Belarusian boy decides to join the Soviet Army opposing Nazi Germany during World War II.

7. The crew of a German U-boat suffer incredible hardships in ___ ____ as they attempt to stay alive.

36. PRIVATE INVESTIGATORS

The shadowy world in which the movie P.I. tends to operate can have a seductive appeal for an audience. P.I.s travel light, play both sides as necessary, and will make their own rules. They're free spirits, answering to nothing but their own personal morality.

ACROSS

2. After marrying beautiful heiress Nora (Myrna Loy), former detective ____ _____ (William Powell) is repeatedly drawn back into the criminal underworld.

5. Mickey Spillane's ____ _____ is brought to life in all his brutal, misanthropic glory in *Kiss Me Deadly* (1955).

6. Chevy Chase's iconic creation, _____, is a sublimely indifferent fruitcake of a detective.

8. A sort of revisionist or neo noir, *The Long Goodbye* transposes Raymond Chandler's illustrious detective _____ _____ from his 1940s natural habitat to the more pessimistic 1970s.

9. One of Jack Nicholson's seminal performances sees ____ _____ embroiled in a complicated murder plot related to the Los Angeles power elite.

10. Bob Hoskins seems to have a whale of a time as Roger Rabbit's toon-hating and extremely reluctant partner _____ _____.

DOWN

1. Bogart gives arguably the quintessential portrayal of the private dick as ____ _____ in this John Huston classic.

3. Mickey Rourke crackles with charisma as _____ _____, a downtrodden and bedraggled detective hired to find a long-forgotten musician.

4. Robert Mitchum plays ____ _____ in the archetypal "you can't escape your past" film noir, with director Jacques Tourneur and writer Daniel Mainwaring infusing the movie with a palpable foreboding doom.

7. Although the character's origins were seemingly forgotten as he morphed into James Bond over the course of the sequels, ____ _____ was originally a private dick fighting injustice on the streets of Harlem.

37. MAD SCIENTISTS

Playing God seems to be the prevalent pastime of the mad scientist. Probably inspired by forerunners such as Archimedes and the mythological Daedalus, the mad scientist can exist almost anywhere on the good/evil spectrum with no prerequisite to be villainous, though trouble will inevitably result from his unholy tinkering with the nature of things.

ACROSS

3. Dr._____. This former Nazi scientist's big idea is to move civilization underground in the face of a nuclear threat from Russia.

8. In *Mad Scientist: The College Years*, a series of experiments that begin with student doctor _____ ____ reanimating a dead cat leads to him decapitating a lecturer and bringing the head back to life.

9. Topol's eccentric Hans _____ is concerned by the strange weather conditions on Earth, so he builds a spaceship in order to investigate a distant star system he believes to be the source of the storms.

10. Loony Dr._____-_-_____, a self-proclaimed "sweet transvestite from Transsexual, Transylvania," becomes jealous when his creation prefers the company of Janet (Susan Sarandon).

DOWN

1. Like a tragic, goth Pinocchio, Edward Scissorhands was made to be like a real boy by the mercurial _____ (one of Vincent Price's last roles).

2. The sinister Dr. _____, head of research at the heartless Clamp corporation, gets his hands on Gizmo, the lovable Mogwai.

4. Dr._____ _____'s iconic DeLorean time machine is a symbol of the 1980s, much like the denim ensemble worn throughout the movie by Marty McFly.

5. Dr. Michael _____'s complicated love life has already seen him widowed and then married, but his real troubles start when he falls in love with a brain in a jar.

6. Charles Laughton played the eponymous character in the original and best take on H.G. Wells's *The Island of Dr._____*.

7. Having succeeded in creating human life in miniature, Dr._____ is eager to work with Dr. Frankenstein and further develop his ideas.

38. MARTIAL ARTS MOVIES

Two people taking it in turns to kick each other isn't an inherently interesting spectacle for most moviegoers. But the martial arts genre has much more to offer, particularly if one delves into the best its Asian homelands have to offer, which is what we have done, along with a few very fine Western examples, in this puzzle.

ACROSS

4.   In what is easily Chuck Norris's best movie, he plays eponymous Texas Ranger ____ ____ _____, a man out to avenge the death of his partner.

7.   In ____, Nameless, the prefect of a small territory in ancient China, arrives at the palace of ruler Qin, who has been subject to a series of assassination attempts by his rivals, but Nameless claims to have beaten each in combat.

8.   In _____, it might seem like David Mamet is out of his comfort zone with this story about a skilled martial arts trainer who vows never to fight again.

9.   After being left for dead by her partner and colleagues, a supremely talented assassin sets off in search of retribution in ___ ____, Tarantino's epic tale.

10. Fast-paced, action-packed, and brimming with charm, _____ _____ is essentially a traditional crime caper but with Jackie Chan in top form.

DOWN

1.   Threads involving forbidden love, the theft of a priceless sword, bandit kidnappers, honor, and vengeance are all successfully juggled by Ang Lee in _____ _____, *Hidden Dragon*.

2.   Through judo, Sanshiro (Susumu Fujita), a youth with an attitude problem, learns about what's important in life in Akira Kurosawa's ____ _____.

3.   Stephen Chow's ____ __ _____ is a manic cross between the cartoons of Chuck Jones, classic martial arts cinema, and the Three Stooges.

5.   *The Legend of* _____ _____, Jackie Chan's last significant Hong Kong movie before his focus switched to a spell in Hollywood, is chock-full of his trademark slapstick.

6.   Featuring villainous hopping zombie-vampires that can be stopped only by kung fu or a sticky note to the forehead, __. _____ is a fine example of the wacky imagination in the Hong Kong action cinema of the 1980s.

39. MOVIES ABOUT CELEBRITY

Although fascination with celebrity seems to have reached some sort of zenith in recent times, filmmakers have been preoccupied with analyzing and deconstructing the nature of fame for decades. That in itself shows us the desire to be famous has probably been a problematic phenomenon for far longer than many of us realize.

ACROSS

5. ____ __ _____ was made when both Scorsese and star Robert De Niro were at the peak of their powers.

6. A vapid wannabe novelist tries to penetrate celebrity cliques in order to raise his own stock and enjoy the advantages of the rich and famous in _____.

9. In _____ _____, teenage music fan and wannabe writer William Miller lands a dream assignment covering an up-and-coming rock band for *Rolling Stone* magazine.

10. Inspired by the career of Elvis Presley, ___ ___ _____ uses a musical comedy format to examine the nature of fame.

DOWN

1. *The* _____ ____ is the true story of a group of fame-obsessed Californian students who took to burgling the homes of Hollywood stars.

2. The movie __ _____ ____ spends a week following Rome-based gossip magazine columnist Marcello Mastroianni.

3. Gloria Swanson plays Norma Desmond, once a giant of the silent film era but now largely forgotten, in _____ *Boulevard*.

4. In __ ___ ___, an ambitious TV weather girl hatches a plan to kill her husband, who she perceives is standing in the way of her success.

7. The fictional documentary _'_ _____ ____ follows Joaquin Phoenix as he claims to be retiring from acting to pursue his real dreams.

8. *Bright* _____ _____, Evelyn Waugh's account of the 1930s "it crowd," was adapted from his second novel, *Vile Bodies*.

40. PRISON MOVIES

Whether examining the nature of prisons or merely using incarceration as part of a dramatic structure, prison movies provide all sorts of opportunities to present exciting escape attempts, oppressive regimes, social conflict, and more. Although technically a different genre if we're being pedantic, P.O.W. movies are included here.

ACROSS

7. Republican inmates of Northern Ireland's notorious Maze prison embark on an ideological hunger strike led by Bobby Sands (Michael Fassbender) in _____.

8. _ _____. Nineteen-year-old Algerian Malik El Djebena is sentenced to six years in a French prison for attacking police officers.

9. *La* _____ _____ is a philosophical look at life in a German P.O.W. fortress during World War I.

10. Dieter Dengler, a German pilot serving the United States in the Vietnam War, is shot down and held captive in the jungles of Laos in _____ ____.

DOWN

1. _____ _____ is the terrifying true story of Billy Hayes (Brad Davis), an American tourist caught trying to smuggle hashish out of Turkey.

2. The first feature-length movie from *Wallace and Gromit* creator Nick Park, _____ ___ sees a farm full of chickens intent on escape.

3. William Holden, an American sergeant, runs all the scams in World War II P.O.W. camp _____ *17*.

4. *Female Prisoner 701:* _____. Framed by her lover, a corrupt cop, Nami Matsushina becomes a liability in the prison to which she's sentenced.

5. *Escape from* _____. Although officials like to say nobody ever escaped from this prison, there's a good chance Frank Morris (here played by Clint Eastwood) managed it.

6. Andy Dufrasne (Tim Robbins), an innocent man jailed for the murder of his wife, finds solace in friendship with a fellow inmate in *The* _____ *Redemption*.

41. SHOOT-OUTS

The great French director Jean-Luc Godard once observed, "All you need for a movie is a gun and a girl." While there's possibly a touch of hyperbole to the statement, there's also some truth. The gun is the ultimate dramatic device. Introduce one to a scene, almost any scene, and the dynamic changes.

ACROSS

3. Uncovering a cult in a quaint English town, cops Simon Pegg and Nick Frost discover the conspiracy goes deeper in ___ ____.

4. Robert De Niro wants to make one last big hit before retirement. Caught in the act, he is pursued by cop Al Pacino in the brilliant ____.

7. With a guitar case full of guns and determined to avenge the death of his loved one, el Mariachi shoots his way from saloon to saloon in _____.

8. Fat Sam's Speak Easy hosts the chaotic showdown between rival gangs in _____ _____. Bullets are replaced with custard.

10. Neo (Keanu Reeves) and Trinity (Carrie-Anne Moss) spring their leader Morpheus (Laurence Fishburne) from the Agents in ___ _____.

DOWN

1. In ____ '__ __, Mr. Smith saves a heavily pregnant woman from a hit man, only for the hit man's reinforcements to arrive as the woman goes into labor.

2. In *The* _____, the gunfight on the steps of Chicago's Union Station builds to the infamous "baby carriage catch."

5. From the opening frames of *The* ____ _____, the viewer senses this is how it has to end. Pike (William Holden) fronts the final stand against a corrupt element of the Mexican army after one of his posse is murdered.

6. In one three-minute take in ____ _____, two cops take out a small army of gun smugglers hiding out in a hospital. Scenes like this gave director John Woo his reputation for being the foremost action filmmaker of his generation.

9. Dying of cancer, former gunslinger John Books (John Wayne) decides he has unfinished business in *The* _____.

42. CONCERT MOVIES

Although not the mainstream mainstay they once were, concert films are still the purest means of combining music with moving imagery. And, with such a diverse and extensive back catalog, they will always be of value to music and movie fans alike.

ACROSS

1. The likes of Bob Dylan, Van Morrison, Neil Young, Eric Clapton, and Muddy Waters join the Band for their 1976 farewell live concert, *The _____ _____*.

3. *Neil Young: _____ __ _____*. During an emotionally charged summer for Neil Young (his father had just died), concerts at the Ryman Auditorium in Nashville were filmed by concert film legend Jonathan Demme.

4. Shot over three nights at the Pantages Theatre in Hollywood, *Stop _____ ____* helped revolutionize the way sound is recorded for movies.

7. The final stage of the Rolling Stones' 1969 U.S. tour is chronicled by eminent documentarians Albert and David Maysles in _____ _____.

9. *The Concert for _____*. Some of the biggest stars of the day are brought together by Beatle George Harrison for a benefit concert.

10. *The _____ _____ Under Great White Northern Lights*. At the height of their popularity, the band play a series of gigs across Canada. The relationship between band members Meg and Jack White is as fascinating as their unique performing style.

DOWN

2. _____ _____ *and the Spiders from Mars* was recorded at London's Hammersmith Apollo in July 1973.

5. Ethereal Icelandic post-rock peddlers Sigur Rós play a triumphant series of homecoming shows over the summer of 2006 in _____.

6. _____ ___, featuring Otis Redding, Jimi Hendrix, and the Who, provides a snapshot of life at the heart of the counterculture when optimism was still its dominant force.

8. After several failed attempts to pin down a Led Zeppelin gig on film, *The Song Remains ___ ____* was finally nailed over the summer of 1973.

43. PERFORMANCES BY CHILDREN

Whether or not young children can genuinely act, or are merely following instructions, is a question such performers have always faced. Can children truly understand character motivations and emotions? When the end result is as good as these, does it even matter?

ACROSS

3. As the angelic orphan _____ _____ is paired with another top-notch child performance in Anthony Newley's Artful Dodger.

6. In *Interview with the Vampire*, the eternally young _____ is saved from a grim death at the hands of the plague when she is bitten by, and turned into, a vampire.

8. Jodie Foster's lauded performance as child prostitute ____ in *Taxi Driver* is a touchstone for all young actors.

9. In the 1980s, if you needed a cocky but appealing youth to do some light charming, you went to Corey Feldman, as epitomized by his performance as Clark "Mouth" _____ in *The Goonies*.

10. In *The Fallen Idol*, _____, the son of a French diplomat in London, idolizes butler Baines, but when Baines's wife dies in an accident witnessed by the boy, he wrongly forms the impression that the butler killed her.

DOWN

1. _____ is a troubled child searching for a father figure. She finds one in the unlikely form of Leon, who just happens to be a mob hitman.

2. With mother, stepfather, and teachers unable, or unwilling, to offer _____ _____ the simple affection the troubled adolescent needs, we must watch a profound tragedy unfold in *The 400 Blows*.

4. Haley Joel Osment was nominated for a Best Supporting Actor Academy Award for his sensitive portrayal of ____ ____.

5. The children of Midwych start to exhibit strange characteristics. The deeply creepy _____ _____ spearheads the campaign to destroy those who challenge them in their mysterious objectives.

7. Precocious _____ _____ drives the narrative in *Little Miss Sunshine*, this quirky tale of a family of misfits on a road trip to a child beauty pageant.

44. SPIES AND SECRET AGENTS

Spies come in many guises. Cold War agents sneaking microfilm across borders, swaggering action men leaping from trains, and desk-bound suits pulling strings from afar. The shadowy world of espionage is an excellent breeding ground for fascinating movie characters.

ACROSS

3. There are pretenders to _____ _____'s throne, but for the last 50 years nobody has managed to topple him. If anything, his appeal is stronger than ever.

5. Before the *Bourne* series, movie spies were usually either Cold War relics or unconvincing suave operators. With its incredible characters that avoid black-and-white moral classification, _____ _____ reinvented spy movies.

6. Based on the novel by legendary author John Le Carré, Burton won a BAFTA for his hypnotic performance as ____ _____.

8. In the improbable story of a husband and wife who are both freelance spies/assassins, Angelina Jolie plays the wife, ____ _____.

9. In East Berlin, the Stasi monitor anyone with values different from their own, but Hauptmann ____ _____ begins to question whether the playwright he is assigned to spy on might be fighting for a worthy cause.

10. Disillusioned C.I.A. analyst _____ ___, played by John Malkovich, is sacked, divorced, and then blackmailed by a moronic personal trainer who believes they have acquired a data disk of national importance.

DOWN

1. Although offered up as a sort of working-class, down-to-earth James Bond, _____ _____'s first adventure in *The Ipcress File* is every bit as far-fetched as those of his better-known colleague.

2. Gary Oldman's performance as _____ _____, the head of the British secret service who must discover the identity of a Soviet mole, is superb.

4. Cary Grant isn't the most convincing of spies, but that does nothing to harm Hitchcock's 1946 classic *Notorious*, in which he plays T. R. _____.

7. In one of the most memorably chilling performances in cinema from Angela Lansbury as ___. _____, *The Manchurian Candidate* suggests even the family matriarch can be corrupted beyond recognition by communism.

45. MOVIES ABOUT MOVIES

Navel-gazing is a favorite pastime of filmmakers, so perhaps it's no surprise that there have been so many great movies made about the industry. More surprising is the way most of them paint it as caustic and exploitative, regardless of where and when they were made.

ACROSS

2. In the film *8½*, _____, a successful filmmaker (Marcello Mastroianni) has "director's block" and is lacking enthusiasm for his latest movie.

3. _____'_ *Travels* is an intelligent and commercial movie about the difference between making intelligent movies and commercial ones.

5. _____ _____. Woody Allen's film about a filmmaker who is plagued by accusations that his new films aren't as good as his old.

7. *Sunset* _____ is one of the most beloved movies to emerge from the Hollywood studio system. The craving for attention of a forgotten silent era star becomes a biting allegory for the sham that is fame and celebrity.

9. *A* ____ ___ ___ *Story*—Winterbottom's approach to filming *Tristram Shandy*, the famously unfilmable novel, is to make a movie of the attempt to make a movie.

10. In ___ _____, Altman ruthlessly skewers Hollywood types for their lack of creativity and honesty—it's hard to see how the director ever worked again.

DOWN

1. Hollywood of the late 1920s is the setting for musical comedy masterpiece _____' __ ___ ____. It wasn't initially a success, with audiences taking their time to discover the charms of Gene Kelly's centerpiece routine.

4. Fans of Tim Burton might be surprised by this subdued and affectionate tribute to __ ____, the cross-dressing World War II hero who arguably made the worst movies in history.

6. Sharing a similar setup to *Singin' in the Rain*, ___ _____ also touches on the same issues. This bittersweet love story took home seven Oscars.

8. The famously baffling _____ *Drive* sees enthusiastic Betty (Naomi Watts) reduced to an emotional wreck by her attempts to crack Hollywood.

46. VISUAL EFFECTS SEQUENCES

Visual effects are the processes used to create imagery "out of camera," i.e., not live on a set (special effects). This puzzle focuses on modern methods, which essentially means computer generated imagery (C.G.I.), although other techniques can be involved.

ACROSS

5   There are showier sequences in *Jurassic Park*, but the scene in which the human characters first see a long-necked _____ is unforgettable.

6.   In *The Abyss*, early C.G.I. is used to show the _____, a nonterrestrial intelligence using water to form shapes and faces.

8.   Several sequences from Alfonso Cuaron's majestic space drama _____ could qualify. But the opening 13-minute shot of debris crippling a space shuttle stands out for its beauty and technical complexity.

DOWN

1.   In *Inception*, as Ariadne starts to understand the control she wields over a dreamscape, she literally folds the city of _____ into a cube before our eyes.

2.   Even those disappointed to the point of being offended by the *Star Wars* prequels reserve praise for the ___ ____ in *Episode 1: The Phantom Menace*, where Lucas indulges his love of motor racing in this action sequence.

3.   We watch with bated breath in _____ 2 as a metallic humanoid shape strides from the flames, demonstrating how effective a tool C.G.I. is.

4.   This fairly forgettable movie, _____ ___, has one legendary V.F.X. sequence at its center—the scene in which Kevin Bacon's Sebastien Caine first becomes invisible, one grisly layer of tissue at a time.

6.   In _____ _____, the sequence in which the eponymous port is attacked by Japanese forces during World War II is most definitely a standout scene.

7.   The first film to use C.G.I. extensively, *Tron* was ruled ineligible for an Academy Awards effects nomination, but the heavily stylized _____ _____ race sequence is still visually stunning and utterly exciting.

8.   A rare example of a real actor contributing at least as much to a C.G.I. character as the computer wizards, Andy Serkis's physical portrayal proved essential to the appeal of the wretched _____.

47. MOVIES ABOUT ALIENATION

Loneliness is a complicated and powerful emotional response, but it's one that can be well suited to being explored by cinema. These run the gamut of characters defined by their estrangement from conventional society.

ACROSS

3. Two girls spend the summer after high school trying to decide who they are going to be in _____ _____. They have a few unremarkable adventures, face difficulties getting on in life, and challenges to their friendship.

4. Humphrey Bogart was known for playing cynical characters, but with his realistic portrayal of an alcoholic murder suspect, he won uncommon plaudits for his work in *In a* _____ _____.

5. Hermann Hesse's abstract tale of alienation is not always completely successful. But there is enough of the great author's metaphysical analysis to make _____ a powerful and engrossing experience.

6. Travis Bickle is among the most notorious of cinema's alienated souls. This disillusioned Vietnam veteran freewheels aimlessly around New York in _____ _____.

7. Supposedly about a loner left to care for his child, the reality is David Lynch doesn't care about _____'s narrative.

8. On a whim, journalist David Locke (Jack Nicholson) assumes the identity of a recently dead arms dealer in *The* _____.

DOWN

1. River Phoenix and Keanu Reeves form a strong bond as they attempt to earn a living for themselves as street hustlers in *My Own* _____ _____.

2. An almost dialogue-free mixture of animation and live action, *Pink Floyd—*_____ _____ is an introspective nightmare of a movie.

4. A bestial circus strongman buys a naïve young girl to keep him company and help with his act in _____ _____.

6. After a chance meeting in Tokyo, two isolated Americans become friends. The loneliness is palpable in Sofia Coppola's *Lost in* _____.

48. COOLEST CHARACTERS

The cool kid in school had nothing on this mixture of confident, stylish, and unnaturally appealing characters. To avoid making the other men and women in this puzzle seem a bit drab, James Bond is deliberately excluded.

ACROSS

3. Aging flight attendant _____ _____ oozes the nonchalant class that can only come from experience, even when dealing with a vicious gun dealer.

5. Lauren Bacall was just 19 when she made her debut in Howard Hawks's adaptation of Ernest Hemingway's novel, playing free-spirited American ____ _____ roaming Martinique.

7. In *Fight Club*, _____ _____ is confident, good-looking, stylish, cool, and tough, all qualities that a modern emasculated man might project onto a fantasy persona. Which, funnily enough, is just what has happened here.

8. _____ _____ is a dynamic, young petty thief who, after stealing a car, kills the policeman pursuing him. Murder isn't cool, but in *Breathless*, Jean-Paul Belmondo can do what he likes.

9. ____ _____ is the charismatic, gregarious billionaire genius behind the *Iron Man* superhero and has the coolest of Avenger colleagues.

10. The casual indifference with which _____ _____ greets supercilious city officials, intolerant professors, or disorderly ghosts is the basis of his profound cool.

DOWN

1. Jive-talking, afro-wearing karate expert _____ somehow manages to make even Bruce Lee look uncool in *Enter the Dragon*.

2. It's hard to quantify cool, you just know it when you see it, and Alain Delon's ____ _____ in *Le Samourai* has got more of it than anyone else.

4. If we skip his psychotic penchant for torture, the gritty nonchalance makes Vic Vega a.k.a. Mr. _____ in *Reservoir Dogs* the coolest character.

6. During the day ____ _____ is an easily forgettable high school kid in small-town Arizona. But by night he becomes the pirate radio D.J. Hard Harry, committed to exposing the hypocrisy and injustice at his school.

49. CONTEMPORARY BLACK-AND-WHITE MOVIES

Although color movies have dominated the landscape for half a century or so, black and white has never really gone away. Technical and financial limitations no longer necessitate monochrome cinematography, but creative choices apparently still lead to it.

ACROSS

3. Hanake won the Palme d'Or at Cannes for his darkly fascinating portrayal of life in a German village just prior to World War I in *The* _____ _____.

5. Frances Halladay is a struggling dancer living in New York. When her best friend moves out of their shared apartment, she starts an uneventful journey of personal discovery in _____ __.

9. The hugely popular French silent movie ___ _____ (2011) uses monochrome as a means of mimicking the techniques and limitations of the era the filmmakers want to evoke.

10. Ostensibly a story about a prison break, ____ __ ___ is essentially a study of the dynamic between the three protagonists, whose behavior and philosophizing reveal interesting human truths.

DOWN

1. __ _____ had a profound impact on release in its native France, as it examines the lives of young immigrants living in a notorious Parisian housing project.

2. *The Man* ___ ____'_ _____ is an unusually downbeat entry in the Coen brothers' canon.

4. Spielberg's use of the monochrome look in _____'_ _____ is reverential; it's as if he is so respectful of the ordeal that garish color seemed crass.

6. The personal study of the characters and particularly movies that inspired a young Tim Burton echoes the feel of the subject perfectly in __ ____.

7. Cory McAbee's avant-garde space western, *The American* _____, is a strange beast, relying heavily on monochrome photography.

8. Darren Aronofsky's surreal, Kafkaesque debut, __, follows an obsessive number theorist who may have stumbled onto an explanation of mankind's purpose on Earth.

50. WEIRD WESTERNS

Perhaps it's because the western is often considered the core cinematic form that it's been subverted so often over the years. Or perhaps it's because it provides such a good allegorical framework. Whatever the reason, there are some seriously wacky westerns out there.

ACROSS

2. *Tears of the* _____ _____. Beautiful pastel imagery abounds in this stylized and poetic minor masterpiece from first-time director Sasanatieng.

7. *Sukiyaki* _____ _____. Essentially a Japanese western with elements of samurai movies, featuring Quentin Tarantino as an elderly gunman.

9. Loosely based on Hermann Hesse's novel *Siddhartha* and starring electric guitar–wielding gunslingers, _____ unsurprisingly belongs to the subgenre known as "acid western."

10. There's nothing unusual about musical westerns. What makes *The Terror of* ____ ____unique is the exclusively dwarf cast.

DOWN

1. 7 _____ __ __. ___. When the mysterious Chinese circus master Dr. Lao arrives in the small town of Abalone, he introduces the residents to all sorts of fantastical wonders.

3. __ ____ is a legendary slice of far-out flower power craziness. A huge hit on the "Midnight Movies" circuit (thanks to John Lennon's vocal support).

4. *The* _____ has a loyal following thanks to it being the last movie to feature stop-motion dinosaur effects by the legendary Ray Harryhausen.

5. _____ __ ____ sees Elvis Costello, Grace Jones, Dennis Hopper, Courtney Love, and Jim Jarmusch rampage through this bizarre remake of 1967's *Django, Kill!*

6. In _____'_ *Palace* by Robert Downey Sr., Jesse is on his way to Jerusalem when he falls foul of gangster Seaweedhead Greaser and the world is threatened by constipation.

8. _____ ___. This Johnny Depp vehicle is, on one hand, a funny and accessible fish-out-of-water tale. On the other hand, it's a consciously postmodern existential parable infused with the poetry of William Blake.

51. MOVIES THAT'LL MAKE YOU CRY

Be warned, some of these movies go well beyond traditional melodramatic tearjerkers. When profound suffering is documented by filmmakers with exceptional ability, it can prove to be an overwhelming combination. If in doubt, stay well away.

ACROSS

1. *The Diving Bell and the* _____ is a true story of Jean-Dominique Bauby, who suffers a massive stroke that renders him unable to move. Using just his left eye, he manages to develop a system of communication.

4. __ ____ ___ is the true story of Christy Brown, the Irish artist who was born with a form of cerebral palsy. Daniel Day-Lewis won his first Academy Award for this movie.

6. Destined to become Great Prince of the Forest, _____, about a good-natured fawn, is Disney's classic tearjerker.

7. In _____, we are drawn into the tragic love affair between working-class Jack Dawson and upper-crust Rose DeWitt Bukater.

8. Widely criticized for being emotionally manipulative and overly sentimental, ____ _____ follows Jenny and Oliver, a young couple in the throes of true love, until they discover Jenny is terminally ill.

10. Farm boy Travis Coates reluctantly adopts a yellow-coated mongrel stray that saves the family from various threats. But after ___ _____ is bitten by a rabid wolf, the family faces a heartbreaking dilemma.

DOWN

2. ____ __ _____ is the story of a father trying to make life in a World War II concentration camp bearable for his young son.

3. Nicolò (Cary Grant) and Terry (Deborah Kerr) meet and almost instantly fall in love but are already in relationships in *An* _____ __ _____.

5. A young boy in a small Italian town is enchanted by the cinema and forms a close friendship with the local projectionist. Grown up and a successful filmmaker, he returns to the town in _____ _____.

9. In *Grave of the* _____, an abandoned brother and sister struggle to survive during World War II in the firebombed remnants of the city.

52. HENCHMEN

If James Bond movies have taught us nothing else, it's that every memorable villain needs an equally engaging henchman. Someone to do the dirty work . . . and be killed by the hero in the middle of the third act.

ACROSS

2. Gary Busey played the unforgettable, and slightly crazy, __. _____, whose final showdown with Mel Gibson's Riggs is among the most exciting fight scenes of the era.

3. If you are of a certain age, __. ____ is likely seared into your consciousness. He channels something genuinely unnerving in *Innerspace*.

6. The result of an attempt to clone Austin Powers's nemesis, Dr. Evil, and despite being under 3 feet tall, ____-__ got Britney Spears's phone number.

8. Any number of the henchmen to have faced off against James Bond could have made this puzzle. But ____ ____ is the most intriguing thanks to his undoubted intelligence and a penchant for manipulating even his boss.

9. Although ____ ____'s part is small, it's memorable. When Lee Van Cleef's Colonel Mortimer strikes a match on the hunchback's hump, a tense round of one-upmanship ensues.

DOWN

1. _____ _____ is instrumental in the plans of corrupt corporation president Dick Jones (Ronny Cox) in *Robocop*.

4. Originally meant to be more humanlike, budget constraints led to the _____'_ bizarre look. In spite, or perhaps because, of their appearance, they proved hugely successful with fans in *Despicable Me*.

5. In *North by Northwest*, Martin Landau plays _____, who works for James Mason and is unforgettably charged with killing Cary Grant.

7. Henchman to Ming the Merciless, expert in brainwashing, genius intelligence, and a fondness for torture: _____ had it all.

10. Making his second appearance as a henchman, this time as memorable mohican-sporting biker punk ___, Vernon Wells lights up the screen as he brings all kinds of crazy to *Mad Max 2*.

53. COMING-OF-AGE MOVIES

Offering a guide through the impenetrable jungle of adolescence, coming-of-age movies can be a valuable touchstone for young teens. As a result, they can become emotionally charged and take a special place in our hearts, with a lifelong sentimental power over us.

ACROSS

2. Often cited as an inspiration for the hit sitcom *Happy Days*, _____ _____ is George Lucas's sentimentalized account of teen life in early 1960s small-town California.

5. A dying Texas town is the setting for *The Last _____ ____*. Centered around a pool hall and cinema, a group of young friends try to enjoy their last summer of adolescence.

7. _____ ____, a moody, monochrome look at the troubled lives of a gang of street thugs, gave opportunities to Matt Dillon and Mickey Rourke.

10. During the summer of 1987, college grad James Brennan (Jesse Eisenberg) is forced to work at a rundown theme park, _____, in order to raise money for school.

DOWN

1. Starring James Dean as Jim Stark, *Rebel _____ _ _____* is as pertinent now as it was in 1955.

3. Once in a while a coming-of-age movie comes along that defines an epoch, which is probably the case with this tale of ____ (Elliot Page) and Paulie (Michael Cera), who must deal with an accidental pregnancy.

4. Among the most controversial coming-of-age movies, ____' naturalistic depiction of sexually active drug-using teens caused a furor on release.

6. Two girls feel trapped by the Swedish town in which they live in ____ __ ____. They fall into a relationship and find they're stronger together.

8. In 1959, four 12-year-old friends set off on foot to find a dead body rumored to be nearby in _____ __ __. On their journey they are nearly killed more than once and face particular challenges from local bullies.

9. *The Squid and the _____*. Two parents subject their sons to hypocritical pseudo-philosophy as a means of helping them deal with their divorce.

54. ANIMATED CHARACTERS

With nothing but imagination to limit their appearance and portrayal, many animated characters have inevitably become among the most memorable and enjoyable committed to screen.

ACROSS

6. One of Disney's most memorable characters and certainly greatest villains. _____ __ ____'s desire to butcher dozens of puppies for their skins is a remarkably dark plot.

7. Born with strange cryokinetic powers that enable her to produce ice and snow, Princess ____ has seen *Frozen* spawn a series of successful sequels.

9. _____, the gentle forest spirit (and mascot of legendary Japanese animation house Studio Ghibli), helps and inspires two young sisters.

10. Everyone's favorite breezy bear, _____, is a lesson in characterization. Instantly likable, and with an endearing instinct to protect young Mowgli.

DOWN

1. ____ _____, Space Ranger was designed as a contrast and modern equivalent to Woody the cowboy. The chemistry the two share became the basis of the film series's phenomenal success.

2. Described as one of the most influential people of the last quarter century, the epitome of American humor and everything that's good about TV, _____ _____ was first seen on *The Tracey Ullman Show*.

3. ____ _____, a.k.a. the Pumpkin King of Halloween Town in *The Nightmare Before Christmas*, is not a bad guy, he just needs his enthusiasm for Halloween back.

4. Much of this foil-wielding feline's appeal lies in Antonio Banderas's excellent voice work, which reveals ____ __ _____ as a cocky but lovable matador type.

5. In post-apocalypse Tokyo, _____ leads a biker gang that gets tangled up in a government conspiracy.

8. Clearly the brains in this human–dog relationship, _____ shares his master's love of cheese.

55. KISSES

Special mention should be made of *Cinema Paradiso* (1988). With the local church demanding the eradication of all kisses from movies played at the town theater, the projectionist spends years editing together each excised embrace. When the compilation is finally run—in one of the most moving scenes in cinema—we're presented with a blizzard of unadulterated passion.

ACROSS

1. "Is it still raining? I hadn't noticed." Whether _____ and _____ kissing is the scene of a romantic swept up in an amorous clinch, or an irritatingly banal stereotype getting wet, is up to the viewer.

5. Baz Luhrmann's spirited Shakespeare tribute features a young couple, _____ and _____, of such celestial perfection it almost seems wrong for them to kiss.

8. In Disney's ____ *and the* _____, the image of the two main characters eating spaghetti and, unwittingly, locking lips over a shared strand has become shorthand for romantic attraction.

9. Murray, ___, surprising Johanssen, _____, with a kiss, is a surprise deliberately saved for the final take of *Lost in Translation*.

DOWN

1. A misunderstanding over what a young girl saw leads to a lifetime of misery as _____ (Keira Knightley) and _____ (James McAvoy) kiss.

2. In *Guess Who's Coming to Dinner*, the fact it addressed the issue of race so acutely, make this a powerful moment when ____ and ____ kiss.

3. After spending the whole film sparring with one another, _____ and ____ finally embrace . . . but only after they've found her cat.

4. Leaving to take part in the Civil War, _____ doesn't think he'll be back. _____ is furious because she shares his concern, making the kiss they also share so poignant.

6. When sheepherders _____ and ____ finally meet up again after years apart, the passion is palpable and the kiss intense.

7. This perennial tale of forbidden dancing, and even more forbidden love, crackles with _____ and ____'s chemistry.

56. HAMMER HORROR

This small British production house had varying success producing a range of traditional fare from the mid 1930s into the late 1950s. But it was a string of sci-fi and horror hits starting with *The Quatermass Xperiment* in 1955 that steered it in the direction for which it will be forever remembered.

ACROSS

2.   The *Curse of* _____ was Hammer's first big horror hit. It departs from the Universal series in terms of the use of color.

3.   Although not well received at the time, _____ _____ (1972) is now widely recognized as a successful attempt to breathe new life into the horror genre.

5.   *The Plague of the* _____. An outbreak of strange creatures is causing problems in a Cornish village, could it be something to do with the local squire's recent trip to Haiti?

6.   The third and final installment in the series of movies (there was also a TV series), _____ *and the Pit* sees an alien spacecraft unearthed during work on London's tube network.

9.   *Dr. Jekyll and* _____ ____. You can tell the movies that came toward the end of Hammer's most successful period by their increasingly wacky concepts. The title says it all, frankly.

10.   Bette Davis stars as the psychopathic _____ to a troubled 10-year-old boy.

DOWN

1.   In *The* _____ _____ ___, friends Duc de Richleau (Christopher Lee) and Rex Van Ryn (Leon Greene) become embroiled in a Satanic cult.

4.   *The* _____ _____ was made just as Hammer was finding its feet with monster movies. It's small on monsters, but that's no bad thing when you have Peter Cushing to play with.

7.   *Curse of the* _____. A young Oliver Reed stars as the titular lupine aggressor in this notably severe take on the myth.

8.   *Horror of* _____. Hammer's first stab at the Transylvanian count is a masterpiece of the horror genre in which Christopher Lee excels.

57. ESSENTIAL DOCUMENTARIES

The very best documentaries should highlight some kind of hidden truth, not necessarily in their subject, but perhaps in ourselves. In fact, at this level the subject is largely unimportant, the wider implications of the movie's study being key.

ACROSS

1. ____ __ ____ documents French high-wire artist Philippe Petit's feat in 1974 to walk a rope between the twin towers of New York's World Trade Center.

4. America's first openly gay elected political representative, and the story of his tragic murder, is the subject of this fascinating study, *The Times of* _____ ____.

5. *The* _____ *and the* ____, an account of France's collaboration with Nazi Germany during World War II, is unlikely to be an easy watch for anyone.

7. A peek behind the curtain at a Californian pet cemetery, _____ __ _____ is the perfect example of why the subject doesn't matter when a gifted documentarian stumbles on characters like these.

8. Found guilty of creating "propaganda against the regime," filmmaker Jafar Panahi is under house arrest awaiting news on an appeal. While there, he cleverly sidesteps a ban on filmmaking to make *This Is* ___ _ ____.

10. *The* ____ ____ ____ is an investigation into the killing of a Dallas police officer and resulted in the killer being completely exonerated.

DOWN

2. In *The* _____, the spotlight is shone on the work of three "reformed thugs charged with defusing tension in violent inner-city communities."

3. Winner of the 2007 Academy Award for Documentary Feature, *Taxi to the* ____ ____, Gibney's examination of the United States' policy on torture, is a sobering experience.

6. Eminent documentarian Barbara Kopple is on comfortable ground with _____ _____ *U.S.A.*, a look at the 1973 "Brookside Strike."

9. Still cited as an inspiration to bands like Metallica, this film is a touching tribute to Canadian rockers _____, who never made it in the music charts.

58. MOVIES ABOUT MORTALITY

Movies have long been a means of addressing the elephant in the room, that ticking clock that we know will slowly wind down and mandate our eventual death. Movies that look at how we deal with this inevitability can offer profound insights into the value of life, and suggestions for what we might do with it.

ACROSS

3. Recently retired insurance actuary Warren Schmidt (Jack Nicholson) sets off on a road trip with the aim of stopping his daughter marrying the fiancé he deems unsuitable in _____ _____.

6. *The* ___ _____. Quadriplegic Ramón Sampedro (Javier Bardem) campaigns for euthanasia to be legalized in his native Spain.

8. Will Smith is Tim Thomas, an engineer so grief-stricken after causing the deaths of seven people, he literally dedicates his life to saving seven others in _____ _____.

9. While making the long journey to an awards ceremony in his honor, cantankerous Professor Isak Borg (Victor Sjöström) starts to reminisce on his life in ____ *Strawberries*.

10. In *A Matter of* ____ ___ _____, Heaven has cocked up the paperwork when Squadron Leader Peter Carter's (David Niven) Lancaster bomber goes down, and Carter is given another chance at life.

DOWN

1. When his long-estranged brother Lyle (Harry Dean Stanton) suffers a stroke, elderly Alvin Straight (Richard Farnsworth) drives his mower 240 miles to see him in *The* _____ _____.

2. In _____ *Story*, a retired couple from rural southwest Japan visit their adult son and daughter in bustling Tokyo.

4. Monty Python's final movie, *The* _____ ___ ____, is a series of amusing sketches tied together by the themes of life and death.

5. *The* _____ ____. Returning from the Crusades, a Swedish knight encounters Death and challenges him to a game of chess.

7. After being diagnosed with cancer, a middle-aged bureaucrat sets out to build a park for local children in the Japanese movie _____.

59. WORST VIDEO GAME ADAPTATIONS

Without wanting to wallow in negativity, it's no small wonder movies adapted from video games have such a bad reputation. It's even debatable whether a first-class movie has ever resulted from a game. But in a sea of subpar cinema, there are some that plumb particularly bewildering depths.

ACROSS

2. What was once a video game with niche appeal became a movie with no appeal when *Wing* _____ swooped onto the big screen.

5. _____ _____ *Bros.* features Bob Hoskins and John Leguizamo as Brooklyn plumbers who must rescue Princess Daisy from evil King Koopa.

8. *Mortal Kombat:* _____ manages to drop all the balls its predecessor, *Mortal Kombat,* just about managed to keep in the air.

9. Based on a title that even non-gamers might have affectionate memories of, _____ _____ is a martial arts movie that is aimed squarely at the kids. That won't help your enjoyment of it, regardless of age.

DOWN

1. ____ _____ is a New York detective investigating the murder of his wife and child. The movie is a confused mess of police-procedural-meets-revenge-fantasy-with-elements-of-film-noir-and-supernatural tones.

3. _____. Uwe Boll churns out nonsense like this 2005 period-vampire fiasco every few months.

4. Coming along years after the ____ craze had passed, the movie of the classic first-person shooter missed the boat in terms of finding its audience.

5. _____ _____. At the time, this garish calamity became a byword for overblown, star-driven disasters. Unable to tap into the martial arts or video games market, it's now almost disappeared from memory.

6. *Alone* __ ___ ____ (2005) sees a paranormal detective searching for a murderer, and possibly marks the apex of Boll's diabolical filmography.

7. With both the game and lead actress boasting megastar credentials, it's no surprise that *Lara Croft:* ____ _____ was a hit. Despite this, it's a first-degree stinker with a leaden script, clichéd action, and ridiculous plot.

60. TOUGH GUYS

A classic movie tough guy needs to be more than just capable of winning a fight. Technical skill and canny strategizing are not what it's about (hence no Bruce Lee). But a tough guy must have an imposing presence, be able to take anything you throw at him, and possess a steely determination in confrontational situations.

ACROSS

4. Lee Marvin as _____ shows he can keep order among one of the most deplorable groups of reprobates ever assembled in the *Dirty Dozen*.

7. Chuck Norris might be the only actor in history who would stand a chance against the fictional names on this list. The all-American Uzi-wielding _____ _____ is possibly his toughest character.

10. It's hard to pick the toughest character the Duke has played, but you definitely wouldn't want to mess with _____ _____ in *Red River*.

DOWN

1. In *The Magnificent Seven*, most sign up to protect a Mexican village from bandits because they need the money; James Coburn's _____ does so because he fancies a fight.

2. Danny Trejo spent the last 40 years largely playing Hollywood villains, but ironically found his greatest success as the heroic _____, a socially conscious Mexican outlaw.

3. Clint Eastwood plays orangutan-owning _____ _____, a truck driver who makes money on the side in bare-knuckle brawls.

5. After an injury puts paid to his football career, ___ "_____" _____ turns to bounty hunting for a living until a hit is put out on his life.

6. _____ _____ demonstrates in *Death Wish* how almost anyone can be a tough guy when inner rage overcomes physical limitations.

8. Bolo Yeung was the go-to guy if a production needed an intimidating Asian villain, though it was his heroic role as _____ ___, a Chinese Hercules, that gave him his signature character.

9. _____ has been around since the 1930s in various books, TV shows, and comics. But it's Schwarzenegger's muscle-bound iteration of the sword and sorcery poster boy that personifies the character for most.

61. MACGUFFINS

"Macguffin" is a term popularized by Alfred Hitchcock and used to describe any plot device, such as an object, a person, or a piece of information, that is desired by the movie's protagonists. It might be a briefcase full of money being sought by both police and criminals. Or it could be plans for a weapon being fought over by rival agents; it doesn't really matter.

ACROSS

2. In *Repo Man*, Los Angeles repossession companies compete to locate and recover a 1964 _____ _____, driven by a mysterious man.

8. The _____ _____ is a combination machine and chemical process that reorganizes matter on a planetary scale in *Star Trek II*.

10. The treacherous ___ ____, formed by the dark Lord Sauron to gain dominion over the free peoples of Middle-earth, is sought by many.

DOWN

1. As war looms in Europe, the balance of power could depend on who gets hold of the _____ _____, in Hitchcock's *The 39 Steps*.

3. Monty Python's take on the legend involving recovering the ____ _____, the chalice into which Christ bled, is every bit as preposterous as you'd expect.

4. With Hitler instructing his agents around the world to round up every important artifact they can find, the race is on to discover the location of the ___ __ ___ _____, which stores the Ten Commandments.

5. With the rich environment Tarantino creates, it's easy to forget what actually drives the plot. But whatever is in crime boss Marcellus Wallace's _____, it must be very important.

6. In the 16th century, the Maltese Knights Templar gifted Charles V of Spain a priceless gold statue of an eagle, the _____ _____. Four hundred years later, San Francisco crooks are killing to get their hands on it.

7. When the ride to his new job is stolen, Antonio (Lamberto Maggiorani) searches high and low for it with increasing desperation in _____ *Thieves* (1948).

9. Private Eye Mike Hammer is one of many parties chasing a valuable and dangerous ___. All we know for sure is that it can kill and nobody connected with it can be trusted.

62. CAR CHASES

With so many great movie car chases to choose from, and two or three so comprehensively dominating the landscape, there was need for some brutal culling here.

ACROSS

2. The complicated chase in __ ____ ___ ___ *in LA* was made more difficult to film by virtue of it taking place against oncoming traffic.

5. The mysterious Frank (Jason Statham) demonstrates his incredible skills behind the wheel when he acts as getaway driver for three bank robbers in *The _____*.

7. Former race car driver Kowalski makes a bet that he can drive from Denver to San Francisco by 3 p.m. the following day in _____ _____ (1971).

8. *In Tomorrow _____ ____*, James Bond (Pierce Brosnan) is under fire from evil media tycoon Elliot Carver's (Jonathan Pryce) goons and uses the car's remote control to evade capture.

9. Out for revenge on crime boss Herman Reyes, street-racing bandits Dom (Vin Diesel) and Brian (Paul Walker) tear through the streets of Rio dragging a safe containing much of his cash in ____ ____.

10. In *The Bourne _____*, nods to *The Italian Job* are inevitable as Bourne careers around Zürich in a Mini Mayfair.

DOWN

1. Professional car thief Vicinski Pace has just one car left to steal in order to meet a highly profitable order in *Gone in 60 _____*.

3. Trinity and Morpheus bend metal, and the laws of physics, trying to escape from Agents in *The _____ _____*.

4. With long, unbroken shots and the camera mounted low on the car, we feel as if we're on board as it screams around the twisty roads of the south of France in _____ (1998).

6. Tarantino pays homage to the 1970s exploitation movies he loves with this retro chase in _____ _____.

63. MUSICALS FOR PEOPLE WHO DON'T LIKE MUSICALS

While it seems inconceivable anyone could not love musicals, rumor has it such people are out there somewhere. This puzzle is designed to bring them around slowly. Each one is a bona fide musical, but is generally free from much of the genre's cliché and cumbersome pageantry.

ACROSS

2. _____ _____: *Bigger, Longer & Uncut.* The foul-mouthed kids found success on the big screen with their maiden musical outing.

6. Songs like "The Candy Man Can" and "Pure Imagination" helped _____ _____ *& the Chocolate Factory* to an Academy Award nomination.

7. _____ _____. Musical styles are mashed together remorselessly in this chaotic explosion of color and sound featuring Nicole Kidman and Ewan McGregor.

8. _____, The Who's take on the musical, follows the mixed fortunes of a deaf, mute, and blind kid who happens to be a pinball wizard.

9. *Everyone Says* _ _____ _____ is one of Woody Allen's usual tales of men and women falling in and out of love, this time with Paris and, of course, music.

10. _____ is a touching tale of an unnamed Irish busker (Glen Hansard) who falls in love with an also unnamed immigrant (Markéta Irglová).

DOWN

1. On a mission from God to raise money for the orphanage in which they grew up, Jake and Elwood Blues (John Belushi and Dan Aykroyd) go on a musical odyssey in *The _____ _____.*

3. The musical is just one of many genres *The _____ _____ Picture Show* can claim to belong to. But, with songs like "Sweet Transvestite" and "Planet Schmanet Janet," it's a musical like no other.

4. Based loosely on the Beatles song written by Lennon and McCartney, _____ _____ details the Fab Four's mission to rid Pepperland of Blue Meanies.

5. In *The Happiness of the _____,* the owners of a quiet hotel in rural Japan face a quandary when their only guest dies.

64. MEMORABLE DEATHS

How important a character is, and whether their death is significant, are not factors relevant to this puzzle. Funny, horrific, profound, or unexpected, all that matters is that the character met an unforgettable end.

ACROSS

6. Having been attacked by an alien life-form that impregnated him, _____ is sitting down to his first meal for days when he goes into "labor."

7. Using the unusual method of painting the entire body gold so it can't breathe, _____ _____ is murdered for her indiscretion with Bond.

9. Holed up in a farmhouse trying to avoid the zombie apocalypse, ___'s cool head and quick thinking sees him survive the night. Until a mob of locals mistake him for one in *Night of the Living Dead* (1968).

DOWN

1. After living on borrowed time just a little too long, _____ ___ _____ (Paul Newman and Robert Redford) are cornered by the Bolivian army.

2. Following a meal fit for several kings, the grotesquely obese __. _____ declines the meal's denouement: a wafer-thin mint.

3. Although it's not clear why _____ _____ doesn't clamber onto the same piece of floating debris that saves Rose (Kate Winslet), his death by drowning in icy waters is no less poignant as a result.

4. You know there's something odd about the framing of the shot as Samuel L. Jackson's executive, _____ _____, stands by an access port in an underwater research station.

5. Atop a high balcony that opens up onto his tasteless mansion, _____ _____ sprays an invading mercenary army with bullets.

8. Intending to merely demonstrate his telepathic capability to assembled guests, this unnamed "_____" is unwittingly engaged in a psychic battle with the far stronger Darryl Revok (Michael Ironside).

10. Shot by a rival officer, we last see Sgt. _____ on his knees, arms aloft, as the Viet Cong approach from all sides.

65. TIME TRAVEL MOVIES

With literally endless possibilities, and no two movies agreeing on how the law of causality is affected by it, there is a plethora of opportunities for movies to explore time travel. As a result, there's a bit of everything here.

ACROSS

4. In ___ _____, Godefroy de Papincourt (Jean Reno) is a medieval knight accidentally sent over 800 years into the future by an incompetent sorcerer.

8. _____'s inventive premise has criminals in the future sending assassins back through time to be disposed of.

9. Dwarves steal a map from the Supreme Being and use it to find hidden passageways through time in order to steal treasure in the ____ _____.

10. Four computer scientists stumble onto the means to travel through time in _____ (2004).

DOWN

1. In *Army of _____*, our hero Ash (Bruce Campbell) is sucked through a vortex and dumped into the Dark Ages with nothing but a chainsaw, a shotgun, and a 1973 Oldsmobile Delta 88.

2. James Cole (Bruce Willis), a convicted criminal, is sent back through time to learn about a virus that wiped out 99 percent of Earth's population and forced the survivors underground in _____ _____.

3. Kurt Vonnegut's surreal antiwar novel *Slaughterhouse-____* was adapted, to the author's great satisfaction, in 1972.

5. Three friends return to a favored old haunt for a night of drinking. But, wouldn't you know it, their hot tub malfunctions and takes them back in time in *Hot Tub ____ _____*.

6. In ____ ___ ___'s *Excellent Adventure*, when two moronic high-school kids look set to fail history, a time traveler from the future takes them to witness some of history's key moments.

7. A future war between man and machine spills over into 1984 when a ruthless android is sent back through time to kill the mother of a freedom fighter in *The _____*.

66. SAMURAI MOVIES

Samurai movies (known in Japan as *chanbara*, an onomatopoeic reference to the sound of clashing swords) were, and to an extent remain, hugely popular in Japan. *Chanbara* play a similar role within Japanese culture as the Western does in the United States, with both likely to investigate themes of honor, revenge, responsibility, and loyalty.

ACROSS

2. _____ (1962) is a simple story about a young ronin obliged to commit seppuku (suicide by self-disembowelment).

4. A modern take on the classic Japanese legend of the blind swordsman, _____ finds director/writer/producer/star Kitano in playful mood.

7. *Samurai* _____. Two of chanbara's biggest stars (Mifune and Tatsuya Nakadai) share the screen in this touching tale about a local daimyo (lord) ordering the son of one of his samurais to turn over his wife to him.

10. In *The _____ __ ____*, Ryu Tsukue is a villainous samurai of extraordinary ability who rejects Bushido, provoking his descent into madness.

DOWN

1. Chan-wook Park's vengeance trilogy, ____ _____ is the stylish tale of a now-adult woman conceived and born purely to seek revenge.

3. *The _____ Samurai* (2002). Director Yôji Yamada might think he was born into the wrong age: his samurai movies belong to the 1960s heyday.

5. Footage from this first entry in the legendary *Lone Wolf and Cub* series, *Sword of _____*, was cut together with the second and released as *Shogun Assassin* (1980).

6. In *13 _____*, Takashi Miike's most critically praised recent offering, political machinations lead to a strike force of top samurai being gathered together to assassinate the sadistic half-brother of the shogun.

8. After *Seven Samurai*, _____ is probably the best, and best known, of master filmmaker Akira Kurosawa's chanbara.

9. When a ruthless clan master kills a village of peasants in order to cover up his theft of a shipment of gold, one of his samurai is determined to see him pay in _____.

67. GANGSTERS

The screen gangster may have evolved since the likes of Paul Muni and James Cagney ruled the roost with flashy, stylish performances. But even as they have become generally more believable, and even vulnerable, the gangster's ultimate appeal has remained undimmed.

ACROSS

4.   ___ _____ is the main antagonist in *Once Upon a Time in America*, an epic, sweeping take on the rise of organized crime in New York.

6.   In rapper Ice Cube's first film role, low-level hood _____ saunters around with a bottle of booze in one pocket and a gun in the other.

7.   Set in a French prison, *A Prophet* follows young Algerian _____ __ _____ as he becomes embroiled in a gang, and then ascends through the ranks.

9.   ___ _'_____ is the head of an Irish-American mob organization in Prohibition-era America. But his judgment is starting to slip, and he ends up in a needless turf war in *Miller's Crossing*.

10.   Martin Scorsese's remake of the Chinese thriller *Infernal Affairs* (2002) beefs up the role of the top gangster somewhat, but that's only sensible when you've bagged Jack Nicholson for the role of _____ _____.

DOWN

1.   Successful London gangster _____ _____ (Bob Hoskins) is trying to legitimize his business interests. On the brink of securing major overseas investment, a series of bombings and murders seem to target his empire.

2.   Joe Pesci's second collaboration with Martin Scorsese (after *Raging Bull*) sees him in his defining role, the doomed mafioso _____ _____.

3.   Rico a.k.a. _____ _____ (Edward G. Robinson) is a small-fry gangster who moves to Chicago and sets his sights on becoming the big fish.

5.   Prolific character actor Henry Silva has played a lot of gangsters over the years—but he'd never been given the sort of chance he was in *Ghost Dog: The Way of the Samurai* as ___ _____.

8.   James Cagney was the ultimate gangster in the genre's ultimate era. Bootlegger ___ _____ rises up through the world of organized crime.

68. MILITARY MEN

Whether preparing for it, trying to avoid it, or just wanting to survive it, war is an inherently dramatic event on which to hang a story. And, like any high-stress situation, it has a habit of creating fascinating characters.

ACROSS

4. In *Dead Man's Shoes*, _____ is discharged from the British army and returns to his hometown of Matlock, Derbyshire, to learn that his younger, mentally impaired brother has been subjected to bullying by a local gang.

7. Arriving as replacement team leader of a bomb-disposal unit in Iraq, Sergeant _____ _____ soon gains a reputation for recklessness that puts his tight-knit team on edge in *The Hurt Locker*.

10. Taking charge of a demoralized American II Corps in North Africa during World War II, General _____ S. _____ soon whips them into shape.

DOWN

1. The stiff R.A.F. Captain _____ is one of the three roles played by Sellers in the black comedy *Dr. Strangelove*.

2. In the World War I trenches, _____ ___ (Kirk Douglas) commands a regiment of French troops who are handed a politically motivated suicide mission.

3. Former U.S. Marine R. L. Ermey was initially hired as a technical advisor until director Stanley Kubrick saw a tape of what he could do. He won a Golden Globe for his role as Gunnery Sergeant _____.

5. The principled Colonel _____ loses sight of what's important in a Japanese P.O.W. camp during World War II.

6. The iconic Lieutenant Colonel William _____ is a man who loves the smell of napalm in the morning.

8. Captain _____ _____ "the Cooler King" (Steve McQueen), despite being the token American in British favorite *The Great Escape*, is also the most memorable character.

9. Failed cab driver ____ _____ (Bill Murray) joins the army expecting training to be like a stay at a fitness resort in *Stripes*.

69. WOMANIZERS

In some ways it's interesting to chart the progress of women's rights through the depiction of the on-screen womanizer. While a Lothario of the 1960s and 1970s was generally complimented on his prowess, by the 1990s and beyond he is seen as an almost tragic, emotionally immature figure.

ACROSS

3. In *Boomerang*, smarmy advertising executive _____ _____ keeps a string of girlfriends on call.

6. When disc jockey ____ _____ picks up a woman in a bar, he becomes the target of her crazed obsession. She stalks him, vandalizes his house, and threatens to kill his girlfriend in *Play Misty for Me*.

7. _____ T.J. _____ is a minor celebrity in the male self-help world, selling videos and giving talks that explain "how to pick up women." Tom Cruise stepped way outside his comfort zone to play this narcissist.

8. Cockney chancer _____ (Michael Caine) sidles from relationship to relationship with little thought for the women involved.

10. Beverley Hills hairdresser _____ _____ takes full advantage of his charms and opportunities by bedding a string of clients in *Shampoo* (1975).

DOWN

1. In *School for Scoundrels*, pleasant young Henry Palfey always loses out in love to roguish cad _____—until he discovers a school that teaches seduction techniques.

2. *Black* _____. This comedic throwback to the blaxploitation movies of the 1970s features an exaggerated version of the sort of Lothario such movies tended to glorify.

4. ____, once a reasonably successful actor, and old college buddy Miles head off on a tour of California wine country prior to the former's marriage.

5. ____ _____ runs into more than he bargained for with his latest squeeze, Randy (Molly Ringwald).

9. *Fellini's* _____ is less a biopic of the legendary Italian heartbreaker than an examination of the quandaries caused by a life of unrelenting pleasure.

70. TWIST ENDINGS

To enjoy a good revelation, it's obviously vital not to be aware what it is. It's always going to be difficult to discuss a twist without exposing it, so consider this a spoiler-heavy puzzle, the details of which should be avoided by anyone who hasn't seen the movies in question.

ACROSS

3. Apparently a typical slasher movie setup (kids holidaying on an isolated island are picked off by an unseen killer) in _____ _____ ___ .

5. Domineering patriarch Noah (John Huston) and his highly strung daughter Evelyn (Faye Dunaway) share a terrible secret in _____ .

7. _____ _____'s unexpected twist only helped its appeal, as we discover that the two main characters are actually one and the same.

9. In the near future, the state rations _____ _____, an artificial foodstuff, but what is it made of?

10. Believing he is stranded on a distant planet, astronaut George Taylor (Charlton Heston) stumbles on a collapsed Statue of Liberty, and realizes he is actually on Earth but in some terrible future in *Planet of the* ____ .

DOWN

1. Fans still debate whether Kevin Spacey's unassuming conman, "Verbal" Kint, really is Keyser Soze in *The* _____ _____ .

2. In _____ , it's hard to imagine anyone isn't aware of the twist. Norman Bates's (Anthony Perkins) mother is long dead, and he isn't quite the gentle boy he seems.

4. A young family move to the _____ , where their adopted son goes missing. After spending months searching the whole country, the mother discovers a hidden door, blocked by building equipment, to a basement.

6. *Les* _____ (1955). A domineering schoolmaster is murdered when his mistress and wife take against him. When he reappears, weeks later, in a ghoulish resurrection that scares his wife to death, we learn the truth.

8. Psychological thriller *The* _____ ____, set against the backdrop of Northern Ireland's Troubles, examines a succession of weighty subjects.

71. ACTOR-DIRECTOR PARTNERSHIPS

Occasionally a director and actor capable of getting the very best from each other are lucky enough to strike up an ongoing relationship. Sometimes they share a common ethos, sometimes there's a chasm between them, and it's the conflict that produces the magic.

ACROSS

4. _____ and De Niro first worked together on 1973's *Mean Streets*. But it was *Taxi Driver* that propelled both into the higher strata of Hollywood.

6. _____ and _____ collaborated before, during, and after their relationship, on such classics as *Annie Hall, Manhattan,* and *Radio Days*.

8. Although their relationship deteriorated significantly, Alec _____ and David _____ produced magic such as *The Bridge on the River Kwai* and *Lawrence of Arabia*.

9. Setsuko ____/Yasujirô ___. The former usually played the daughter in the latter's films, often about the everyday challenges facing ordinary families in a changing Japan.

10. When _____ attended a talent competition staged by Toho, the biggest Japanese studio of the day, _____ was mesmerized. The two men would make a series of films including *Seven Samurai*.

DOWN

1. Together John _____ and John _____ forged the most identifiable screen persona in American cinema from *Stagecoach* to *The Quiet Man*.

2. Max Von Sydow and Ingmar _____ mined the bleakest depths of the human condition. Judd Apatow and Seth Rogen might be making very different movies without them.

3. Jack _____ and Billy _____ made many of Hollywood's best comedies, including *Some Like It Hot* and *The Apartment*.

5. Federico _____ cast Marcello Mastroianni in two of the most important films of the 1960s—*La Dolce Vita* and *8½*.

7. The mercurial, uncontrollable Klaus _____ and the impulsive, determined Werner _____ had one of the most explosive friendships in cinema. Each collaboration resulted in sworn testimonials they would never speak again.

72. POP SONGS IN MOVIES

Sometimes you just need to think of a movie, and a song inextricably linked to it will be stuck in your head for the rest of the day. To allow some other people a chance, Quentin Tarantino, the arch master of this phenomenon, has been excluded from the puzzle.

ACROSS

3.   In David Lynch's *Blue Velvet,* Roy Orbison's ethereal recording, "__ _____," takes on a sinister quality in the darkly oppressive atmosphere of the film.

4.   Donovan's usual folk style on "_____ _____ Man" was discarded in favor of the exotically hypnotic sound of this 1968 hit tune in David Fincher's *Zodiac.*

6.   An immediate hit in the UK, "_____ Rhapsody" initially failed to find success in America until its legendary use in *Wayne's World.*

8.   "__ __ ____" kicks in on a slow-motion glide up to the face of Harvey Keitel's Charlie. Cut to De Niro's Johnny Boy.

9.   Tom Cruise jumping on his parents' sofa in his underpants in *Risky Business* is not the most intellectually rewarding use of "___ ____ Rock & Roll" by Bob Seger, but it's certainly memorable.

DOWN

1.   *Whisper of the Heart,* a lesser-known anime from Studio Ghibli, reflects the curious love many Japanese share for the John Denver tune "____ __ ____, Country Roads."

2.   Played over the opening titles to Danny Boyle's tale of heroin addiction in late 1980s Edinburgh is the thundering sound of "____ ___ ____."

3.   "_ ___ ___ ____." If you ever travel to Punxsutawney to report on a weather forecasting rodent and get stuck in a time loop, pray this isn't the song you wake up to every morning.

5.   The image of John Cusack standing in front of his ex-girlfriend's house with a boom box above his head is unforgettable. As is the Peter Gabriel favorite "__ ____ ____" blasting over the soundtrack.

7.   It might be a bit on the nose, but the use of John Lennon's anti-war classic "_____" is unforgettable for those who have seen *The Killing Fields.*

73. MOVIES ABOUT FASHION

There have been surprisingly few dramatic movies that tackle the fashion world directly. Most successful attempts to get under its skin have used the documentary format, perhaps because the industry features real people who are just as colorful as those we invent.

ACROSS

2. Carrie Bradshaw (Sarah Jessica Parker) perseveres with her seesawing love life in this adaptation of the popular TV show ___ __ ___ ____.

4. *The* _____ _____ *of Petra von Kant* is a fictional drama about cruel and abrasive fashion designer Petra von Kant (Margit Carstensen), who falls in love with aspiring model Karin (Hanna Schygulla).

8. *Who Are You,* _____ _____? Our subject is an American supermodel being followed around Paris by a documentary crew.

9. In _____ ____, Audrey Hepburn is Jo Stockton, a bookshop clerk who inadvertently ends up in the background of a fashion photographer's shoot.

10. This biopic of model ___ Carangi marks Angelina Jolie's first lead performance as the stunning model who shot to stardom in the late 1970s but was blacklisted after cocaine and heroin problems affected her behavior.

DOWN

1. A documentary on the effort involved in producing *The* _____ *Issue*, *Vogue's* most important of the year, and focusing on Grace Coddington.

3. In *The* _____ _____ _____, a naïve girl bags her dream job as assistant to the irascible editor of a fashion magazine.

5. ____ *Before Chanel* (2009) is a biopic of the designer, starring the irrepressible Audrey Tautou.

6. _____: *The Last Emperor* (2008). The documentary covers a year in his life, including a retrospective of his work for the new show.

7. The fashion world is sent up mercilessly in this riotous spoof about the rivalry between two superficial male models. Derek _____ is at the top of the tree when newcomer Hansel MacDonald knocks him off his perch.

74. MOVIES DEALING WITH EXISTENTIALISM

Existentialism can be a tricky term to define and seems to mean different things to different people. Here it's taken to refer loosely to any attempt to make sense of our place within a seemingly meaningless universe, or perhaps a way of examining our personal experiences as individuals and how they make us what we are.

ACROSS

2.	In *The* _____ _____ (1998), a man discovers his entire life is a TV reality show.

3.	The crew of a space station orbiting the planet _____ (1972) fall prey to psychological problems.

5.	In *The* _____ _____ (1985), all but a few of mankind are wiped out when an experiment into energy sharing goes wrong.

9.	In _____ _____, Lester Burnham (Kevin Spacey) is having a midlife crisis and becomes obsessed with his teenage daughter's best friend.

10.	In _____ __ _____, a middle-aged Iranian man decides to kill himself but needs to find someone willing to bury him.

DOWN

1.	With a nuclear satellite causing widespread contamination, two men with a machine that can read brain impulses hole up in an Australian cave with other survivors in *Until the* ___ __ ___ _____ (1991).

4.	_____ _____ sees Robert Redford's directorial debut. When the oldest son of an affluent family dies, his brother, father, and mother all struggle to deal with the fallout.

6.	Existential detectives Bernard and Vivian Jaffe (Dustin Hoffman and Lily Tomlin) must solve why environmental campaigner Albert sees the same stranger three times in one day in *I Heart* _____.

7.	In *Au hasard* _____ (1966), farm girl Marie (Anne Wiazemsky) and her donkey lead comparable lives—both are exploited and abused.

8.	*Being John* _____ (1999). Puppeteer Craig Schwartz (John Cusack) discovers a portal straight into the mind of the actor.

75. GREEDY DEVILS

Avarice is a concept central to more movies than might immediately come to mind. But although greed might be the catalyst for most plots involving crime, a movie won't make this puzzle unless it specifically addresses the subject of greed.

ACROSS

4. Sergio Leone's epic western offers three men's distinct approaches to money. "Blondie" is good, "Angel Eyes" is bad, and _____ is ugly.

5. *The Wolf of Wall Street* is the true story of Long Island stockbroker _____ _____, who swindled millions out of investors in a securities scam.

6. *There Will Be Blood* tells the story of an oilman interested in nothing but money. Daniel _____ symbolizes the dark side of the pioneer spirit.

7. In the all-star caper movie *It's a Mad Mad Mad Mad World,* dying bank robber _____ _____ reveals the location of his spoils to four passing motorists, and the scramble to find the loot begins.

9. In the late 16th century, civil war is raging and the army of cruel lord Shibata is marauding, so there are too many deadly perils for Japanese villagers _____ and _____ to become preoccupied with greed.

DOWN

1. In *A Christmas Carol,* the wonderful Alastair Sim plays the seasonal grouch _____, who learns the perils of greed on a snowy Christmas Eve.

2. In *Trading Places,* Randolph and Mortimer a.k.a. "___ ____" make a bet as to whether a tramp could perform as well as their managing director, Winthorpe, if given the same opportunity.

3. _____ _____ is the character who, more than any other, has come to represent the cancerous greed of amoral stockbrokers, with his motto, "greed is good."

8. In *The Treasure of the Sierra Madre,* three Americans strike gold. One of them, _____, is so busy worrying about the threat his colleagues pose that he doesn't notice his own paranoia and greed.

10. _____ buys a winning lottery ticket and becomes so obsessed with money that she prefers to live in poverty than spend any.

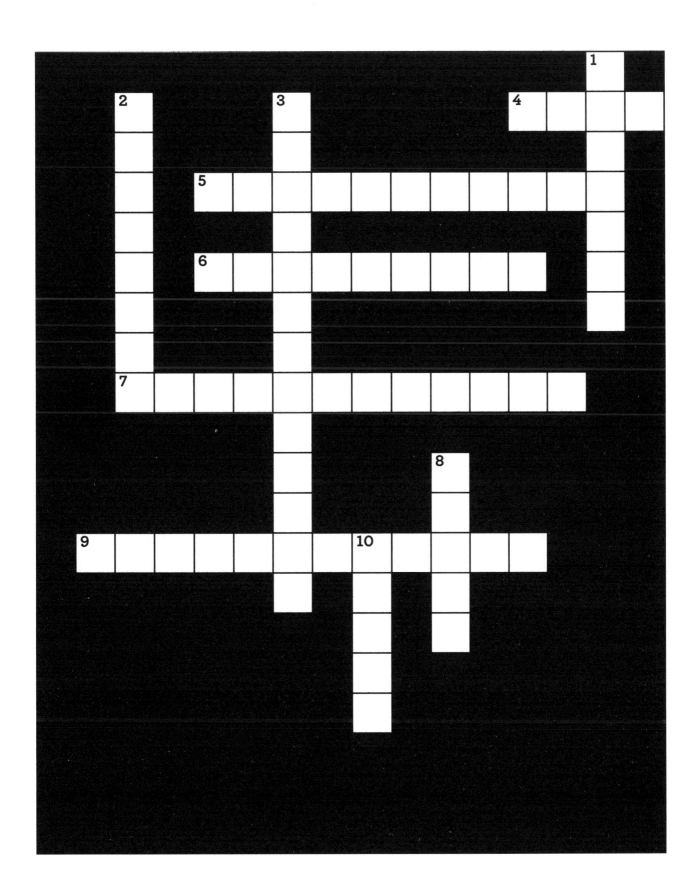

76. COUPLES

Not all the couples here have enjoyed a classic love story. But each is uplifting in its own way and inspiring to one degree or another, a reflection of the power cinema has to involve us in the emotions of two fictional people enjoying a fictional relationship.

ACROSS

2. Across three films and 18 years, director Richard Linklater created two characters, _____ and _____. In the first film, *Before Sunrise*, they meet and spend a romantically charged night in Vienna.

3. *West Side Story* is a thinly disguised take on *Romeo and Juliet*, with New York gangs replacing the feuding Veronese families, and ____ and ____ as the tragic lovers.

4. _____ Butler, a wealthy older bachelor, overhears _____ O'Hara express her love to Ashley.

8. The doctor, ____, and housewife, ____, meet by chance at a railway station and develop an instant attraction. Although both are married, they continue to see each other, leading to nothing but heartache.

9. Can a man and a woman be friends without sex getting in the way? _____ (Billy Crystal) and _____ (Meg Ryan) spend years researching the answer.

10. Every generation needs its iconic young couple who face terrible challenges to their love. A recent pair are _____ Swann and _____ Cullen, who just happens to be a vampire.

DOWN

1. An industrialist trying to force the Sycamore family from their home sees his son ____ (James Stewart) fall in love with their daughter _____ (Jean Arthur).

5. _____, from a family of proud Greeks living in Chicago, falls in love with ____, a non-Greek she knows her father will not accept.

6. Mike Leigh's *Another Year* follows middle-aged couple ____ and _____ Hepple over the course of a year.

7. _____ is a teenager obsessed with death. _____ is a 79-year-old who is preoccupied with enjoying life. Theirs is an unusual but delightful romance.

77. CONTROVERSIAL MOVIES

Given that moral standards differ significantly throughout the world, it's intriguing how a handful of movies have managed to create almost universal international controversy.

ACROSS

3. Refused a home video release in the UK until 1999, The _____ caused much upset with its head-spinning, foul-mouthed little girl.

7. Even on release, _____ __ _ _____ was considered morally reprehensible, with its actors in blackface playing African Americans as ignorant and aggressive, while the Ku Klux Klan are presented as heroes.

9. ____, or *The 120 Days of Sodom,* is a uniquely depraved arduous watch, focusing on the debauched antics of four powerful fascist libertines in World War II-era Italy.

10. _____ of the Will, covering the 1934 Nuremberg rally, is respected by filmmakers, but at the same time its politics is universally despised.

DOWN

1. Among the nastiest of obnoxious horror movies to come out of Italy in the period, _____ *Holocaust* managed to upset just about everybody.

2. Controversy swept the world over the final scene of *The_____ _____ of Christ,* in which Christ descends from the cross, marries Mary Magdalene, and lives a mortal life.

4. The Passion Play is central to the faith of many Christian denominations, yet Mel Gibson's movie version, *The_____ of the Christ,* provoked accusations of anti-Semitism, despite its massive success in the United States.

5. At the heart of the controversy over _____ __ _____ was the perception that Christ himself was being mocked by the Monty Python team.

6. ____ _____ *in Paris.* At the time, it was unheard of for major stars to appear in a movie so sexually explicit, but that one should be involved in the now-infamous "butter scene" was unthinkable.

8. Lars von Trier uses a horror movie to inflict as much unpleasantness on the audience as possible in _____ (2009).

78. BARS IN MOVIES

A hotbed of illicit activity, the place where lovers meet, the scene of raucous partying, a hangout for reprobate degenerates—movie bars have seen it all. Whether you'd like to actually drink in any of these gin joints is a matter of personal preference.

ACROSS

3. In *A Clockwork Orange*, the _____ eschews traditional beverages in favor of milk laced with drugs. It also attracts quite a cross-section of society.

4. In the only movie Eddie Murphy made with his hero Richard Pryor, the two men play a father and (adopted) son running a speakeasy and gambling joint, ____ _____ ___, in Prohibition-era New York.

6. With the most cryptic of staff and a clientele of waltzing ghosts in the Overlook Hotel, the ____ ____ will not be for everyone.

8. Believe it or not, the real _____ ____ is pretty much the same as the movie version. Half-naked women dance on the bar, sing, and do anything they can think of to get patrons to part with their cash.

9. In 2084, ___ ____ _____ is an underground bar in Mars's red-light district. It doubles as a front for revolutionaries seeking to overthrow the cruel governor, Vilos Cohaagen.

10. _____'_ is a typical old west saloon with a particularly unpalatable proprietor in *The Unforgiven*.

DOWN

1. ___ _____ Cantina, a disreputable bar at the center of "the most wretched hive of scum and villainy," has interesting customers, freedom from droids, and regular outbursts of theatrical violence.

2. On Pleasure Island, naughty children can do whatever they want at the ____ ____ (this was 1940). Just don't make a jackass of yourself.

5. The ____ _____ seems a particularly welcoming place. But the gay bar is full of mustachioed, leather-clad clichés, so if you're a macho police cadet it might not be quite up your street.

7. Classier than anything we'd know today, ____'_ ____ Americain featured a piano bar and casino where a tuxedoed Humphrey Bogart kept order.

79. DYSTOPIAN FUTURES

A dystopia is essentially any society in which we wouldn't want to live. Usually that means it's governed by some sort of oppressive, totalitarian regime. Or perhaps it has witnessed a nuclear holocaust or been decimated in some other terrible fashion. But a society that is outwardly pleasant but inwardly devoid of art, humor, personal freedom, etc. can be just as much a dystopia.

ACROSS

2. _____'s dystopia is a world in which all humans are unavoidably divided into five factions based on certain human virtues.

3. With society hanging by a thread after oil supplies run out, the wife and son of ___ ___ (Mel Gibson), a tough but disillusioned cop, are murdered by marauding bikers and he seeks vengeance.

4. The life of a low-level bureaucrat spirals out of control when he tries to correct a simple error. Terry Gilliam's _____ has one of most fantastically idiosyncratic futures the movies have yet to depict.

5. The ingenious idea that drives _____ supposes a world 500 years in the future in which human life has intellectually regressed, so when an average Joe frozen in 2006 wakes up, he finds himself a genius.

7. _____ (1927) is the movie that has surely influenced this subgenre more than any other.

8. In author Ray Bradbury's future, Guy Montag (Oskar Werner) is a firefighter tasked with burning every book. Inevitably, he starts to glance at them and wonders if he's doing the right thing in _____ _451_.

9. _ ___ ___ ___ ___ sees Vic (Don Johnson) communicate telepathically with his dog Blood (Tim McIntire) as he searches for food in the wasteland.

DOWN

1. Clearly inspired by _Blade Runner_, _____'s future Tokyo is a beautifully ugly battleground seemingly populated by rival biker gangs.

2. Convicted of a crime for which he's innocent and placed in cryogenic status, John Spartan (Sylvester Stallone) is thawed out to save the future from a threat of the past in _____ ___.

6. _____ _____ is an immersive experience centering on Rick Deckard (Harrison Ford), a kind of official bounty hunter.

80. VAMPIRES

Thanks largely to the *Twilight* series of novels by Stephenie Meyer, vampires have experienced something of a renaissance. But for those who think the bloodsucking succubus is best personified by a perpetually teenage centenarian heartthrob, read on for some even more interesting immortals.

ACROSS

4. _____ _____'s relationship with Bella Swan is credited with attracting the sort of young girls who had shown little interest in the genre.

7. With the rights to *Dracula* prohibitively expensive, director F. W. Murnau decided to simply change the character's name to ____ _____.

8. For many, ____ _____ is still the definitive Dracula. Although undoubtedly a supremely memorable and effective portrayal, it's also stagey, stiff, and undeniably dated.

9. Another modern take, *The Hunger*, starring David Bowie, sees Catherine Deneuve as _____ _____, a beautiful serial killer with a hunger for more than just blood.

DOWN

1. Ingrid Pitt, the first lady of Hammer horror, makes her vampire debut in *The Vampire Lovers*, where she plays the beautiful _____ Karnstein.

2. The first of nine occasions in which _____ ___ would play Dracula, Hammer's original movie, *Dracula: Prince of Darkness*, made the actor's name while simultaneously typecasting him for life.

3. The vampire myth is updated for the Spielberg generation in the black comedy *Fright Night*, about a vampire, _____ _____, who moves to the suburbs.

5. *Let the Right One In.* This dark, understated Swedish movie is a unique take on the subject, supposing vampires such as ___ live undetected among us and face the same struggles we do.

6. _____ is evicted from his castle by the Romanian government, which plans to turn it into a gymnastics training center in *Love at First Bite*.

10. The curious little movie _____, from horror maestro George Romero, suggests vampirism as the possible result of mental illness.

81. COMEDY TROUPES AND DOUBLE ACTS

With few things more subjective than humor, establishing a "house style" is uniquely valuable for a comedy act. Fans are assured they will get what they're looking for when they buy their ticket, and a guaranteed audience gives the act confidence and security.

ACROSS

4. Many of the Christopher _____ Troupe first got together for Rob Reiner's 1984 classic *This Is Spinal Tap*.

7. The first double act to achieve megastar status, _____ ___ _____ defined not only a style of comedy but the physical dynamic of the double act.

9. The British triptych of Edgar Wright, _____ ____, and Nick Frost started out together in TV's *Spaced* and have taken Hollywood by storm since their "zomromcom" *Shaun of the Dead*.

10. Successful stage shows and records led to a big-screen debut for these counterculture pinups, _____ and _____, whose *Up in Smoke* was the smash hit comedy of 1978.

DOWN

1. Richard Pryor's belligerent stage persona and ____ _____'s sensitive acting style don't suggest themselves as ideal bedfellows.

2. The alternately surreal, satirical, dark, and ridiculous humor of the British comedians _____ _____ found them the greatest international success of any comedy act for decades.

3. After struggling as a nightclub singer, ____ _____ teamed up with stage comic Jerry Lewis in 1946.

5. The kings of slapstick, the _____ _____ made literally hundreds of shorts over a career that also took in vaudeville, TV, comic books, novelty records, radio, and even video games.

6. From impoverished childhoods the ____ brothers became big screen legends, but Groucho, the most successful, remains immediately recognizable and extensively quoted.

8. Once again the vaudeville stage proves a stepping-stone to Hollywood, with _____ and _____ becoming possibly the most popular comedy act of the 1940s and 1950s.

82. BATTLES

The movies have always been preoccupied with military conflict, both historical and fictional. It offers great dramatic possibilities while presenting easy-to-understand good/bad morality, and it can make for the most thrilling of climaxes.

ACROSS

3. In *300*, every technical trick in the book is deployed to amp up the drama as a small band of battle-hardened Spartans attempt to see off a huge Persian army determined to conquer them at the Battle of _____.

7. An undermanned, underarmed Allied parachute brigade tries to take and hold a crucial bridge in the Dutch town of _____ in *A Bridge Too Far*.

9. In *Star Wars: A New Hope*, the attack on the _____ ____ is a real corker, where we clearly understand what the rebels need to do to win.

10. The film *Ran* is a tale of the downfall of a once-powerful Sengoku-era clan, and features the spectacular Battle of the _____ clan.

DOWN

1. The Battle of _____ Bridge was one of the bloodiest battles of the First War of Scottish Independence, which saw victory for William Wallace's forces both in real life and in the movie *Braveheart*.

2. The Battle of the Hornburg (a.k.a. _____'_ _____) sees a vastly outnumbered Rohirrim army retreat to the fortress to face evil wizard Saruman's Uruk-Hai force.

4. The climax to *Duck Soup* is a chaotic war scene as _____ declares war on neighboring Sylvania.

5. The breathtaking opening scene in *Saving Private Ryan*, the _____ _____ landing, is as effective today as it was on release.

6. During the Anglo-Zulu war a small British detachment find themselves hemmed in with 4,000 Zulus approaching as they face the Battle of _____'_ _____.

8. It's easy to take scenes like the Charge of the _____ in *Waterloo* for granted. The epic scale is the result of employing 20,000 extras and some exceptional filmmaking.

83. COPS

For this puzzle we're not interested in how accomplished a cop might be, how many citizens they've rescued, or the number of robberies they've solved. It's purely about how much we enjoy watching them.

ACROSS

2. ___ _____ (Sean Connery) Irish cop signs up to become part of Elliot Ness's (Kevin Costner) elite Untouchables, a special unit dedicated to catching Al Capone.

4. Redesigned from the vaguely effective police sergeant of *Police Squad!* TV series, Sergeant _____ _____ of the *Naked Gun* movies is an inept dimwit.

5. Gruff, violent, racist, and alcoholic, Detective _____ _____ is a dedicated New York cop on the trail of a huge heroin shipment in *The French Connection.*

8. If the world-class incompetent Inspector Jacques _____ solves a case, chances are it's by accident.

9. In *The Departed,* the highly capable Captain _____ _____ marks another scene-stealing role for Alec Baldwin.

10. New York cop ____ _____ must call on all his resourcefulness to overcome a team of exceptional thieves posing as terrorists in *Die Hard.*

DOWN

1. Street-smart Detroit cop ____ _____ becomes embroiled in a smuggling racket when an old friend is murdered and he follows a lead to California.

3. _____ _____ is different. As if a pleasant, homely lady from a quaint town doesn't seem vulnerable enough when facing hardened killers, writer/directors the Coen brothers made her heavily pregnant.

6. By the time *Touch of Evil* was mooted, Orson Welles's reputation was in tatters. But he was able to convince Universal Pictures to let him write and direct, and he made his character, ____ _____, even more unpalatable.

7. Detective _____ _____, a well-respected African American homicide detective, is passing through Sparta, Mississippi, when racist police chief Bill Gillespie (Rod Steiger) arrests him for murder.

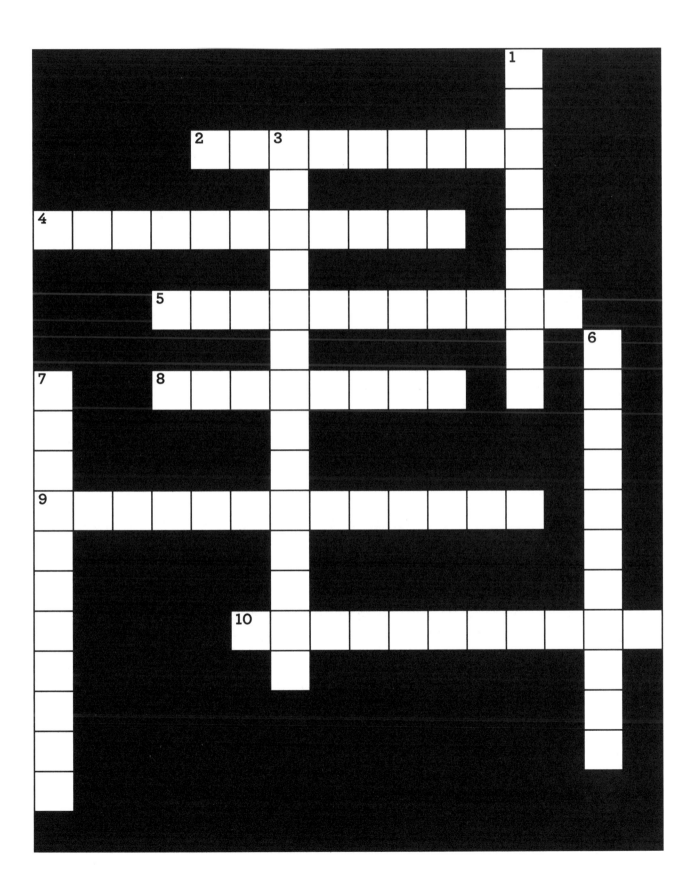

84. MOVIES FEATURING ROAD TRIPS

On your own or in a party. Allegory or straight story. Motorcycle or lawn mower! There's little to link these movies beyond the ever-effective device of centering them around a journey.

ACROSS

6. *The _____ _____* sees Kermit head off to Hollywood in search of stardom. On the way, other well-loved Muppets join him in his quest.

8. In *The _____ Story*, elderly Alvin uses the only means at his disposal, a lawn mower, to travel to visit the brother he hasn't spoken to for years.

9. Having smuggled a quantity of cocaine into Los Angeles from Mexico, bikers Wyatt and Billy are flush with cash in _____ _____ and decide to make the long trip to the Mardi Gras in New Orleans.

10. Neal Page is desperate to get home to his family in Chicago at Thanksgiving. Del Griffith might be heading the same way but has rather less urgency about him in *_____, _____ and Automobiles*.

DOWN

1. In *_____ and _____*, a housewife and a disillusioned waitress decide to hit the road. But when one of them kills a man who attempts to rape her friend, things get serious as they meet their fate in the Grand Canyon.

2. Ellie, a wildly spoiled heiress, absconds from her family to marry a gold-digger of whom they disapprove. Making the journey to him in *It Happened ___ ____* proves more difficult than expected.

3. When limo driver Lloyd believes his client has mistakenly left her bag at the airport, he and his equally imbecilic friend Harry vow to return it to her as they travel from Rhode Island to Aspen in *_____ and _____*.

4. A pair of drag queens and their transsexual cohort Bernadette head off into the Australian desert in their bus in *_____, Queen of the Desert*.

5. Believing he's won a sweepstakes, pensioner Woody Grant convinces his estranged son David to drive him to collect his winnings in *_____*.

7. Ernesto "Che" Guevara's 1952 travels through South America are often cited as a formative tale for the future revolutionary in *The _____ Diaries*.

85. FEMME FATALES

Although present in all sorts of genres and mediums, the femme fatale (fatal woman) is most closely associated with film noir. Her most vital feature is the ability to ensnare and then lead a man to his doom, either moral or actual.

ACROSS

2. _____ Dietrichson is intent on collecting a big insurance payout by having her husband bumped off in *Double Indemnity*.

4. *Brick* places the action in an American high school. _____ _____ already has an inauspicious air about her before we discover her criminal actions.

5. Tapped-out cashier Chris Cross falls for con artist _____ _____ who, believing him to be wealthy, wrings every penny she can from him.

7. Ruthless weather girl _____ _____ Maretto wants to be rid of her loving husband Larry. She convinces high school student Jimmy Emmett and his friends to kill Larry.

8. _____ _____, the animated nightclub singer and wife of Roger, isn't bad, she's just drawn that way.

9. _____ Tramell's frequent state of undress, not to mention Michael Douglas's bare bottom, are the only features that distinguish *Basic Instinct* from the classic noirs it apes.

10. Emotionally torturing Jimmy Stewart should be a crime, but it's her role in the murder of an industrialist's wife that sets _____ _____ on the path to doom in *Vertigo*.

DOWN

1. Advertising executive _____ _____ is found shot dead in her apartment. But when she reappears, the identity of the dead woman needs to be reexamined and she becomes the prime suspect.

3. A sultry call girl, _____ _____, is deployed by the perpetrators to compromise the investigation in *L.A. Confidential*.

6. In post–World War II Vienna, Harry Lime is apparently killed in an accident, leaving his best friend to investigate. Lime's girlfriend, _____ _____, appears to know more than she will admit.

86. PSYCHOPATHS

This puzzle should demonstrate just how great a movie psychopath can be. Whether quietly deranged or ostentatiously firing both barrels of crazy, these characters are among the most chilling in cinema.

ACROSS

1. Unnervingly rational _____ (Tom Waits) is one of the eponymous *Seven Psychopaths* in this excellent satirical black comedy.

3. The savage, remorseless, and utterly terrifying _____ _____ (Dennis Hopper) in *Blue Velvet* is one of the most memorable film characters ever.

7. In *American Psycho*, the superficial excesses of the 1980s are lampooned brilliantly in this study of psychopathic investment banker _____ _____ (Christian Bale), who finds his recreation in grisly murder.

10. Having convinced himself he's doing God's work by killing women, phony preacher _____ _____ (Robert Mitchum) ingratiates himself into the lives of the family of his former prison cellmate.

DOWN

2. Seven years after the death of his wife, Aoyama (Ryu Isibashi) falls for the serene _____ _____ (Eihi Shiina) who, on realizing he was once married, snaps and poisons him, before revealing a fondness for torture.

4. Just one of the destructive forces hemming in protagonist Renton, the witless _____ (Robert Carlyle) is a hysterically aggressive lunatic.

5. With no apparent motive, ____ _____ (Rutger Hauer) drifts across America hitching rides before killing the unsuspecting drivers.

6. Kathy Bates's most famous role is the unhinged literary fan _____ _____, who captures and imprisons her favorite author because she's unhappy with the latest turn taken in a series of his novels.

8. _____ (Tadanobu Asano), a sadomasochistic enforcer for the Japanese mob, both delivers and receives a series of terrible injuries in *Ichi the Killer*.

9. The excellent Sir Ben Kingsley as ___ _____, who bullies retired crook Gal Dove (Ray Winstone), is the best thing about *Sexy Beast*.

87. COMEDY HORROR MOVIES

What at first might seem an illogical blend of genres makes some sense when you consider how much more palatable horror can be when tempered with humor. Our brains respond in a similarly instinctive way to being scared and amused, so it's a perfect synergy between the genres.

ACROSS

5. Herbert West (Jeffrey Combs) is a brilliant student doctor who has devised a means to bring the dead back to life in __-_____.

6. A fairly run-of-the-mill "kids in peril from beasties" B-movie is elevated to a greater status by perfectly judged tongue-in-cheek moments featuring a swarm of killer _____s in a parody of *Jaws*.

7. _____ is essentially a zombie art-house comedy based on the *Dylan Dog* comics.

9. Prior to his success with *The Lord of the Rings,* director Peter Jackson wrote _____ a.k.a. *Dead Alive.*

10. Like Peter Jackson, Sam Raimi started out making nasty but silly horror movies before becoming a household name. ____ ____ *II* is the perfect blend of horror and preposterous humor.

DOWN

1. _____ is intriguing for the way it satirizes callous corporations. Though lacking in subtlety, this British movie sees an office outing to a remote Hungarian forest end with murderous attacks.

2. _____ __ ___ ____ is a lovingly crafted ode to George Romero. This "zomromcom" sees unambitious Londoner Shaun (Simon Pegg) attempt to win back his girlfriend while fighting a zombie apocalypse.

3. Wes Craven here deconstructs the slasher genre to hilarious effect in _____, as Sydney becomes the target of a mysterious killer named Ghostface.

4. *The* _____ __ ___ _____ attempts to be the last word on the titular cliché. As American students spend their weekend in a deserted cabin, they become victims of a bizarre experiment.

8. *An American Werewolf* __ _____ starts with two American backpackers attacked by a werewolf on the Yorkshire moors in England.

88. DANCING IN THE MOVIES

Hollywood in particular has produced many musicals featuring fabulous dance numbers. But quality routines appear in dramatic and comedic movies too, and so this puzzle focuses on dance scenes not from musicals that are often overlooked.

ACROSS

3. In _____, the eponymous blind swordsman makes his way through a brutal feudal-era Japan in a taciturn gloom. The last thing we expect at the end of the movie is a bravura tap-dancing routine!

8. _____! sees pilot Ted Striker don the infamous white suit and dance to a sped-up version of the Bee Gees' "Stayin' Alive."

9. The "Nonsense Song" performed by Charlie Chaplin in _____ _____ is a largely improvised piece using random words from various languages.

10. In _____ _____, there's just no arguing with the emotional power of Johnny and Baby's climactic dance scene.

DOWN

1. On their quest for the ____ _____, King Arthur (Graham Chapman) and his knights finally reach Camelot, where—after witnessing the ridiculous "Camelot Song" and dance—Arthur decides it is a silly place and moves on.

2. In The _____ ____, the scene where Parry (Robin Williams) and Lydia (Amanda Plummer) meet becomes an extensive waltz.

4. The brilliantly fun opening sequence to the third Austin Powers movie, _____, consists of a succession of gags danced to Quincy Jones's "Soul Bossa Nova."

5. In _____ Frankenstein, Dr. Frankenstein decides to prove his creation can do anything a real human can . . . a stage show in top hat and tails ensues!

6. Mob enforcer Vincent Vega is challenged by gangster's moll Mia Wallace to win a jive competition. The electric scene in ____ _____ is played out to Chuck Berry's "You Never Can Tell."

7. In _____ _ ____ (1962), three friends give an impromptu performance of the Madison dance in a French café. The atmosphere crackles with unconstrained joie de vivre.

89. RED MENACE MOVIES

In the 1950s, Hollywood expertly tapped into America's growing fear of communism with a succession of sci-fi movies built around the same simple allegory. In place of communists, aliens became the unknown evil invaders, and one of the most identifiable and formulaic subgenres exploded into life.

ACROSS

3. After seeing a meteorite land nearby, teenager Steve Andrews (Steve McQueen) and his girlfriend become embroiled in an attempt by a globule of gelatin, called ___ _____, to take over the world.

4. In *X the _____*, a radioactive beast terrorizes a Scottish army base, getting bigger and stronger as it absorbs more energy.

5. *20 _____ _____ to Earth* sees an American spaceship return from Venus carrying a small lizard-like creature, which immediately starts to grow.

8. One of the most important movies of the red menace wave was *Invasion of the _____*, directed by Don Siegel.

9. *The _____ Xperiment* a.k.a. *The Creeping Unknown*. The lone human survivor of a spaceship crash begins mutating into a terrible monster.

10. In *The Thing from _____ _____*, scientists at an Arctic research station are besieged by an alien monster after accidentally thawing it out.

DOWN

1. H.G. Wells's celebrated story about an alien invasion in Southern England is successfully transposed to rural California in *The ___ of the _____*.

2. In *Earth vs. the _____ _____*, Dr. Russell Marvin (Hugh Marlowe) launches a series of satellites that mysteriously fall back to Earth. When he captures the event on a strange recording, he realizes why.

6. *Invaders from _____* features a popular concept in these movies, whereby ordinary people are changed into emotionless automatons as aliens either replace or take control of them.

7. In *This _____ _____*, aliens seeking our help in an intergalactic war turn out to be less trustworthy than we expected.

90. BEST ADAPTATIONS OF A TV SERIES

Attempting to adapt a successful TV series for the big screen is a notoriously tricky prospect. It's not just about making something that works at 60 minutes or less do the same over the course of a couple of hours. Audience expectations change when they pay money to sit in a darkened theater.

ACROSS

2. In *Three* _____ _____, Shiba (Tetsuo Tamba) falls in with a pair of samurai charged with recovering the kidnapped daughter of a magistrate.

7. _____ *and* ____-____ *Do America* (1996). The juvenile delinquents wake up one morning to discover their TV stolen.

10. Harrison Ford is Dr. Richard Kimble in *The* _____. He is wrongly convicted of his wife's murder and escapes to track down the real killer.

DOWN

1. _____: *The Movie* features most of the original cast of the TV series, including Johnny Knoxville, Bam Margera, and Steve-O.

3. _____ *Bebop: The Movie* (2001). In 2071, a deadly virus is released on Mars as part of a wave of terrorist attacks, and the bounty hunter crew of the spaceship *Bebop* is dispatched to catch the culprits.

4. Fans have decried the variable quality of ____ ____ movies for over 30 years, so it was a pleasant surprise when J.J. Abrams's reboot, featuring Chris Pine and Zachary Quinto, proved so popular.

5. Lieutenant Frank Drebin of Police Squad must foil an attempt to kill Queen Elizabeth II on American soil in *The* _____ ___.

6. The crew of the _____, a "Firefly-class" spaceship, close ranks to protect one of their own when a genetically engineered assassin is sent after her.

8. The British satirical TV series *The Thick of It* is reworked into a feature film, __ ___ ____, that sort of bridges the gap between the original show and its U.S. incarnation, *Veep*.

9. _____ is determined to show the audience every link in the chain of the cocaine trade. The movie is based on an equally successful British TV series, *Traffik*, which focused on a similar system in Europe and Pakistan.

91. FRENCH NEW WAVE FILMS

This vague term loosely groups together a generation of iconoclastic filmmakers who brought a then-unique immediacy to the medium. They often addressed the political and social issues of the day and pioneered a style that made extensive use of real locations, natural light, radical editing techniques, naturalistic acting, and tropes more common in documentaries.

ACROSS

2. Jean-Paul Belmondo plays a charismatic criminal on the run with a beautiful woman in tow in _____. And it doesn't end well for him.

4. Ferdinand runs away with his babysitter, Marianne. They drift south on a crime spree, then separate. Years later they meet again, but things are not the same in _____ __ ___.

8. __ ____ __ ____ is the story of Nana (Anna Karina), a beautiful young woman who abandons her husband and child in order to become a famous actress. Unsurprisingly, things don't end well.

10. *Last Year at* _____. This divisive film toys with time, identity, and reality. None of the characters are named and a deliberate lack of information leaves the audience unsure whether what they're seeing is real.

DOWN

1. Alain (Maurice Ronet) leaves the Versailles clinic at which he's being treated in ___ ____ _____, intent on enjoying one final night of revelry before ending his life.

3. A misunderstood and neglected young boy slips through the cracks of society to become another victim of an uncaring system in *The 400 _____*.

5. In *Hiroshima ___ _____*, actress Elle, who is in Hiroshima to film an anti-war movie, has an affair with architect Lui and they philosophize on war.

6. *The _____ of Cherbourg* is told entirely through song. It's the story of young lovers, separated by war, who eventually find happiness with others.

7. _____ ___ ___ is the story of a shy writer from Austria and a more extroverted Frenchman. The many shapes of love are investigated in this part-frothy, part-gloomy classic starring Jeanne Moreau.

9. In __ _____, a small French community is gripped by a series of violent murders of young women.

92. SLASHER MOVIES

What exactly is a slasher movie? Generally speaking, it must feature a psychopath who systematically kills a sequence of victims in a particularly gruesome fashion. They are almost always American movies, and the killer will generally be a masked male who uses some sort of bladed weapon.

ACROSS

2. *When a _____ _____*. High school student Jill (Carol Kane) is babysitting for neighbors when she receives intimidating phone calls, only to discover the calls are coming from . . . inside the house!

5. In _____ _____, a young girl sees summer camp as a way to start to get over the trauma after her family is killed in an accident. Bad idea.

7. In *The _____*, the caretaker of an upstate New York summer camp is terribly burned when spoiled kids play a prank on him.

10. _____ ____. A group of teen friends wind up in a creepy museum full of mannequins. The reclusive owner has telekinetic powers and can control the mannequins.

DOWN

1. Set around _____, dangerous psychopath Michael Myers has escaped, and a group of teenage friends are terrorized by a masked killer.

3. *The _____ _____ ___ Massacre*. Although it's on the edge of what qualifies as a slasher, it's just such a well executed movie that it deserves mention.

4. Generally considered the first slasher movie, the simple premise of _____ _____ sees a crazed killer picking off the girls of a sorority house.

6. __ _____ *Valentine*. The first Valentine's Day Dance in 20 years is due to take place in Valentine Bluffs. The reason for the hiatus is soon revealed when we learn an accident left five miners dead two decades before.

8. More than three decades after a man in full World War II combat gear brutally murdered a young couple at a dance, the same sinister killer seems to be back in *The _____*.

9. American summer camps seem to be the most perilous environment in the world. Their reputation takes another battering in _____ *the 13th*.

93. WOMEN IN A MAN'S WORLD

This puzzle if populated by female characters who perform a role more generally associated with men, and do so better than those men might usually manage. They don't need to be tomboys, just good at what they do.

ACROSS

6. Like the serial killer she is sent to interview, _____ Starling is both capable and perceptive.

8. _____ _____ of the clan Dunbroch is to be betrothed to the son of one of her father's allies against her will. When none of the suitors can match her in an archery contest, it sets off a chain reaction.

9. The Whangara of New Zealand believe the spirit of their mythical ancestor Paikea is present in each of their chiefs, who have all been males until ___, an 11-year-old girl who sets out to convince them otherwise.

10. The buzz of testosterone-charged newspaper offices lure former reporter _____ _____ back into the mire in this comedy starring Cary Grant.

DOWN

1. *Zero Dark Thirty*, a fictionalized account of the hunt for Osama Bin Laden, sees C.I.A. operative _____ _____ thrown in at the deep end.

2. _____ _____ is a warrant officer aboard the *Nostromo* when an unknown creature infiltrates the ship, and the race begins to find and kill it before it kills the whole crew.

3. Unassuming, heavily pregnant police chief _____ Gunderson in *Fargo* (1996) must be one of the most popular of all female movie characters.

4. On the outskirts of a miserable old west town, the vivid _____ juggles the disparate groups of outlaws, cattlemen, and assorted lowlifes who frequent her saloon in *Johnny Guitar*.

5. Set in the distant future after "Seven Days of Fire" have left much of the world a toxic wasteland, _____ is an ecologically minded fable.

7. One of nine collaborations between Katharine Hepburn and Spencer Tracy, *Pat and Mike* is the lighthearted story of gifted sportswoman ___ _____'s struggle to be taken seriously.

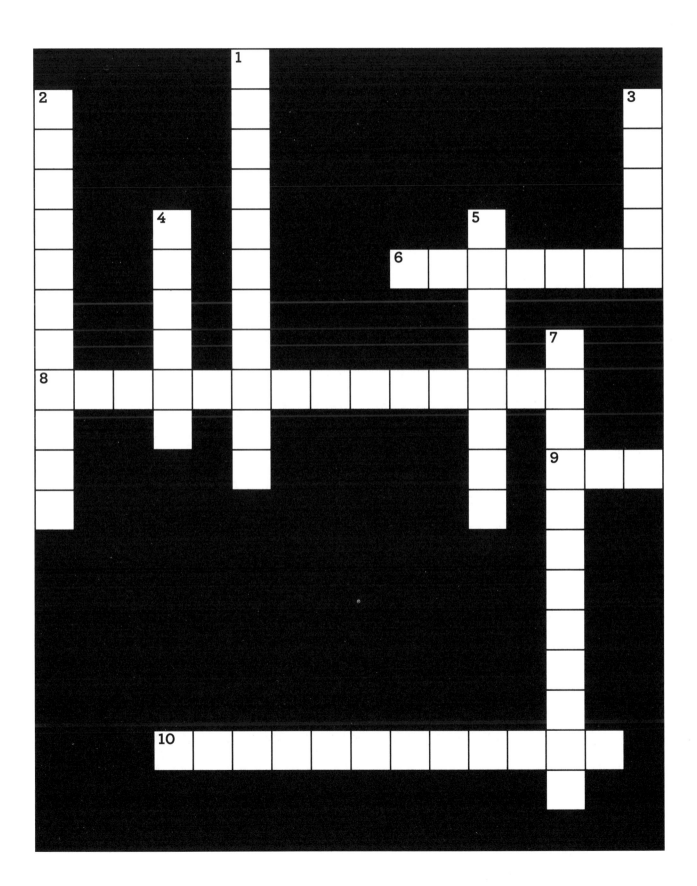

94. CAMEOS

The ultimate movie in-joke has to be the cameo. Sometimes it's such an in-joke that fans don't even know it's happened, as with Cate Blanchett's uncredited turn as a fully masked forensic pathologist in 2007's *Hot Fuzz*.

ACROSS

3. In *The Player*, two screenwriters pitch a script, but are horrified when asked to cast it with stars. By the end of the movie, it becomes obvious that they are happy to sell out, as _____ _____ bursts onto the stage.

4. After battling their way to Hollywood in search of movie stardom, the Muppets gain an audience with Lew Lord, a brilliantly cast _____ _____.

6. *Cannonball Run II*. Not the most impressive movie for Frank _____ to end his career with, but at least he's funny in it.

8. _____ _____ was one of many stars to request a part in *Fear and Loathing in Las Vegas*. The spin he gives the character, adding an unscripted request for a kiss from Johnny Depp's Raoul Duke, makes the scene.

9. A montage showing us the origins of the X-Men features Charles Xavier and Eric Lensherr recruiting mutants. In a bar they find Wolverine (_____ _____), but are rudely dismissed.

10. Alvy Singer is incensed at a pseudo-intellectual who misinterprets the analysis of renowned media philosopher Marshal _____, so Alvy produces the real person.

DOWN

1. In *Dodgeball* the team forfeits the a match and the judges vote on whether they can continue. Thankfully, the casting vote belongs to _____ _____.

2. A band of zombie apocalypse survivors decide it would be fun to hide out at _____ _____'s house, until he pretends to be a zombie as a practical joke.

5. Rob Gordon is obsessed with two things: music, and his ex-girlfriend Laura. His inability to relate to women leads to an imagined conversation with Bruce _____.

7. A silent movie about Hollywood producers trying to make a silent movie. When the director telephones to offer Marcel _____ a role, the famous mime artist utters the only word of dialogue: "Non!"

95. ASSASSINS

It's curious how movie assassins often have the most clearly defined morality of any character type. It might not be a morality we share, but it's usually a well-developed and rigid system to which they will adhere at any cost. Which is more than you can say for some heroes.

ACROSS

1. Jim Jarmusch offers a meditative take on the killer for hire, his _____ ___ being philosophically inclined and inspired by *bushido*.

4. In *Grosse Pointe Blank*, Cusack is brilliant as _____ _____, a killer at a school reunion who gives in to nostalgia and grows a heart.

5. A teen junkie winds up in prison, from where she is reluctantly recruited to be an assassin for a secretive government agency known as the Center, in _____.

7. Director Joe Wright shifted gears dramatically from his trademark literary adaptations to make _____, a frenzied action thriller about a 16-year-old girl trained as an assassin.

9. In *Le Samouraï* ___ _____ is the melancholic character who oozes French style as he goes about his business with meticulous precision.

10. The most intimidating, remorseless, and determined _____ _____ is an iconic creation, which instantly elevated Spanish star Javier Bardem to the Hollywood A-list.

DOWN

2. This westernized mishmash of the first two *Lone Wolf and Cub* movies is probably the best introduction to the celebrated samurai killer _____ ____.

3. *The Green Man* is a comedy about a British assassin, _____, who suffers a series of farcical episodes while attempting to knock off a politician.

6. Bounty hunters, outlaws, and starving villagers fight it out among themselves in the bleak landscape of Utah's Great Blizzard of 1899. _____'s ultimate opponent, Loco (Klaus Kinski), is a memorable killer.

8. In John Woo's contract-killer classic, __ ____ is disillusioned with his life and determined to help an innocent bystander he mistakenly blinded.

96. SPACESHIPS

It's well over 100 years since Georges Méliès's *A Trip to the Moon* saw a group of enthusiastic astronomers launch their makeshift spaceship. By the late 1960s, more advanced techniques eventually allowed photorealistic work in sci-fi films. The computer revolution has left imagination the only limiting factor, with incredible C.G.I. creations within reach of even budget productions.

ACROSS

1. Mankind is colonizing deep space and it's the job of the _____ _____ crew to go on ahead and destroy any unstable planets.

4. Originally a light freighter, the _____ _____ has been heavily modified for use as a high-speed smuggler's ship, but it ends up playing a vital role in the victories of the Rebel Alliance.

6. The *Star Trek* mythology has seen about a dozen versions of the U.S.S. _____, most of them eventually destroyed.

7. With its endless dank chambers and dark corridors, the industrial mining ship _____ proves to be an ideal habitat for the eponymous *Alien*.

8. In Mel Brooks's *Star Wars* spoof, the role of the *Millennium Falcon* goes to _____ 5, a battered Winnebago R.V. spaceship.

9. *The* _____ __ _____ is powered by an Infinite Improbability Drive that connects the logic circuits of a Bambleweeny 57 Sub-Meson Brain to an atomic vector plotter suspended in a Brownian Motion producer. Naturally!

10. _____'_ _____, a classic saucer-shaped craft, causes mass hysteria when it lands in Washington, D.C., in *The Day the Earth Stood Still*.

DOWN

2. The ungainly Firefly-class _____ is home to a band of renegades attempting to earn a living while evading the rulers of the future galaxy.

3. Earth is devoid of all plant life, the only remaining examples kept alive in giant glass domes orbiting Saturn. The _____ _____ is a commercial freighter to which six such domes have been attached.

5. Every detail of the _____ ___ is based on actual or theoretical (in 1968) science. The engines are gaseous core nuclear reactors, and the ship's systems are controlled by a central computer that's in constant contact with machines on Earth.

97. SO BAD THEY'RE GOOD

There is no shortage of low-budget exploitation movies that could fit this puzzle. But because there are so many, and because it's more fun to mock a disaster that has no excuse, this puzzle favors movies that had the potential to be better.

ACROSS

1. _____ is an action movie about an American champion gymnast called on by his country to win a martial arts tournament for some reason.

5. _____ _____ was always intended to be the gloriously campy tongue-in-cheek kitsch that it is as Ming the Merciless is intent on destroying Earth.

6. ___ ___ __. An *E.T.* rip-off that came too late and forgot to be any good, even though it features Jennifer Aniston.

7. While the director of the atrocious *He-Man* adaptation, *Masters of the _____*, had the good grace never to helm another movie, the lead actors—Dolph Lundgren and Courteney Cox—fared rather better.

9. Commander Ace Hunter (seriously) is the heroic leader of _____, an elite military unit charged with riding motorcycles and shooting big guns at baddies in this explosion of 1980's tackiness.

10. _____ *Earth*. Terl, leader of the Psychlos, has enslaved the human race and is stripping Earth of its resources. What we need is a hero. And a script that makes sense.

DOWN

2. Directed and starring Tom Wiseau, ___ _____ is a relative latecomer to the so-bad-they're-good movie landscape. But this is almost certainly the worst movie ever made.

3. _____ _____ *2: The Colombian Connection*. In this second foray for Chuck Norris's Special Forces unit, they are deployed to South America.

4. Essentially *All About Eve* with strippers, _____ is either one of the most hilariously bad movies ever made or a hyper-real meta-analysis of modern movie tropes.

8. _____ *2*. No trolls, a dentist non-actor for a leading man, and a director who didn't speak English—what could go wrong?

98. SUPERHERO MOVIES

Historically, comic books and movies lived in close quarters but seldom met. TV shows and Saturday serials (TV's cinematic predecessor) dabbled, but Hollywood was slow to grasp the potential of adapting comics for the big screen. Things have clearly changed.

ACROSS

4. Half-vampire _____ (Wesley Snipes) works to rid the world of evil bloodsuckers.

6. Sam Raimi was considered an odd choice for the highly anticipated 2002 _____-___ adaptation, but this hugely popular movie launched Raimi into the directing A-list.

8. It's not immediately obvious how a smug, alcoholic, arms-dealing billionaire is one of the most popular movie characters of the age in ____ ___.

10. The long-awaited zenith of superhero medleys, _____ Assemble, finally arrived in 2012, and didn't disappoint fans.

DOWN

1. With his audience on the ropes after wowing them with Batman Begins, Christopher Nolan delivered a knockout punch with the sequel, The ____ _____.

2. The first significant and successful superhero movie, _____ is still revered today as one of the best of its type, with Christopher Reeve as Clark Kent and his alter ego.

3. The _____ is Pixar's take on the superhero movie. It revels in showing us the post-retirement lifestyle of a couple of heroes and their talented children.

5. The age of the modern superhero mega-hit began with Marvel's _-___ (2000) centering around Professor Xavier's school for gifted children.

7. Although 1978's Superman had already taken the comic book aesthetic seriously, it still kept one toe in the camp pool. _____ changed everything.

9. The movie that made Brandon Lee a star is also, tragically, the last he made. ____ _____, set in a bleak Detroit, sees Eric Draven, a musician who is killed by a vicious gang of thugs, resurrected by a supernatural force.

99. MOST STYLISHLY DRESSED CHARACTERS

It's often lamented that these days there's a touch less style up on the screen than there used to be. Whether true or not, we'll give more recent movies a helping hand by ruling out the eternally stylish likes of Humphrey Bogart and Audrey Hepburn.

ACROSS

1. In *Casino*, hustler _____ _____ makes a living from looking good, so it's no surprise she has the effortless elegance of a Grace Kelly or Elizabeth Taylor. At least that's how she starts the movie.

6. The stunning Catherine Deneuve (_____ Serizy), spends much of *Belle de Jour* looking like a model who's just stepped off the Paris catwalk.

9. Dressed throughout *Gentlemen Prefer Blondes* like the showgirl she plays, Marilyn (_____ ___), shows off some of the most glamorous costumes imaginable.

10. In *The Talented Mr. Ripley*, Jude Law is styled to within an inch of his life as he plays the character _____ Greenleaf.

DOWN

2. With the extravagant frocks matched by the equally excessive hairpieces, Kirsten Dunst, playing the titular character Marie _____, looks like an extra from an Adam Ant video for much of the movie.

3. Colin Firth, as _____ _____, is a man who looks very much at home in the exquisitely tailored 1960s suits he sports in *A Single Man*.

4. The 1970s drug-dealing New York pimp look isn't for everyone. But Ron O'Neal as _____ in *Super Fly* can pull it off like a pro.

5. Many of _____ _____'s real suits were used for reference in this biopic of the American business magnate, but how many other actors could make them look as good as DiCaprio?

7. The traditional high-collared dresses worn by __ __-____ throughout *In the Mood for Love* are almost a character in their own right.

8. This whole film is more concerned with superficial appearance than substance, so it's no surprise the protagonist, _____ ___ (Richard Gere), is one of the best dressed in the movies.

100. GREAT COMEDY MOVIES YOU MAY NOT HAVE SEEN

With humor so subjective and exposure to movies dependent on so many factors, it's hard to meet the demand of this puzzle's title. Some may be familiar or even well known, but then a list of unobtainable curiosities is no good to anyone.

ACROSS

3. *The Discreet Charm of the* _____, Luis Buñuel's great masterpiece, is an absurdist assault on the pretension of Europe's chattering classes.

4. The illegitimate scion of the upper-class D'Ascoyne family sets out to bump off the eight relatives that stand between him and a fabulous inheritance in ____ _____ *and Coronets.*

5. _____ _____. Mike Judge, the man behind *Beavis & Butthead* and *King of the Hill*, makes his live-action feature debut with this satire about office drones getting one over on the boss.

6. In *World's* _____ ___, Lance (Robin Williams) finds his obnoxious 15-year-old son dead after an autoerotic asphyxiation accident.

8. In _ _____ ___, the sequel to *If...*, Mick Travis has left school and entered the job market, becoming a traveling coffee salesman.

9. Xi (N!xau), a Kalahari Bushman who has never had contact with the outside world, finds an empty Coke bottle in the desert in *The Gods* ____ __ _____.

10. In the largely forgotten farce _ ___ ____, spoiled Henry Graham (Walter Matthau) winds up penniless and decides to marry money.

DOWN

1. ____ __ ____, Jacques Tati's directorial debut, features himself as a postman in rural France, where residents of his district are being visited by a traveling fair.

2. The cult British comedy _____ ___ _ follows two out-of-work alcoholic actors as they escape London for a few days in a primitive country cottage.

7. _____ _____ *a.k.a. Pocket Money* is a French film directed by François Truffaut about the struggles and yearnings of children in a French town.

101. FAUX DOCUMENTARIES

Documentaries have seen a conflict between the need to be both authentic and entertaining since scenes were first staged for 1921's *Nanook of the North*. Faux documentaries eschew claims to authenticity but can still inform us, though more usually they just amuse.

ACROSS

1.   *Waiting for* _____. With a rumor that Broadway talent scout Mort will attend the opening night of their new play, the amateur dramatics society of Blaine, Missouri, gets carried away with excitement.

3.   _____ _____. Peter Jackson's touching tribute to his long-forgotten cinematic idol, Colin McKenzie, is no less entertaining as a result of the man never having existed.

5.   _____ is a bleak, theoretical presentation of the effect of nuclear war on a typical Northern English community.

9.   In ___ _____ ___, a thief is approached by a film crew wishing to follow him around and document his life.

10. Relating the reality of nuclear war, *The* ___ ____ was considered so effective that for 20 years it remained off limits to TV broadcasters for fear it would spread panic.

DOWN

2.   Superficially, _ ___ ____ asks why an original artwork, such as a painting by a great master, should be worth more than an indistinguishable copy.

4.   Whether it's turning it up to 11, smuggling a cucumber through a metal detector, or recounting the various demises of a string of former drummers, ____ __ _____ ___ is full of memorable jokes.

6.   *Exit Through the* ____ ____. Anonymous street artist Banksy maintains a mysterious air with his movie debut by focusing on people and events.

7.   In *Incident at* ____ ____, eminent documentarian and filmmaker Werner Herzog plays himself as part of a team sidetracked looking for the monster.

8.   Woody Allan directs and plays his eponymous character Leonard _____, in this story of a man with the uncontrollable ability to transform his appearance to match those around him.

102. THIEVES, PICKPOCKETS, AND BURGLARS

The movies have done much to elevate our view of the larcenist. When necessary, they are vilified, but often charm is the only differentiator when it comes to celebrating the daring of a cat burglar or denouncing the dishonesty of a common thief.

ACROSS

1. Not an obvious choice, but throughout the *Hobbit* series _____ _____ is referred to as "the burglar."

4. _____ (James Caan) has become a successful jewel thief by being extremely careful and methodical about his work.

6. After breaking out of prison, a bank robber embarks on the elusive last big score. George Clooney's ____ _____ has the charisma to simply talk his way into a bank vault if necessary.

9. The archetypal gentleman thief, ____ _____ is retired to the French Riviera when a cat burglar imitating his style causes him unwelcome attention from the authorities.

10. Professional gambler ____ _____ is left penniless and desperate when his luck finally runs out, so he starts putting a gang together to rob a casino in *Bob le Flambeur*.

DOWN

2. Batman has always been used to address issues of duality. To that end, _____ ____ a.k.a. Catwoman is presented as a reflection of Batman himself.

3. The sinister ringleader of a gang of criminals who pull off a security van heist, _____ _____ (Alec Guiness) is better suited to dealing with hardened thugs than he is a little old lady.

5. This first in the *Pink Panther* series focuses less on the popular Clouseau (Peter Sellers) than it does his antagonist, ___ _____ (David Niven).

7. The _____ _____ (a.k.a. Jack Hawkins) is the mythical leader of a gang of pickpocket orphans who terrorize London in this Charles Dickens adaptation.

8. In director Robert Bresson's film, a young man, _____, slides into criminality when he joins up with a gang of highly coordinated pickpockets.

103. REMAKES BETTER THAN THE ORIGINALS

Hollywood studios are said to be prone to copying proven ideas rather than pursuing original ones, but is it that simple? If a good movie fails to find an audience because, for example, it's subtitled, is it really that wrong to remake it and tailor the idea to the audience?

ACROSS

3. Michael Mann adapted his own small-scale TV movie, _____, for the big screen just six years after the original, *L.A. Takedown.*

4. The 1937 version of _ _____ __ _____ is excellent, but Judy Garland does something special with the role in the later one.

7. A young girl seeking revenge for the death of her father hires a cantankerous U.S. Marshal to help her in _____ _____ (2010), a remake of the John Wayne classic.

9. *Invasion of the* _____ _____ sees Donald Sutherland discover that humans are being replaced by alien duplicates.

DOWN

1. ___-___, William Wyler's version of the fable of a Jewish prince sold into slavery, is the most successful of many, complete with chariot race.

2. Movies with a great concept but flawed execution are prime candidates here. _____'_____ is a good example of this, with the original (starring Frank Sinatra and the Rat Pack) failing to make us care about proceedings.

3. Howard Hawks's legendary light touch with comedy is demonstrated wonderfully in ___ _____ _____, a remake of *The Front Page* (1931).

5. ___ ___. Both movies feature a scientist transformed into a fly, but that's about the extent of the similarity.

6. Unsatisfied with his first attempt, Alfred Hitchcock decided to remake his own movie, *The Man Who* _____ ___ _____, which tells the story of a complicated assassination plot.

8. In _____ _____, a remake of *La Totale* (1991), secret agent Harry Tasker (Arnold Schwarzenegger) has to reveal his true profession to wife Helen (Jamie Lee Curtis) when both are kidnapped by terrorists.

104. FISTFIGHTS

If drama is conflict, you can't get much more dramatic than two characters beating each other senseless. Like the wandering ronin of Kurosawa's movie *Yojimbo*, this puzzle takes the view that an honorable fight cannot be waged with firearms.

ACROSS

5. As it's revealed one lead character is just an invention of the other's fractured mind, we see scenes play out as they really happened, not as we initially saw them in _____ ____.

7. No additional reason is needed to seek out *Bad Day at Black Rock*, an expertly played, supremely taut thriller. But if some icing on the cake is required, it features a one-armed Spencer Tracy (_____) doing karate.

10. In *The Quiet Man*, tension over an unpaid dowry erupts into old-school fisticuffs. While marauding through an Irish village, combatants ____ _____ and Will Danaher stop for a pint, and inevitably end up friends.

DOWN

1. In *The Legend of Drunken Master*, the fight demonstrates Jackie Chan's extraordinary athleticism in ____ ___-____'s final fight scene.

2. Sacha Baron Cohen and Ken Davitian stage a fight between _____ and _____ that will define the aesthetic of early 21st-century fight scenes.

3. The only time Bruce Lee and Chuck Norris appeared together on screen. Who would have won the fight between Dragon and ____ if the contest were real is still hotly debated by fans and experts today.

4. In *Any Which Way You Can*, these two brawlers, _____ _____ and Jack Wilson, are clearly destined to be pals.

6. Although Bob Barker is a kindly legend of U.S. TV, he proves to be one of the most badass in this puzzle. _____ _____ doesn't stand a chance in this scuffle—the result of Barker criticizing his golf game.

8. In *From Russia with Love*, producers wanted a villain who shared Connery's imposing stature. Robert Shaw as ___ _____ was certainly that man.

9. In *They Live*, ____ wants Frank to put on special glasses that reveal the world as it really is. Frank doesn't want to put the glasses on.

105. 1970s EXPLOITATION MOVIES

With the relaxation of censorship allowing more graphic content, the 1970s saw a revolution in exploitation cinema, a hitherto fairly benign genre. Parents who had fretted over the previous era's toothless monster movies were suddenly faced with something far more depraved.

ACROSS

5.   In *The _____ _____ on the Left*, the killers of a teenage girl seek refuge with her parents, who soon catch on and exact their revenge.

6.   *Master of the Flying _____*. Martial arts master Wang is pursued by an evil assassin seeking revenge for incidents in this movie's predecessor.

8.   _____ _____ took full advantage of the newly relaxed rules. Its popularity among the middle-class mainstream was unexpected and led to a wave of so-called porno chic movies.

9.   _____: *She-Wolf of the SS* is one of the more curious exploitation subgenres, mixing softcore nudity with cartoonish Nazi authority figures.

10.   _____ _____ (Pam Grier) seeks revenge for the death of her boyfriend. Grier was the queen of Blaxploitation.

DOWN

1.   Featuring footage of human deaths and tragic accidents masquerading as a documentary, _____ __ _____ draws few mainstream defenders.

2.   _____'s success saved the M.G.M. studio from bankruptcy, kick-started the Blaxploitation phenomenon, and changed the way theme music was used.

3.   Sweden wasn't exactly a powerhouse behind the wave of exploitation movies that swept through the 1970s. But it did produce *They Call Her ___ ___*, a favorite of Quentin Tarantino.

4.   _____ ___ _____. This intricately plotted period samurai movie (or *chanbara*) is the first of a series featuring Hanzo (Shintaro Katsu).

7.   _____ _____ *2000*. Thirty years in the future, the sport of the moment is a cross-country road race offering extra points for running people down. The significant kitsch appeal led to a 2008 remake.

106. MADE-FOR-TV MOVIES

What can make TV movies interesting is the creativity stemming from the limitations the medium imposes on them. Rules dictate the language, violence, and sexual content that can be used, and they must adhere to a structure providing for regular commercial breaks and a set running time.

ACROSS

4. _____ _____ is the true story of U.S. Army Captain Jeffrey MacDonald and the murder of his wife and child. But suspicion he was the killer led to a series of contradictory trials.

5. ___ ___ _____ was part of a wave of nuclear apocalypse movies in the 1970s and 1980s. By focusing on a typical Kansas community, it spoke to a huge audience, with 100 million Americans seeing its first airing.

6. _____'_ ____ is another true story, about football player Brian Piccolo (James Caan), who is stricken with cancer.

8. In _____ *and I'll Come to You,* Professor Parkin (Michael Hordern) vacations in a near-deserted, windswept coastal village. After finding a bone whistle, he's terrorized by surreal sounds and visions.

9. Steven Spielberg's sort-of debut, ____ is the story of a motorist terrorized by a trucker.

10. *The* _____ __ _____. Based on Susan Hill's gothic novella, this British TV adaptation precedes a more recent version starring Daniel Radcliffe.

DOWN

1. *The* _____ _____ is perhaps best known now as the inspiration for *The X-Files.* It follows a fairly standard TV mystery formula but with more imagination.

2. __ _____ _____ was one of the first movies to address the AIDS crisis. Homosexual lawyer Michael (Aidan Quinn) discovers he has AIDS and encounters uninformed prejudice as he attempts to deal with it.

3. In many ways way ahead of its time, *Special* _____ uses the then-unusual device of presenting the narrative as a series of news reports.

7. *Don't Be Afraid* __ ___ _____. One of those simple horror movies that stuck in the mind of all who saw it at the time.

107. MOVIES FEATURING PETS

It's impossible to know how many browbeaten parents have been cajoled into pet ownership after their children watched one of these movies. If you fear such a fate, avoid anything with cute dogs and convince the kids to see more dinosaur movies.

ACROSS

4. Although the TV series is now legendary, some may not remember the movie that preceded it. After being rescued by young Sandy, _____ chooses to remain with him and his Ranger father.

6. Rodent gourmet Remy (voiced by Patton Oswalt) has charm, culinary talent, and a burning desire to cook in _____.

9. Although played by many chimps (and even a few humans), one ape in particular found great success as _____'s comic relief.

10. It might be a bit of a push to call a whale a pet, but the strength of the bond between him and 12-year-old Jesse in ____ _____ makes it so.

DOWN

1. _____ is another reason not to give pets as Christmas presents. It's a shame, though, because Gizmo is an unfeasibly cute critter . . . just don't feed him after midnight.

2. In _ ____ _____ _____, career criminal and devout animal lover Ken Pile adores his collection of exotic fish. In fact, he loves one so much he's prepared to give up the proceeds of a jewel heist to prevent her being eaten!

3. _____ _____'s faithful feathered friend, Hedwig, a female snowy owl, is integral to the mythology of the series.

5. Best known for ___ ____ ___ detective comedy, Asta, a wire fox terrier played by Skippy, was one of the first movie pets to grab the imagination of audiences.

7. So popular was Jack the dog that there were petitions to award him an honorary Academy Award alongside ___ _____, crowned best film.

8. When three tiger cubs are orphaned, naturalist Joy Adamson rears them as best she can in ____ ____. But she forms a strong bond with the smallest, Elsa, and decides to try and rehabilitate her into the wild.

108. STRANGEST MOVIES (THAT ARE WORTH SEEING)

There are plenty of bizarre movies out there, but delving into the surreal can be more irritating than rewarding. This puzzle covers the full spectrum of crazy; the only common feature is that these movies are well outside the mainstream—but well worth seeing.

ACROSS

5. *The* ____ _____. A thief lies in a desert with flies covering his face. He is befriended by a footless, handless dwarf.

9. Peter Jackson's puppet-based (very adult) behind-the-scenes look at a TV variety show, ____ ___ _____, has been described as "violently surreal" and "*The Muppets* on acid."

DOWN

1. Although there is a plot (concerning the theft of a machine that allows the user to enter people's minds), _____, a Japanese sci-fi thriller anime, is really an exercise in style.

2. In *The* _____ __ _____, we jump about in time and place, starting with a statue kicking a soldier and ending on a close-up of an ostrich.

3. In ____ _____ by David Lynch, there is a murder... probably. Someone did it... probably. It features Fred Madison (Bill Pullman... sometimes).

4. _____ ____. Through a secret door in her basement (and, subsequently, a large intestinal tract), a young girl finds herself in the sixth dimension.

6. Hiroshi Teshigahara's _____ descends into hypnotic surreality as the lead character and his son wander into a ghost town to join other lost souls.

7. A group of people pretend to be mentally impaired and cause mayhem everywhere they go. Only superficially is ___ _____ a strange movie.

8. _____ _. A mysterious stranger moves in with a dysfunctional Japanese family. It's shot on videotape and comes from the highly prolific modern master of weird, Takashi Miike.

10. _____. After running down a metal fetishist in his car, a Japanese man starts turning into metal.

MOVIES
WORD SEARCH
PUZZLES

For the following word search puzzles, look for the words in **bold**. Whether they're upside down, back to front, right side up, or diagonal—the words in these puzzles will have you searching till you're cross-eyed.

1. ANTIHEROES

```
H  B  E  L  K  C  I  B  S  I  V  A  R  T  N
J  C  F  J  Q  T  L  G  N  T  K  E  G  H  I
I  N  X  K  Y  Y  R  B  B  B  K  I  I  E  K
Y  Q  O  U  S  E  A  D  H  O  W  Y  L  B  S
U  X  Q  S  H  B  U  J  R  U  V  G  D  A  S
F  P  E  V  K  H  K  C  V  I  F  E  C  N  I
K  O  K  O  O  C  E  B  Y  C  V  L  A  D  L
J  X  E  W  Z  I  A  B  J  P  C  E  D  I  P
R  R  N  L  U  B  J  Q  L  T  S  R  T  E
F  E  R  R  I  S  B  U  E  L  L  E  R  H  K
Q  S  A  P  N  K  X  B  Q  K  P  C  P  A  A
L  H  A  Q  O  G  J  Z  V  L  U  Z  K  E  N
C  T  W  D  N  B  U  H  Q  N  M  L  D  L  S
R  E  L  B  A  R  T  S  Y  N  N  H  O  J  Y
E  M  A  N  O  N  H  T  I  W  N  A  M  V  O
```

1.	MAN WITH NO NAME	6.	FERRIS BUELLER
2.	THE BANDIT	7.	TRAVIS BICKLE
3.	LUKE JACKSON	8.	DRIVER
4.	SNAKE PLISSKIN	9.	OH DAE-SU
5.	JOHNNY STRABLER	10.	CHARLIE CROKER

2. MANIC PIXIE DREAM GIRLS

```
X  Y  F  K  Q  T  J  I  S  A  M  N  E  F  L
N  O  L  C  D  F  T  U  B  R  H  P  C  V  D
R  E  W  T  D  A  G  B  T  F  T  N  N  Y  B
U  C  O  M  H  A  K  L  G  B  W  S  A  B  N
B  I  R  Z  R  G  N  I  O  L  E  H  V  D  B
L  K  A  K  I  B  I  N  G  N  G  S  N  O  N
O  T  A  J  D  G  N  L  I  T  Q  R  A  F  H
C  N  X  I  U  N  M  T  O  E  Q  V  S  X  B
E  Z  N  Q  W  U  N  M  B  G  H  E  U  L  O
R  P  N  C  Q  E  D  M  X  V  Y  A  S  F  K
I  P  I  C  M  A  D  I  S  O  N  L  L  T  M
A  Z  L  E  Y  T  C  J  O  N  E  U  L  L  J
L  V  L  Q  A  U  P  F  H  X  A  N  H  O  P
C  C  A  T  H  E  R  I  N  E  E  F  W  N  H
T  O  N  I  S  I  M  M  O  N  S  O  V  Z  P
```

1.	SUGAR KANE	6.	SAM
2.	CATHERINE	7.	HOLLY GOLIGHTLY
3.	CLEMENTINE	8.	ANNIE HALL
4.	MADISON	9.	TONI SIMMONS
5.	SUSAN VANCE	10.	CLAIRE COLBURN

3. SPORTING MOMENTS

```
C B I K X Q I J S I M G S F H
E X B N U L F U E T U L F E U
P C K B X G Y R J C K L M N N
E M N F S Y O J M R O A S I D
K X A A Q T U B O G G V Y L R
Q O Z H T R B D G G F O F G E
D D Z J C S U N N H G Y O N D
L I J T W Y I O F G L I V I M
I I L V I D L D V D A M P S E
V B U U O E D E E X K J R S T
E S I L H Z I S K H B A S O E
M G P T B D T O L I T H M R R
A X M V E I U V L G L Y K C S
E H C E E P S S E H C N I E F
T H G I F O T G N I O G U X U
```

1. **UNLIKELY CHAMP**
2. **IF YOU BUILD IT**, HE WILL COME
3. **THE DISTANCE**
4. THE **INCHES SPEECH**
5. **EXPLODING GOLF** COURSE
6. OVERCOMING **TEAM EVIL**
7. PLAYING **THE LONG GAME**
8. **CROSSING** THE **LINE**
9. DANIEL LARUSSO'S **GOING TO FIGHT?**
10. ABRAHAMS WINS THE **HUNDRED METERS**

4. QUESTS

```
R  M  B  E  U  T  K  X  E  U  W  G  J  C  P
E  D  N  B  C  R  E  A  K  A  U  M  L  A  H
T  J  C  E  A  E  W  L  W  K  Y  N  R  N  Y
I  E  M  U  W  A  E  O  D  F  Q  K  C  T  U
P  U  Q  O  Y  S  V  L  D  O  C  Q  O  G  M
U  F  B  H  O  U  E  N  F  O  R  O  C  N  P
J  Z  O  V  A  R  U  I  V  N  B  A  A  V  G
I  M  D  L  T  E  E  E  S  E  E  D  D  M  J
E  V  G  U  A  P  N  H  T  V  R  D  G  O  G
Z  R  G  K  L  A  H  A  T  G  N  P  L  N  Q
T  H  E  O  N  E  R  I  N  G  M  H  L  O  O
O  L  G  T  Z  I  W  J  P  L  C  P  C  T  G
M  D  Y  N  P  Y  I  P  T  A  H  Q  L  J  Q
N  O  S  R  E  D  N  A  A  L  E  M  A  P  V
E  D  P  C  M  Y  G  L  B  C  E  L  R  R  O
```

1. FIND **A WAY HOME**
2. **TREASURE**
3. THE **GOLDEN FLEECE**
4. **THE ROOM**
5. **THE ONE RING**
6. **PIRATE BOOTY**
7. **PAMELA ANDERSON**
8. MYSTERIOUS SIGNAL FROM **JUPITER**
9. **EL DORADO**
10. THE **ARK** OF THE COVENANT

5. CARS

```
E  R  I  X  U  U  G  P  O  M  K  J  S  I  E
K  L  C  O  Z  B  T  V  R  J  U  R  W  C  A
M  E  L  I  B  O  M  S  E  U  L  B  T  F  Y
I  O  T  H  Q  X  Z  J  T  M  A  O  G  V  O
P  J  E  G  F  Q  R  P  H  T  O  V  A  G  P
W  E  V  I  F  H  C  A  M  N  U  Z  P  I  U
S  I  N  H  E  L  Y  O  E  N  N  D  V  Z  A
V  J  L  W  U  Y  B  C  G  H  R  W  S  U  Q
M  P  O  N  T  I  A  C  T  R  A  N  S  A  M
H  Q  C  X  L  D  E  L  O  R  E  A  N  W  E
K  K  N  E  I  T  H  E  R  B  I  E  N  B  B
N  N  I  L  O  X  W  Q  K  D  V  F  M  F  F
W  K  L  D  O  D  G  E  C  H  A  R  G  E  R
C  A  O  U  Y  B  N  P  T  I  H  K  H  T  O
C  F  L  L  G  R  E  G  N  E  L  L  A  H  C
```

1. BATMOBILE
2. ECTO ONE CADILLAC
3. CHALLENGER
4. HERBIE
5. DODGE CHARGER
6. THE **MACH FIVE**
7. PONTIAC TRANS AM
8. **LINCOLN** CONTINENTAL MKIII
9. THE **BLUESMOBILE**
10. DELOREAN

6. HAUNTED HOUSES

```
Y H T O C T F N G X G E T S C
X O A H N B S N W Y U S I N K
A B R U O A I R M Z L U J D I
P Q H X N R Y B N Y L O G M O
W O X Z U T P U F R C H S I G
J O L J C M I H U Y O L R W W
I U N T H R Y N A S T L E N M
Y O L V E I L K G N T E H H Q
C G W E E R K J L P A H T F I
S T S O H G G S D Y G G O O N
M F O L C Y N E N Q E L E R D
S T N E C O N N I D P Y H C W
N B Z O C B R Z Z S B Z T C H
R G E G D U R G E H T Q E L Q
V Z W W Z E C S J P O R R R P
```

1.	THE **CONJURING**	6.	13 **GHOSTS**
2.	THE **ORPHANAGE**	7.	**THE GRUDGE**
3.	**THE OTHERS**	8.	**GULL COTTAGE**
4.	THE **HAUNTING**	9.	THE **INNOCENTS**
5.	**POLTERGEIST**	10.	**HELL HOUSE**

7. HIGH SCHOOL MOVIES

```
B  I  B  B  X  F  E  S  V  D  D  C  E  N  T
F  R  I  H  W  T  R  O  O  X  R  Y  A  C  E
F  T  E  A  Z  E  W  I  J  C  A  H  I  L  N
A  V  D  A  H  V  W  H  R  C  O  C  R  U  T
J  G  E  T  K  A  V  U  M  F  B  D  M  E  H
Y  F  A  I  A  F  S  W  A  L  K  D  S  L  I
J  E  O  W  P  H  A  C  V  X  C  L  C  E  N
H  N  F  T  M  N  S  S  N  P  A  V  F  S  G
C  W  L  O  M  Y  A  I  T  G  L  S  V  S  S
X  L  R  Y  P  C  Y  C  R  C  B  D  L  G  I
C  E  W  F  K  O  G  E  I  B  L  O  C  R  H
S  L  R  I  G  N  A  E  M  R  Z  U  W  Y  A
P  F  T  F  Z  S  D  Z  D  I  E  F  B  M  T
Q  M  D  B  E  Z  Y  I  F  K  P  M  Z  O  E
E  L  E  C  T  I  O  N  F  J  W  M  A  T  Q
```

1. HEATHERS
2. ELECTION
3. THE **BREAKFAST CLUB**
4. CLUELESS
5. RUSHMORE
6. MEAN GIRLS

7. AMERICAN PIE
8. BLACKBOARD JUNGLE
9. TEN THINGS I HATE ABOUT YOU
10. GREASE

8. MONSTERS

```
E  T  A  B  E  F  P  E  G  O  K  U  P  O  Q
P  H  C  B  B  Y  A  A  H  G  E  H  R  U  K
N  E  K  A  R  K  E  H  T  Z  V  J  C  H  P
T  M  C  Z  Z  I  I  G  O  D  Z  I  L  L  A
A  O  K  H  Y  X  C  N  N  I  J  P  I  T  A
H  N  P  Y  X  Q  N  B  G  I  J  R  Z  T  E
S  S  C  O  O  Z  T  S  L  K  L  P  J  T  R
D  T  V  A  O  T  N  D  J  S  O  W  Q  U  I
I  E  E  N  H  I  S  I  M  N  R  N  A  Z  T
O  R  U  Z  L  P  I  Q  V  J  K  B  G  R  R
B  X  O  M  H  F  X  E  R  R  E  V  O  L  C
A  C  E  Y  L  F  E  L  D  N  U  R  B  X  G
R  R  T  A  F  H  X  Y  J  B  F  G  N  C  F
G  I  A  N  T  T  R  O  L  L  S  D  W  R  L
L  S  O  Z  P  N  N  Q  I  X  G  Q  H  C  H
```

1. GRABOIDS
2. GIANT TROLLS
3. THE **CRAWLING EYE**
4. GREMLINS
5. THE KRAKEN

6. GODZILLA
7. KING KONG
8. BRUNDLEFLY
9. THE MONSTER
10. CLOVER

9. FAMILIES

```
L  I  F  E  I  S  S  W  E  E  T  R  I  E  H
G  Y  K  S  L  T  O  S  G  X  O  J  O  T  O
E  R  B  B  Y  N  E  E  R  C  S  S  R  E  O
M  B  I  M  A  I  X  N  S  V  K  M  R  W  V
Y  K  W  S  E  W  N  E  E  W  N  A  F  V  E
N  K  P  H  W  T  N  U  Y  N  A  D  R  S  R
P  Q  T  W  A  O  R  J  Y  M  B  D  A  O  S
E  J  K  G  E  P  L  B  Z  F  R  A  Q  X  P
M  V  F  L  N  I  B  D  A  M  E  V  U  U  I
M  O  R  F  O  B  F  U  S  G  W  V  Z  M  I
A  O  V  S  T  O  O  S  N  O  S  P  M  I  S
C  I  Y  G  F  G  R  K  N  N  T  Q  O  G  I
P  K  K  E  A  Y  G  W  P  W  E  R  R  O  O
D  G  U  J  C  S  R  B  J  M  R  Y  O  K  J
A  X  L  D  S  R  E  Y  W  A  S  F  P  N  A
```

1. THE **TENENBAUMS**
2. THE **SIMPSONS**
3. UNIDENTIFIED FAMILY IN **LIFE IS SWEET**
4. THE **HOOVERS**
5. THE **GRISWOLDS**
6. THE **CORLEONES**
7. THE **ADDAMS**
8. THE **BREWSTERS**
9. THE **SAWYERS**
10. THE **BANKS**

10. AVENGERS

```
L  G  S  T  X  Y  G  P  W  B  S  Q  M  P  B
E  E  L  A  J  M  U  E  G  H  U  A  A  A  G
W  R  L  E  D  I  R  B  E  H  T  U  T  S  Z
R  L  I  E  M  J  U  K  L  T  L  M  D  T  I
N  E  H  Z  N  E  H  C  I  K  A  E  I  R  T
S  W  R  O  N  A  O  E  E  N  C  A  W  W  E
H  I  E  Y  Z  F  R  R  L  X  K  A  O  K  B
Q  C  F  O  F  O  S  S  J  N  S  L  I  R  G
B  E  I  Y  S  E  Y  I  E  C  P  M  A  U  M
B  K  N  S  Y  E  R  O  E  L  B  I  G  L  B
X  W  N  A  Z  O  C  C  X  S  R  D  Y  S  U
Z  X  E  C  T  V  N  C  X  O  Y  A  A  V  P
H  G  J  V  C  V  W  M  J  X  Y  K  H  H  E
O  H  K  C  D  I  O  W  I  F  O  M  N  C  K
S  U  M  I  C  E  D  S  U  M  I  X  A  M  C
```

1. MATTIE ROSS
2. CHEN ZHEN
3. THE BRIDE
4. JENNIFER HILLS
5. COFFY
6. GEUM-JA LEE
7. MAJOR CHARLES RANE
8. PAUL KERSEY
9. MAXIMUS DECIMUS MERIDIUS
10. BATMAN

11. HEISTS

```
T H E I T A L I A N J O B T F
D O G D A Y A F T E R N O O N
E N T V J E R N T N U M M C C
E N A H X U P W Q Q N S L E H
E A V M E L Q M X K L X L A U
H M Y I E K T X C C O H I N B
H E I Z R D I D V X L I H S Z
Z D D C O X N L D I A V R E G
A I J I H U D O L Q R O E L B
M S V R Q T J P H I U H D E U
V N O N H C T A N S N G N V G
R I F I F I M E J U A G E E G
N Q L T F V R X K H P C V N O
Z N A M R B A H F B U X A R D
R O Y Y I D K U J P E Z L I Z
```

1. RIFIFI
2. INSIDE MAN
3. CASH ON DEMAND
4. THE **LAVENDER HILL MOB**
5. THE ITALIAN JOB

6. SNATCH
7. DOG DAY AFTERNOON
8. OCEAN'S ELEVEN
9. RUN LOLA RUN
10. THE KILLING

12. PERFORMANCES AGAINST TYPE

```
J  T  R  O  B  I  N  W  I  L  L  I  A  M  S
E  O  P  I  K  C  B  M  O  H  D  D  P  X  A
N  W  A  O  T  Q  A  L  E  Z  N  E  D  G  N
N  E  T  U  F  O  L  V  Y  O  V  T  L  X  G
I  Q  R  P  X  A  B  Q  F  Y  S  V  Y  N  E
F  M  I  K  A  J  E  Y  H  Z  U  J  R  W  L
E  O  C  H  B  W  R  V  X  J  O  G  D  D  A
R  R  K  J  U  N  T  P  L  H  Y  N  M  I  L
A  I  S  V  E  M  B  E  L  S  Y  R  L  N  A
N  S  W  H  K  G  R  R  K  A  P  Q  I  M  N
I  U  A  E  W  A  O  B  Q  T  C  P  D  V  S
S  J  Y  U  K  M  O  A  P  T  M  L  P  O  B
T  Y  Z  R  R  E  K  H  A  R  O  B  E  D  U
O  K  E  Q  P  Z  S  J  N  U  Q  B  K  C  R
N  O  R  E  H  T  E  Z  I  L  R  A  H  C  Y
```

1. HENRY FONDA
2. ROBIN WILLIAMS
3. HYE-JA KIM
4. ALBERT BROOKS
5. CHARLIZE THERON

6. DEBORAH KERR
7. JENNIFER ANISTON
8. PATRICK SWAYZE
9. ANGELA LANSBURY
10. **DENZEL** WASHINGTON

13. FILM NOIR

```
A W P O S T M A N A L W A Y S
T S V Q R Y W Y Y E G T B T Y
H H P Q A J I N V W M Y U I A
E M E H U L U M D T F C T N W
B T W B A A D K R V T G U M H
I T R L I L U O M X U E K E G
G F A O H G T F L Y A Z J D I
C W L O G G S J A L D I V N H
L G L D W I Y L U S L T D I S
O Y U S Z R P A E N I R N E E
C I M I E M L U W E G H Y L V
K T X M Y U P R T E P L W B E
G Q Z P V X F A V G N S E U I
Y L E L X T U O N A M D D O H
H F H E U E P Q Q K N U A D T
```

1.	THE BIG SLEEP	7.	BLOOD SIMPLE
2.	THE **ASPHALT JUNGLE**	8.	GILDA
3.	DOUBLE INDEMNITY	9.	ODD MAN OUT
4.	THE BIG CLOCK	10.	THE **POSTMAN ALWAYS** RINGS TWICE
5.	LAURA		
6.	THIEVES' HIGHWAY		

14. DOCUMENTARIES ABOUT CINEMA

```
E  E  S  E  S  R  O  C  S  N  I  T  R  A  M  C
M  Y  B  E  S  T  F  R  I  E  N  D  R  J  E
B  N  L  U  J  W  L  Q  B  K  W  R  W  W  L
H  H  M  H  A  Q  P  A  N  A  E  T  J  Y  L
W  B  R  L  L  P  P  B  M  O  R  H  R  W  U
G  X  D  P  I  J  O  K  K  A  Y  I  S  F  L
M  J  V  S  T  F  S  C  A  N  N  D  K  D  O
Y  N  D  Y  S  G  F  F  A  C  U  C  X  A  I
V  I  S  I  O  N  S  O  F  L  I  G  H  T  D
V  W  M  H  H  P  L  R  Y  Q  Y  X  O  A  C
Z  J  X  M  O  J  I  I  Y  R  A  P  H  Y  L
D  K  J  S  I  V  L  Y  T  G  O  M  S  G  O
A  R  E  M  A  C  E  I  V  O  M  T  S  E  S
P  E  V  E  R  T  S  G  U  I  D  E  S  V  E
F  M  C  M  A  S  Y  C  S  A  J  C  F  S  T
```

1. **VISIONS OF LIGHT**
2. HEARTS OF DARKNESS: A FILMMAKER'S **APOCALYPSE**
3. THE **CELLULOID CLOSET**
4. MAN WITH A **MOVIE CAMERA**
5. THE **STORY OF FILM**
6. **MY BEST FIEND**
7. A PERSONAL JOURNEY WITH **MARTIN SCORSESE**
8. A.K. **AKIRA** KUROSAWA
9. THE **PERVERT'S GUIDE** TO CINEMA
10. LOST IN **LA MANCHA**

15. ANDROIDS

```
R A I C Y T C V E R L J L I S
O E T P H B P P Y A O N E N I
B P G A I Q K Y X H W Z O G P
B W C N D H T G N P L F A I S
Y T H E I R O N G I A N T G S
T H H V X L Y R A X A X J O D
H R X G I F S T R S N Q I L B
E E Z Z I M T N U J D M I O K
R E Y V R J M K U X D T V J Z
O P E Z W V O F M G J C Q O S
B I G Q V K Z K H P E Z G E L
O O T W O I K U I L P H Y K V
T B T T A P Y Q L E T R T W B
V O O Z I G P A W V D B Y O W
F M A R I A W B D S L B P C A
```

1. THE GUNSLINGER
2. DATA
3. THE IRON GIANT
4. ROBBY THE ROBOT
5. MOTOKO KUSANAGI
6. WALL-E
7. JOHNNY FIVE
8. GIGOLO JOE
9. MARIA
10. THREEPIO

16. SIDEKICKS

```
O  J  C  Y  C  B  I  Z  Y  H  N  J  V  M  E
S  J  J  V  X  O  U  J  S  O  T  F  R  I  E
E  H  E  T  L  M  T  F  T  I  M  K  M  T  G
I  D  O  G  A  R  T  H  A  L  G  A  R  C  M
H  Z  U  R  J  M  G  G  R  H  B  C  E  H  A
C  I  Y  D  T  U  K  L  C  H  S  B  N  M  G
G  R  V  F  A  R  D  D  S  E  I  I  F  I  E
N  V  L  N  Y  N  O  R  L  A  F  K  I  T  S
A  Q  L  Z  D  E  F  U  I  G  B  U  E  C  I
W  A  N  R  Z  Q  O  A  N  S  J  F  L  H  W
C  W  T  M  N  N  Q  G  B  D  M  J  D  E  M
N  O  S  T  A  W  N  H  O  J  R  D  B  L  A
P  E  D  R  O  S  A  N  C  H  E  Z  W  L  S
K  N  D  K  V  F  T  V  J  P  P  S  Z  Y  U
E  A  H  P  B  B  J  W  E  I  G  Z  D  R  O
```

1. SAMWISE GAMGEE
2. CAL NAUGHTON
3. GARTH ALGAR
4. SHORT ROUND
5. HAROLD **MITCH** MITCHELL

6. DR. JOHN WATSON
7. DUDE
8. WANG CHI
9. PEDRO SÁNCHEZ
10. R. M. RENFIELD

17. PARTIES

```
Y  F  S  T  H  G  I  N  E  I  G  O  O  B  E
B  P  D  K  T  T  Y  X  D  X  I  K  J  C  C
X  S  G  L  A  D  O  L  C  E  V  I  T  A  N
C  I  V  K  E  N  X  Y  E  O  H  T  E  L  E
L  F  K  J  D  E  I  T  O  N  D  Y  R  Z  I
K  U  K  O  D  I  Q  M  G  M  E  C  O  J  C
H  Z  U  I  E  N  G  O  A  S  O  H  E  L  S
R  Y  A  C  R  C  A  K  W  L  Z  F  U  O  D
I  T  V  B  E  G  Z  I  B  Y  H  R  W  O  R
F  R  P  Q  U  B  D  V  C  J  Y  O  G  H  I
K  A  M  K  Q  E  M  B  G  M  H  U  U  C  E
Z  P  A  X  S  Z  R  Y  T  E  I  C  O  S  W
T  E  A  H  A  C  M  K  C  M  G  Y  U  D  E
Z  H  U  E  M  Q  P  F  G  S  U  M  X  L  C
U  T  H  I  S  I  S  T  H  E  E  N  D  O  X
```

1. MASQUE OF THE RED DEATH
2. EYES WIDE SHUT
3. ANIMAL HOUSE
4. THIS IS THE END
5. SOCIETY
6. WEIRD SCIENCE
7. THE PARTY
8. LA DOLCE VITA
9. BOOGIE NIGHTS
10. OLD SCHOOL

18. TOUGH GIRLS

```
T  Y  N  H  P  E  B  Y  T  G  R  E  A  X  P
M  O  I  Y  I  A  I  U  V  O  D  I  U  V  H
R  K  E  G  P  E  V  S  N  I  C  M  D  C  I
S  N  G  W  M  F  Q  N  R  P  A  N  H  R  L
J  A  E  O  I  B  O  B  E  Y  Q  I  I  P  H
M  N  A  L  I  C  E  O  D  X  N  T  S  Z  J
I  I  J  Q  H  H  F  A  S  A  Y  U  E  L  D
X  P  I  A  T  B  Y  P  O  E  A  I  G  F  O
O  W  R  N  G  J  Q  B  N  V  L  N  D  H  R
C  A  F  M  Z  X  R  O  J  A  Z  E  P  E  V
S  D  S  P  M  I  Z  B  A  P  K  S  N  L  J
Y  H  T  T  E  P  N  B  W  K  H  L  I  E  T
C  Z  N  N  E  T  T  F  C  Q  P  Y  X  F  F
X  S  O  P  U  R  M  G  X  T  C  P  E  U  Z
W  R  X  S  T  E  D  P  U  Z  K  H  H  R  X
```

1. XIAO MEI
2. ALICE
3. THE BRIDE
4. RED SONJA
5. **MAGGIE** FITZGERALD

6. CHINA O'BRIEN
7. MAY DAY
8. SARAH CONNOR
9. NEYTIRI
10. SELENE

19. SEQUELS AS GOOD AS THE ORIGINALS

```
T  S  B  J  Q  O  C  M  T  D  B  W  S  G  M
S  W  O  E  O  H  Y  T  X  A  E  M  R  E  V
O  K  U  U  I  X  O  O  U  E  F  L  I  Z  J
J  Q  R  G  C  A  B  Y  K  D  R  Z  A  T  V
H  W  N  N  S  M  L  S  X  E  A  C  F  I  R
Q  K  E  D  N  D  L  T  M  H  N  R  F  M  S
S  J  S  I  Y  A  E  O  D  T  K  O  A  E  N
L  M  U  F  T  M  H  R  Z  F  E  A  L  I  T
S  C  P  E  L  P  O  Y  C  O  N  A  A  N  C
T  Z  R  B  B  O  H  V  I  N  S  D  N  C  T
E  F  E  Q  Y  E  Y  U  G  W  T  I  R  H  H
X  Q  M  Q  Z  Q  K  Z  M  A  E  A  E  I  V
Q  Y  A  U  X  S  M  B  I  D  I  C  F  N  P
S  E  C  R  U  O  S  S  E  D  N  O  N  A  M
E  N  Y  W  A  E  V  N  M  O  Q  Z  I  V  X
```

1. 28 **WEEKS LATER**
2. **DAWN OF THE DEAD**
3. **MAD MAX** 2
4. THE **BOURNE SUPREMACY**
5. **TOY STORY** II
6. **MANON DES SOURCES**
7. **INFERNAL AFFAIRS** II
8. BRIDE OF **FRANKENSTEIN**
9. ONCE UPON A **TIME IN CHINA** II
10. **HELLBOY** II: THE GOLDEN ARMY

20. FICTIONAL MOVIE PLACES IT WOULD BE GREAT TO VISIT

```
H U N D R E D A C R E W O O D
J O O W U E L A W H M M N E K
B H G J W I R T J V Q H H N Y
K C T S E A H A V E N R K E E
G N U H M H Z Q W S L L Z T D
P T W A B E T K K F P U G R N
G L Y N Q A A O L V C F D M A
O E S G E I X D O G X E J A L
X X Q R D L T H E N E X U S R
Q S C I I C U D M A T X M Y E
L Y O L H J L C L R D O P S D
N D N A L R E V E N V M W N N
V Z H H L S D C V I T P K N O
K A I B C V V W O A A S P D W
M E N A P L O T I P A C E H T
```

1. TOONTOWN
2. HOGSMEADE
3. NARNIA
4. THE NEXUS
5. SEAHAVEN
6. THE CAPITOL PANEM
7. THE HUNDRED ACRE WOOD
8. SHANGRI-LA
9. NEVERLAND
10. WONDERLAND

21. MISGUIDED BELIEVERS

```
L L E U Q E I D D E R F F N A
N G Y B S B N Z C B R A A B M
H A R R Y P O W E L L R I A A
X A E E X U J H U M F N M R R
I X X J O S J R N R C S I R A
D A K Z R L Z S K O H W G Y L
U K Y I L E L B O N F O P Y O
M F T F K L T P L J N R I N M
F R U Z N I E S Z T H T R Y F
I P A R W R M S I N K H U Y T
E L S I R E M M U S D R O L R
C A R D I N A L R O A R K V C
G N S O S P A O K A N L F M K
N A M Y L O H E H T N O M I S
E K H N O I E C W P H G W V N
```

1. ABIN COOPER
2. REVEREND **HARRY POWELL**
3. SISTER JEAN
4. LORD SUMMERISLE
5. MOLA RAM
6. JIMMY LEE **FARNSWORTH**
7. SIMON THE HOLY MAN
8. CARDINAL ROARK
9. FREDDIE QUELL
10. BARRY

22. HEROES

```
B  H  X  P  Z  R  N  V  R  O  X  D  H  J  S
F  P  C  L  Z  O  N  O  L  Q  M  C  D  E  E
Y  H  U  I  N  A  B  N  U  E  N  A  D  F  N
Q  J  D  H  V  I  Q  Q  N  I  F  F  E  F  O
Y  E  O  R  N  O  W  A  F  D  C  S  E  E  J
L  U  C  H  E  X  K  S  E  B  P  U  O  R  A
L  D  O  S  N  L  U  O  H  A  F  Y  U  S  N
O  O  C  A  L  C  P  T  R  O  V  X  O  O  A
D  S  C  I  I  X  H  T  K  B  S  K  U  N  I
E  Z  W  T  Y  D  A  A  O  V  N  A  S  U  D
E  E  T  D  R  C  S  X  N  Z  O  I  N  J  N
R  A  L  R  U  B  O  X  M  C  V  T  R  N  I
Z  D  Q  S  I  X  C  G  O  Q  E  J  Q  E  A
H  X  G  M  H  C  L  Z  O  J  A  G  D  M  J
C  X  A  D  G  W  R  E  J  D  K  H  N  Z  O
```

1. ERIN BROKOVICH
2. ATTICUS FINCH
3. JEFFERSON
4. SHOSANNA DREYFUSS
5. JOHN CHANCE

6. ROBIN HOOD
7. INDIANA JONES
8. SPARTACUS
9. REE DOLLY
10. WILL KANE

23. BUDDY MOVIES

```
S  T  Y  Z  A  R  C  R  I  T  S  D  W  K  S
E  H  E  A  V  E  N  L  Y  U  U  H  O  E  C
N  Z  W  G  P  I  T  H  N  M  E  E  J  N  A
O  E  Y  R  B  S  E  D  B  E  K  N  J  H  E
T  N  I  K  J  S  A  D  L  O  P  N  Y  P  A
N  F  I  S  E  N  U  S  M  L  P  F  R  X  G
A  B  J  W  C  M  O  S  P  M  P  G  V  Q  O
I  P  F  E  B  N  N  H  N  O  P  B  J  F  N
F  Z  K  E  M  I  D  N  I  G  H  T  R  U  N
E  I  R  E  P  Z  F  U  J  Q  J  J  L  R  E
D  C  A  U  D  Z  L  V  H  Y  F  Y  Q  S  U
A  L  E  T  H  A  L  W  E  A  P  O  N  K  B
S  M  I  D  N  I  G  H  T  C  O  W  B  O  Y
V  Z  P  P  J  I  U  U  I  V  G  H  B  Q  O
F  G  O  T  H  W  V  L  Y  W  S  T  W  N  M
```

1. BUTCH CASSIDY AND THE SUNDANCE KID
2. WHEELS ON MEALS
3. MIDNIGHT RUN
4. STIR CRAZY
5. UP IN SMOKE
6. MIDNIGHT COWBOY
7. LETHAL WEAPON
8. THE **DEFIANT ONES**
9. **DUMB** AND **DUMBER**
10. **HEAVENLY** CREATURES

24. MEDICAL DOCTORS

```
O L L E Z S N A I T S I R H C
M G X X P F P D L Y Q N L E Q
A V A A Y V N H Z Q Y R N C K
L M V V E A K R G T N H H R C
C E T U I N V D O I N H R E B
O S T E P H E N M A T U R I N
L G A W A E Z B C A T Y M P A
M W K V R L K I M B Z U A E O
S C Z H J S Q C R H G D M Y M
A V T T X I J U O U L F S E C
Y W Q L M N T P X L Y C W K H
E X V P N G C E N C B F Z W B
R N N M O N T G O M E R Y A K
O D A N A G I R R A G R D H M
P R O F E S S O R M I L L A R
```

1. DR. **MALCOLM SAYER**
2. DR. **YURI ZHIVAGO**
3. DR. NIKOLAS **VAN HELSING**
4. **DR. BLOCK**
5. PROFESSOR MILLAR
6. DR. **STEPHEN MATURIN**
7. DR. **CHRISTIAN SZELL**
8. **DR.** NICHOLAS **GARRIGAN**
9. DR. **MONTGOMERY**
10. DR. **HAWKEYE PIERCE**

25. UNDERRATED MASTERPIECES

```
L  W  S  Q  S  N  O  D  X  F  Y  Y  H  C  S
A  X  X  R  A  Q  F  E  R  A  N  J  Z  A  G
D  Y  Z  I  E  K  D  S  U  E  D  M  R  B  S
Y  N  C  I  F  M  G  J  O  Y  A  A  F  L  E
V  P  M  X  N  A  R  S  U  I  U  M  O  E  Q
E  Z  M  Q  S  C  P  O  T  U  B  Y  S  G  Q
N  U  Z  B  T  L  R  H  F  E  H  R  Y  U  K
G  H  T  Z  A  O  A  B  Y  S  C  F  F  Y  H
E  R  E  V  E  F  T  H  G  I  N  R  R  W  S
A  Y  A  X  T  H  S  P  A  T  O  A  W  E  A
N  M  I  X  E  A  E  M  I  K  I  T  R  Q  A
C  R  T  G  R  Y  N  O  S  F  E  R  A  T  U
E  B  A  F  R  S  O  J  R  W  J  U  Y  Y  R
O  M  H  C  N  U  L  D  E  K  A  N  F  F  O
E  Y  E  S  W  I  D  E  S  H  U  T  Z  D  M
```

1. LONE STAR
2. DREAMS
3. NOSFERATU THE VAMPYRE
4. LADY VENGEANCE
5. THE GAME
6. TRANSFORMERS: THE MOVIE
7. EYES WIDE SHUT
8. SATURDAY NIGHT FEVER
9. NAKED LUNCH
10. THE CABLE GUY

26. 1980s ACTION MOVIES

```
Z  J  P  O  J  L  Y  U  I  D  A  E  E  U  C
E  U  N  U  F  D  U  R  E  P  S  N  J  B  W
N  K  F  E  H  G  K  L  X  U  A  B  T  C  R
F  O  G  S  V  Z  T  V  O  M  C  R  D  N  F
R  L  P  B  W  A  Y  H  L  D  V  T  W  K  V
A  U  F  A  F  M  D  I  E  H  A  R  D  U  B
M  M  N  O  E  A  L  I  E  N  S  O  M  L  N
B  R  R  N  O  W  U  C  I  K  G  B  O  K  V
O  C  O  R  I  U  L  Z  J  O  Y  O  Q  A  G
E  T  E  T  V  N  F  A  S  E  D  C  W  E  E
K  T  O  Y  A  X  G  W  H  S  G  O  G  P  K
M  L  F  A  V  D  Q  M  P  T  M  P  Y  H  C
A  L  D  I  J  Z  E  O  A  G  E  Z  V  B  K
O  U  X  U  O  F  R  R  W  N  P  L  M  L  O
W  Y  O  B  K  T  H  G  P  H  G  I  R  V  K
```

1. THE **RUNNING MAN**
2. **RAMBO**: FIRST BLOOD PART II
3. THE **DELTA FORCE**
4. **ROAD HOUSE**
5. **DIE HARD**
6. **BLOODSPORT**
7. **ALIENS**
8. **ROBOCOP**
9. **LETHAL WEAPON**
10. **PREDATOR**

27. INSPIRATIONAL MOVIES

```
E  L  S  W  R  V  S  Q  E  D  E  N  H  M  D
F  I  A  T  S  I  N  A  I  P  E  H  T  E  R
I  F  O  Y  C  S  I  O  R  P  N  H  A  K  I
L  E  U  S  H  U  F  N  B  M  D  D  R  Q  B
L  I  Y  V  O  L  I  C  Q  N  P  M  W  A  G
U  S  X  W  O  W  C  X  V  O  T  B  F  X  N
F  B  S  J  L  J  W  E  E  U  U  K  O  I  I
R  E  N  B  O  E  S  T  U  M  N  X  S  G  K
E  A  Q  D  F  I  S  U  S  A  Q  T  E  T  C
D  U  L  Y  R  L  M  K  H  J  Q  D  P  U  O
N  T  T  Q  O  E  C  S  Y  Q  M  E  A  D  M
O  I  L  H  C  M  W  R  A  W  R  M  R  W  A
W  F  D  V  K  A  F  X  D  K  N  N  G  C  X
R  U  M  C  H  K  S  P  L  O  C  C  K  S  I
U  L  W  S  T  O  I  L  L  E  Y  L  L  I  B
```

1.	THE **GRAPES OF WRATH**	6.	**DEAD POETS** SOCIETY
2.	TO KILL A **MOCKINGBIRD**	7.	IT'S A **WONDERFUL LIFE**
3.	**THE PIANIST**	8.	**BILLY ELLIOT**
4.	THE **SCHOOL OF ROCK**	9.	**LIFE IS BEAUTIFUL**
5.	THE **SHAWSHANK** REDEMPTION	10.	**AMELIE**

28. AMBIGUOUS ENDINGS

```
D K C N S Z P R Q Z O D T K S
E S M V D O S G N Y G M U I M
T H T T T M K D N D Y S H N O
I A L B D R P T H L Q U T G K
G N K L P K J P H Y G Q N O I
S E C E I P Y S A E E V I F N
I D Z E S V L W J G Z U R C G
X N X K P H A R B N U Y Y O B
Z H I I K T E W P I H F B M A
I T P S S I I L Z H H W A E R
V B U A M A V O T T J H L D R
Y N C G O R I X N E Y C S Y E
U Y J S S T T C S H R C N C L
R E D R U M Y M O T A N A C S
Y Z B Y O A U G P I U U P G F
```

1.	INCEPTION	7.	TAKE SHELTER
2.	CAST AWAY	8.	ANATOMY OF A MURDER
3.	FIVE EASY PIECES	9.	THE THING
4.	SHANE	10.	LOCK, STOCK AND TWO SMOKING BARRELS
5.	THE KING OF COMEDY		
6.	PAN'S LABYRINTH		

29. FEMALE VILLAINS

```
G  S  F  D  N  I  F  H  I  R  O  T  L  Q  R
Y  R  W  O  O  Q  P  G  N  X  Y  A  Z  J  E
M  E  L  R  S  M  N  K  Y  X  D  B  O  J  K
Z  V  V  E  D  R  U  H  W  Y  F  E  V  H  R
O  N  P  E  U  D  R  P  T  S  A  J  Y  Y  A
Q  A  F  N  H  R  S  R  L  F  Y  H  J  X  P
Y  D  W  L  E  A  E  A  C  K  P  Y  J  V  E
F  S  D  E  N  M  R  H  O  V  S  T  S  J  N
I  R  J  W  A  K  A  R  T  F  C  H  B  L  I
S  M  U  I  J  I  T  L  I  A  E  Z  F  M  R
C  M  N  S  Y  K  C  X  R  N  E  G  E  S  A
Y  E  Q  Y  B  Q  H  W  J  D  G  H  G  P  H
M  A  R  G  A  R  E  T  W  H  I  T  E  P  T
Q  Q  E  A  B  X  D  Y  J  G  Q  W  O  T  A
E  G  R  O  E  G  A  N  I  G  E  R  T  N  K
```

1. CAPTAIN **DOREEN LEWIS**
2. **LADY TREMAINE**
3. **BABY JANE HUDSON**
4. **EVE HARRINGTON**
5. **NURSE RATCHED**

6. **REGINA GEORGE**
7. **KATHARINE PARKER**
8. **MARGARET WHITE**
9. **HEATHER** CHANDLER
10. **MRS. DANVERS**

30. BIOPICS

```
B E Q Y U R Y O D T X B Z O V
J Y L D A K L M J M R E H U Q
E A I E O N A K L G L U N Q L
L F N E P X K O R S M G P A P
P H C R F H C E I G N B V I A
O Y O X N L A L E B X I V V E
E U L E A H O N T D E U V Z Q
P Q N M K P D U T E O T W I Y
Y D O R E O P J N M T O F W M
T O P S Y T U R V Y A A D I F
R Z R R B Q O F U F M N S L F
A E S E T S Z S K U D V U Z E
P M A F E H L S S F N B X F E
K R O W T E N L A I C O S A V
S C H I N D L E R S L I S T Y
```

1. **TOPSY-TURVY**
2. THE **ELEPHANT MAN**
3. **LA VIE EN ROSE**
4. **LINCOLN**
5. **MALCOLM X**
6. THE **SOCIAL NETWORK**
7. **SCHINDLER'S LIST**
8. **PERSEPOLIS**
9. **YANKEE DOODLE** DANDY
10. 24 HOUR **PARTY PEOPLE**

31. FAMILY MOVIES

```
S M I T P I O K G P S A X C U
J P F E Y C S B F P K I K R W
B R I R X T G R Z N H I O R U
F I M R S K Y R O T S Y O T T
F N B E I R K W F E F N B G N
D C W S A T Y A O Z G O E Y F
B E O T H L E F D T W Q L X L
R S V R L M X D R C R B G C A
Z S Y I O U A O A L M O N V F
G B W A H T U R Z W U T U J G
J R E L J S O L I H A F J K B
C I V J E E O T W R A Y L Z O
B D E R A S G N I H T D L I W
H E S R T Q C F F A T G E S X
M X B T Q J B I N X E M A A N
```

1. **SPIRITED AWAY**
2. E.T. THE EXTRA-**TERRESTRIAL**
3. THE **WIZARD OF OZ**
4. **WILLY WONKA** AND THE CHOCOLATE FACTORY
5. **TOY STORY**
6. WALLACE & GROMIT IN THE **WRONG TROUSERS**
7. THE **JUNGLE BOOK**
8. WHERE THE **WILD THINGS ARE**
9. THE **PRINCESS BRIDE**
10. MY NEIGHBOR **TOTORO**

32. ANTI-ESTABLISHMENT MOVIES

```
P  A  U  B  H  H  O  Y  I  E  O  Q  F  L  H
U  U  M  S  W  W  I  F  A  V  S  Y  O  Q  C
T  G  N  D  U  X  L  S  E  P  L  N  Y  U  O
N  O  D  I  S  L  Y  G  Q  V  G  C  C  F  N
E  K  Q  M  S  R  R  E  N  D  D  K  G  M  F
Y  M  B  S  I  H  W  Q  I  T  O  F  Y  C  I
S  J  L  D  Y  F  M  S  I  O  W  O  E  F  G
W  Z  E  E  E  V  T  E  S  X  O  G  O  P  U
O  R  G  D  H  A  K  N  N  S  D  O  B  S  R
P  W  E  O  N  F  E  E  J  T  T  O  V  N  A
E  T  N  C  Q  S  B  T  Z  L  P  H  F  R  T
M  D  E  M  T  M  Z  W  O  H  H  A  G  R  I
Q  B  R  N  N  P  X  O  I  S  D  E  R  F  O
C  P  Q  H  P  Y  S  R  M  B  S  Z  A  K  N
K  L  V  M  E  E  B  K  N  S  L  D  J  C  W
```

1. IF
2. ONE FLEW OVER THE CUCKOO'S NEST
3. THE NINTH CONFIGURATION
4. EASY RIDER
5. NETWORK
6. PUNISHMENT PARK
7. REDS
8. FOOTLOOSE
9. PUTNEY SWOPE
10. THE LONELINESS OF THE LONG-DISTANCE RUNNER

33. VILLAINS

```
K A Z W S H J R T W T Q P X Q
C E D J E P A E X Y B P S Q N
P H E N R Y P O T T E R D P O
T Q I T A G S E M D D G P K O
J L M L Q L P V N M A I S D K
N R L D D V S W Y I X K N P T
E R I I N C Z N S J W O T P Z
Y M M A U M A H A Y A D B W R
L M H U B K P T F H D O E O A
D K J A N I N E C O D Y T U V
G W O U L N A R L H G C A M E
T Z F T M R O J A G E V C C J
Z C J Z O S A X V S L R H N J
L L E Z S R D C X I C P E K Z
A I I N S K K R S Z X Y U G E
```

1. THE **CHILD CATCHER**
2. **SILVA**
3. **JANINE CODY**
4. **SCAR**
5. **HENRY POTTER**
6. **NOAH CROSS**
7. **DR. SZELL**
8. **KHAN** NOONIEN SINGH
9. **EDWIN EPPS**
10. COLONEL **HANS LANDA**

34. SCENE-STEALING PERFORMANCES

```
V  G  X  O  I  W  L  W  L  S  E  H  S  F  N
I  J  J  I  H  J  U  D  I  D  E  N  C  H  O
O  N  Z  R  W  E  E  M  P  X  O  P  I  K  S
L  I  F  P  L  G  A  J  H  N  Q  C  Y  Q  R
A  W  R  A  E  W  Z  T  E  A  S  V  O  U  E
D  D  Y  C  O  T  W  W  H  P  E  D  T  Z  T
A  L  W  I  L  L  E  O  K  L  P  H  M  M  E
V  A  C  D  M  D  X  R  E  E  E  U  V  R  P
I  B  X  A  H  T  V  N  S  R  T  D  H  V  B
S  C  U  H  U  I  E  N  F  E  M  N  G  W  O
N  E  G  J  S  G  O  O  D  E  L  D  L  E  B
B  L  Y  W  U  G  R  O  B  E  P  L  V  R  R
S  A  P  E  J  D  E  Q  J  W  M  Z  E  L  O
F  R  F  H  N  W  O  R  B  H  P  L  A  R  P
G  M  E  P  C  C  Z  F  J  O  J  P  W  X  S
```

1. LEONARDO **DICAPRIO**
2. **HEATH LEDGER**
3. **PETER SELLERS**
4. **BOB PETERSON**
5. **VIOLA DAVIS**
6. MARGARET **RUTHERFORD**
7. **ALEC BALDWIN**
8. **EUGENE LEVY**
9. **RALPH BROWN**
10. **JUDI DENCH**

35. WAR MOVIES WITH A DIFFERENT PERSPECTIVE

```
E  E  J  F  S  Y  J  F  O  R  V  T  C  U  D
N  E  A  N  O  W  U  E  G  R  O  U  N  O  H
E  S  U  M  L  V  D  K  V  O  L  O  W  W  T
M  D  D  R  D  M  Y  N  B  L  R  N  O  K  R
Y  N  G  O  I  M  P  S  O  I  F  L  D  G  A
A  A  C  T  E  Z  A  D  F  A  Y  H  I  I  E
T  E  O  N  R  D  E  O  L  N  Z  J  T  A  D
T  M  Y  O  O  N  S  L  R  B  G  S  X  J  N
H  O  W  V  F  S  O  D  U  K  Q  D  M  C  A
E  C  A  R  O  T  A  R  O  T  A  R  O  T  N
G  U  D  R  R  A  M  I  J  O  W  I  F  H  E
A  H  C  U  A  T  P  T  E  O  H  M  M  Q  V
T  P  Q  Z  N  E  D  W  R  C  D  C  A  O  A
E  U  H  M  G  V  S  H  C  W  G  G  U  O  E
S  Q  F  L  E  Z  I  B  J  K  T  S  E  O  H
```

1.	SOLDIER OF ORANGE	6.	ENEMY AT THE GATES
2.	CULLODEN	7.	DOWNFALL
3.	TORA! TORA! TORA!	8.	IWO JIMA
4.	HEAVEN AND EARTH	9.	COME AND SEE
5.	CROSS OF IRON	10.	DAS BOOT

36. PRIVATE INVESTIGATORS

```
Y  Y  Q  P  R  K  T  H  B  N  D  H  P  M  P
R  A  S  A  J  E  S  K  M  I  I  I  P  E  H
P  R  I  B  A  L  M  N  E  C  M  V  R  G  H
I  H  N  S  K  V  E  M  O  K  J  W  Z  E  O
P  D  I  U  E  W  S  G  A  C  Y  B  E  A  I
H  U  D  L  G  Y  X  F  N  H  C  T  E  L  F
N  H  I  B  I  T  Y  R  L  A  E  X  U  Y  T
F  G  I  A  T  P  F  K  O  R  Y  K  W  W  G
J  O  I  E  T  K  M  A  L  L  X  R  I  U  P
Q  P  T  Q  E  V  A  A  H  E  X  D  R  M  D
E  D  A  P  S  M  A  S  R  S  J  I  Y  A  Q
S  F  W  N  U  Y  C  Q  N  L  N  D  R  O  H
Y  E  L  I  A  B  F  F  E  J  O  H  K  Y  H
G  Y  H  C  I  X  A  C  X  A  W  W  O  M  G
B  T  N  A  I  L  A  V  E  I  D  D  E  J  I
```

1. NICK CHARLES
2. MIKE HAMMER
3. FLETCH
4. PHILIP MARLOWE
5. JAKE GITTES
6. EDDIE VALIANT
7. SAM SPADE
8. HARRY ANGEL
9. JEFF BAILEY
10. JOHN SHAFT

37. MAD SCIENTISTS

```
K  R  N  R  K  V  P  J  W  W  T  I  E  Z  S
R  N  E  O  O  G  M  T  W  S  P  V  W  A  U
R  W  F  T  O  T  G  J  E  V  O  U  R  R  I
U  L  U  E  R  N  N  W  A  L  K  D  D  K  R
H  D  F  X  X  U  T  E  E  M  S  S  G  O  O
U  Q  N  R  S  R  F  G  V  Z  U  T  O  V  T
R  R  I  I  E  J  N  N  M  N  I  A  Y  L  E
H  T  H  B  O  A  U  Z  K  R  I  W  P  K  R
U  V  R  G  R  I  K  T  Q  N  B  E  O  J  P
F  E  G  T  D  R  M  O  R  E  A  U  H  C  P
H  L  S  P  M  G  A  U  M  T  N  R  U  T  S
N  R  E  W  R  I  U  K  F  G  K  K  F  P  Z
D  R  C  A  T  H  E  T  E  R  T  M  O  U  D
N  W  O  R  B  T  T  E  M  M  E  M  Q  V  L
I  A  D  Y  N  H  G  C  S  Y  R  F  N  I  P
```

1. **DR. STRANGELOVE**
2. DR. **HERBERT WEST**
3. DR. HANS **ZARKOV**
4. DR. **FRANK N. FURTER**
5. **THE INVENTOR**
6. **DR. CATHETER**
7. DR. **EMMETT BROWN**
8. DR. MICHAEL **HFUHRUHURR**
9. **DR. MOREAU**
10. DR. **PRETORIUS**

38. MARTIAL ARTS MOVIES

```
L  M  O  W  C  N  S  V  W  J  P  Y  M  T  R
U  O  H  I  B  S  W  T  U  O  R  P  A  I  E
F  O  N  Q  T  F  Q  D  T  O  L  F  J  X  G
V  P  Z  E  D  L  O  C  T  L  K  W  X  F  I
K  U  J  L  W  S  E  S  I  M  O  T  Z  I  T
E  L  O  W  T  O  E  B  R  K  C  G  V  O  G
Y  F  E  O  Z  C  L  V  D  H  D  K  F  T  N
O  C  R  T  I  L  A  F  K  E  X  W  V  M  I
Q  Y  U  L  I  M  N  V  M  O  R  E  H  F  H
V  Z  O  K  P  R  L  Q  Y  C  P  B  B  L  C
B  P  C  I  X  K  V  C  Z  B  Q  B  C  M  U
S  X  R  A  R  T  J  A  X  B  F  U  D  Q  O
Z  E  Y  A  H  F  J  R  U  L  F  E  A  E  R
T  R  E  T  S  A  M  N  E  K  N  U  R  D  C
K  U  N  G  F  U  H  U  S  T  L  E  D  F  E
```

1. LONE WOLF MCQUADE
2. HERO
3. REDBELT
4. KILL BILL: VOL. 1 & 2
5. POLICE STORY
6. CROUCHING TIGER, HIDDEN DRAGON
7. JUDO STORY
8. KUNG FU HUSTLE
9. THE LEGEND OF DRUNKEN MASTER
10. MR. VAMPIRE

39. MOVIES ABOUT CELEBRITY

```
S G N I H T G N U O Y B A C I
X Y O F P B H G M T Y X L A M
T K W D G Q C C M E A G M T S
P O E W J O Q D B W O V O I T
R A D H U C S Y E P B T S V I
H S V I Z C E B B C W R T E L
C B Y Z E B E H F A Y J F C L
J K C K I F H L F T N C A L H
U R O R Q C O Y E H D Q M O E
Q B D C Z C W R Y B P Q O D R
K I U F J Z Q F S T R U U A E
E S D R W F K A R D J I S L S
K I N G O F C O M E D Y T W X
G N I R G N I L B E H T D Y A
S U N S E T B O U L E V A R D
```

1. KING OF COMEDY
2. CELEBRITY
3. ALMOST FAMOUS
4. BYE BYE BIRDIE
5. THE BLING RING
6. LA DOLCE VITA
7. SUNSET BOULEVARD
8. TO DIE FOR
9. I'M STILL HERE
10. BRIGHT **YOUNG THINGS**

40. PRISON MOVIES

```
A O A C F U P L N Z D Q G E A
C P U Q M U T O O A H C A P N
U R R X V S Y J I R F V L U U
O J Q O O U S T S T A W A O R
I W B B P X E H U A U I T E N
W U E X V H A M L C B Y S M E
B C I V U W E N L L R C C J K
U E H N S M I T I A U E O T C
Z I G H A R Q Y E E B I R V I
Q E A R F C Q E D P W I P K H
R N N Z S I A N A Y R I Y C
K E D J O T W G A C M H O H H
W B E D W N L F R S X G N W P
X M V S Q T C Z G E C N S O D
S S E R P X E T H G I N D I M
```

1. **HUNGER**
2. **A PROPHET**
3. LA **GRANDE ILLUSION**
4. **RESCUE DAWN**
5. **MIDNIGHT EXPRESS**
6. **CHICKEN RUN**
7. **STALAG** 17
8. FEMALE PRISONER 701: **SCORPION**
9. **ESCAPE** FROM **ALCATRAZ**
10. THE **SHAWSHANK** REDEMPTION

41. SHOOTOUTS

```
H  E  A  T  D  B  I  F  G  B  E  L  S  F  O
B  O  G  Q  H  E  D  N  C  A  G  Y  E  O  V
R  U  T  T  C  E  S  D  V  C  K  F  L  B  W
E  Z  G  F  E  L  M  P  S  E  A  H  B  M  O
Z  X  H  S  U  N  Z  A  E  A  H  C  A  U  D
N  I  N  J  Y  Z  P  J  T  R  E  U  H  P  D
V  W  M  F  M  M  Z  W  H  R  A  W  C  G  E
C  L  Z  M  V  P  A  C  B  I  I  D  U  L  L
E  B  F  P  L  I  N  L  E  U  F  X  O  I  I
U  T  E  M  V  U  R  P  O  P  I  G  T  C  O
G  L  O  H  B  X  D  M  I  N  U  H  N  A  B
G  E  C  D  X  S  H  O  O  T  E  M  U  P  D
Q  I  L  E  S  R  F  H  M  E  I  Y  D  V  R
H  I  L  W  N  Z  R  H  B  D  Q  Q  P  C  A
W  T  S  I  T  O  O  H  S  E  H  T  C  O  H
```

1. HOT FUZZ
2. HEAT
3. DESPERADO
4. BUGSY MALONE
5. THE MATRIX

6. SHOOT 'EM UP
7. THE **UNTOUCHABLES**
8. THE **WILD BUNCH**
9. HARD BOILED
10. THE SHOOTIST

42. CONCERT MOVIES

```
K H S E D A L G N A B T K E E
D L O G F O T R A E H N W S M
K H R X N M S R B E K H W N A
A L D E O G X Y L D I P F E S
J X X E W X L A N T A G F S E
W G I M M E S H E L T E R G H
Z P G U F T P B E U D O F N T
Z V R V W T L C O I F O A I S
Q B G A G C I R T H M O F K N
W T L D E G S B M R X A A A I
V T O P O P Y E R E T N O M A
Z B K J N T B M W D P W B P M
T S U D R A T S Y G G I Z O E
P D O F Q U H M K R J K Z T R
N O R T H E R N L I G H T S X
```

1. **THE LAST WALTZ**
2. NEIL YOUNG: **HEART OF GOLD**
3. **STOP MAKING SENSE**
4. **GIMME SHELTER**
5. THE CONCERT FOR BANGLADESH
6. UNDER GREAT WHITE **NORTHERN LIGHTS**
7. **ZIGGY STARDUST** AND THE SPIDERS FROM MARS
8. **HEIMA**
9. **MONTEREY POP**
10. THE SONG **REMAINS THE SAME**

43. PERFORMANCES BY CHILDREN

```
T  Q  I  S  F  E  R  D  S  T  W  E  P  X  B
A  S  P  Y  O  Z  W  H  V  E  N  A  B  B  R
P  I  I  W  B  P  R  L  R  I  N  K  I  U  I
B  E  D  W  Q  A  H  M  S  C  S  K  L  Y  R
C  P  L  U  T  E  L  W  O  N  F  G  R  E  U
Z  I  U  S  A  R  Z  L  M  R  J  O  V  M  B
A  L  K  G  W  L  E  J  E  Y  V  O  V  L  Z
Z  L  H  M  Z  S  C  V  N  Z  O  M  T  W  M
I  I  B  O  E  F  S  U  I  H  D  Y  U  A  E
F  H  X  A  H  U  I  O  E  L  S  I  T  Z  Z
D  P  R  K  J  Y  R  V  B  I  O  H  V  U  B
W  X  D  F  B  P  I  I  G  X  I  H  O  A  B
I  J  X  A  K  L  V  Q  R  L  V  W  O  R  D
Z  A  N  T  O  I  N  E  D  O  I  N  E  L  R
N  D  E  V  E  R  E  A  U  X  W  F  M  F  E
```

1. OLIVER TWIST
2. CLAUDIA
3. IRIS
4. CLARK "MOUTH" DEVEREAUX
5. PHILLIPE
6. MATHILDA
7. ANTOINE DOINEL
8. COLE SEAR
9. DAVID ZELLABY
10. OLIVE HOOVER

44. SPIES AND SECRET AGENTS

```
J  X  O  C  E  N  R  U  O  B  S  O  H  G  E
W  A  Y  Z  S  L  B  Q  K  S  E  A  A  E  O
M  G  N  T  Z  Q  V  M  Y  G  O  E  R  O  I
D  G  R  E  I  B  D  E  W  Q  L  G  R  R  P
J  A  M  E  S  B  O  N  D  P  L  M  Y  G  J
E  A  L  R  L  M  X  P  F  N  W  S  P  E  M
A  O  S  E  S  S  I  Q  X  I  D  Z  A  S  Y
S  S  Y  O  C  I  E  T  V  L  K  W  L  M  S
C  C  X  B  N  L  S  I  H  V  V  H  M  I  E
B  C  Y  Z  B  B  E  E  W  E  I  N  E  L  T
Y  X  D  C  C  V  O  A  L  D  Y  U  R  E  U
A  Q  D  F  E  F  U  U  M  I  R  D  U  Y  L
K  R  B  G  D  Q  Y  X  R  A  N  E  I  G  C
I  V  F  Y  L  O  E  V  S  N  S  K  G  C  C
Q  O  N  F  X  G  U  Y  V  L  E  H  J  I  Z
```

1.   JAMES BOND
2.   JASON BOURNE
3.   ALEC LEAMAS
4.   JANE SMITH
5.   HAUPTMANN
     GERD WIESLER

6.   OSBOURNE COX
7.   HARRY PALMER
8.   GEORGE SMILEY
9.   T.R. DEVLIN
10. MRS. ISELIN

45. MOVIES ABOUT MOVIES

```
D  G  E  Z  S  Z  X  P  C  S  Q  C  F  H  D
T  S  G  O  G  G  J  J  O  V  Q  Z  N  C  R
B  S  V  U  A  S  C  L  C  A  J  I  N  D  A
D  E  I  X  L  X  S  F  K  V  Y  D  A  B  V
T  D  C  T  J  X  D  K  B  P  S  G  R  M  E
O  J  Q  T  R  O  Q  T  U  C  J  G  Q  O  L
Z  G  M  N  O  A  L  Q  L  H  E  C  O  E  U
Z  V  N  W  G  X  E  T  L  L  A  Y  B  B  O
L  G  D  Y  V  W  N  H  S  P  Q  A  C  Z  B
R  E  Y  A  L  P  E  H  T  U  J  U  T  H  T
R  L  E  Q  M  J  H  B  O  R  D  L  H  C  E
P  J  I  K  Z  Z  H  E  R  V  L  R  C  M  S
G  K  G  U  R  E  V  R  Y  Q  R  R  A  K  N
P  L  E  C  Z  L  Y  G  E  I  N  S  M  T  U
S  U  L  L  I  V  A  N  T  R  A  V  E  L  S
```

1.	GUIDO	6.	THE PLAYER
2.	SULLIVAN'S TRAVELS	7.	SINGIN' IN THE RAIN
3.	STARDUST MEMORIES	8.	ED WOOD
4.	SUNSET BOULEVARD	9.	THE ARTIST
5.	A COCK AND BULL STORY	10.	MULHOLLAND DRIVE

46. VISUAL EFFECTS SEQUENCES

```
B  P  I  M  Q  S  F  V  P  Z  D  N  T  Q  E
R  E  H  S  U  L  I  O  S  W  Z  H  N  D  C
A  A  O  R  Z  L  Y  Y  G  L  E  T  R  M  A
C  R  L  R  S  V  L  K  A  P  L  O  W  D  R
H  L  D  O  X  F  M  O  S  P  T  T  N  Q  D
I  H  H  F  V  K  Q  E  G  A  D  I  O  Q  O
O  A  A  H  C  I  U  F  N  H  V  O  I  K  P
S  R  B  B  P  D  N  I  M  G  B  V  F  A  E
A  B  E  Z  O  A  M  C  X  E  W  I  T  A  H
U  O  B  P  H  R  N  Q  L  L  X  N  J  X  T
R  R  O  M  E  H  O  L  L  O  W  M  A  N  N
U  D  H  T  C  V  T  N  X  S  R  P  W  D  M
S  E  C  A  R  E  L  C  Y  C  T  H  G  I  L
F  O  L  D  I  N  G  P  A  R  I  S  Z  P  V
Y  T  I  V  A  R  G  Q  O  O  H  Z  O  X  X
```

1.	BRACHIOSAURUS	6.	TERMINATOR
2.	THE PSEUDOPOD	7.	HOLLOWMAN
3.	GRAVITY	8.	PEARL HARBOR
4.	FOLDING PARIS	9.	LIGHT CYCLE RACE
5.	THE POD RACE	10.	GOLLUM

47. MOVIES ABOUT ALIENATION

```
T  A  X  I  D  R  I  V  E  R  I  F  A  O  X
K  N  O  I  T  A  L  S  N  A  R  T  G  L  N
C  E  Y  D  O  M  E  H  O  X  V  U  C  J  Z
L  V  D  L  G  E  T  H  G  R  R  A  A  E  R
Y  L  C  R  N  E  T  R  R  Z  F  D  W  C  E
T  B  A  O  L  L  J  X  Z  E  L  A  S  B  I
F  L  O  W  N  E  P  P  E  T  S  N  W  O  W
V  A  A  T  E  P  W  A  M  F  M  A  C  U  L
I  C  O  S  X  H  H  H  S  C  E  Y  R  P  F
A  P  F  O  T  H  T  A  H  S  X  Q  X  E  V
R  C  G  H  K  R  A  K  F  Y  E  Y  V  T  K
V  Z  C  G  A  L  A  O  F  U  N  N  N  S  D
L  I  A  E  X  I  T  D  T  X  M  L  G  Z  L
S  O  H  A  D  I  E  T  A  V  I  R  P  E  Q
E  C  A  L  P  Y  L  E  N  O  L  D  T  Z  R
```

1. **GHOST WORLD**
2. IN A **LONELY PLACE**
3. **STEPPENWOLF**
4. **TAXI DRIVER**
5. **ERASERHEAD**
6. THE **PASSENGER**
7. MY OWN **PRIVATE IDAHO**
8. PINK FLOYD—**THE WALL**
9. **LA STRADA**
10. LOST IN **TRANSLATION**

48. COOLEST CHARACTERS

```
O  S  S  I  L  M  R  B  X  D  N  G  R  D  P
L  G  E  L  R  I  N  L  E  W  Y  P  R  K  E
L  O  P  A  I  J  S  R  O  M  J  A  V  S  T
E  Q  Q  X  B  M  X  R  A  A  C  X  A  D  E
T  E  D  N  O  L  B  R  M  C  J  T  W  N  R
S  J  O  W  Z  E  K  R  I  U  Y  M  S  L  V
O  R  B  S  I  H  F  O  O  L  J  J  W  O  E
C  P  X  K  U  L  P  N  E  W  Z  B  T  Z  N
F  W  C  N  X  L  L  R  G  C  N  Y  E  K  K
E  A  T  S  E  R  D  I  X  S  V  I  O  J  M
J  E  I  H  B  U  J  W  A  N  N  R  N  Y  A
R  U  C  S  R  W  D  U  U  M  V  U  A  G  N
V  I  X  D  O  B  K  O  V  Q  S  O  R  R  J
M  T  E  T  O  N  Y  S  T  A  R  K  Y  E  T
X  N  A  E  V  Y  L  V  V  B  H  T  K  X  Z
```

1.	JACKIE BROWN	6.	PETER VENKMAN
2.	SLIM BROWNING	7.	WILLIAMS
3.	TYLER DURDEN	8.	JEF COSTELLO
4.	MICHEL POICCARD	9.	MR. BLONDE
5.	TONY STARK	10.	MARK HUNTER

49. CONTEMPORARY BLACK-AND-WHITE MOVIES

```
U  D  V  S  H  D  J  T  R  L  N  G  E  U  H
E  O  A  T  D  Z  O  L  G  O  X  Z  N  N  Z
R  O  P  G  C  B  P  W  B  B  K  M  I  L  V
E  W  W  B  I  U  R  B  N  S  F  I  A  F  G
H  D  Z  D  B  Z  I  A  Z  B  M  O  H  T  T
T  E  I  V  K  R  F  U  K  P  Y  J  A  S  Y
T  M  J  J  E  L  R  K  E  J  L  L  L  P  M
N  I  Z  T  H  E  A  R  T  I  S  T  A  N  N
S  A  I  R  O  G  D  O  V  W  Z  Y  Q  W  I
A  H  S  E  C  N  A  R  F  I  Z  K  W  G  O
W  A  S  T  R  O  N  A  U  T  C  W  D  U  P
O  L  X  Q  T  Z  P  S  G  U  N  Z  O  T  I
H  S  C  H  I  N  D  L  E  R  S  L  I  S  T
W  L  J  D  N  V  Y  M  T  R  E  X  K  D  C
S  O  U  G  O  Y  P  U  L  P  F  R  M  B  U
```

1. THE **WHITE RIBBON**
2. FRANCES HA
3. THE ARTIST
4. DOWN BY LAW
5. LA HAINE
6. THE MAN **WHO** WASN'T THERE
7. SCHINDLER'S LIST
8. ED WOOD
9. THE AMERICAN ASTRONAUT
10. **PI**

50. WEIRD WESTERNS

```
T C A O T A F M T R S U Z J W
A K Q F G E O I O E P I A H E
Z N U D P A N P E G F X C O S
T L A K Y Y X L O I Z Y H W T
D K B M T V M R C T S G A E E
L A H O D P A B G K L M R T R
S Z W I J A L U B C N E I F N
Q N D Q T X E K E A U I A A D
F A C E S O F D R L A O H M J
Y X Z A X L G I H B U B R Z A
I G N A W G F O Y E L L A V N
G R E A S E R S P A L A C E G
R V L S Z Q A V A H R F A L O
L L E H O T T H G I A R T S X
O T P D C C K E Z P S T L S F
```

1. TEARS OF THE **BLACK TIGER**
2. SUKIYAKI **WESTERN DJANGO**
3. **ZACHARIAH**
4. THE TERROR OF **TINY TOWN**
5. FACES OF DR. LAO
6. EL TOPO
7. VALLEY OF GWANGI
8. STRAIGHT TO HELL
9. GREASER'S PALACE
10. DEAD MAN

51. MOVIES THAT'LL MAKE YOU CRY

C V M Q K K N E B B Y Z D O L
O U Y A Y L R U I A R A M G L
V Q L Y G T T M Q M O R S T W
R O E T S T J X C B T T E F X
V J F S E D Z I D I S T I Z U
O K T R M T N U D Y E X L E J
L K F J U A U E G F V N F F N
D L O Z T G E K O I O Y E I I
Y D O I D L U E E X L Z R N Z
E H T I A U D S Q J G I I Z K
L I F E I S B E A U T I F U L
L C I N E M A P A R A D I S O
E M I W F A J Q Y S Y C Q D K
R A F F A I R R E M E M B E R
E R A W X Y M N B O H S W A I

1. THE DIVING BELL AND THE **BUTTERFLY**
2. MY LEFT FOOT
3. BAMBI
4. TITANIC
5. LOVE STORY
6. OLD YELLER
7. LIFE IS BEAUTIFUL
8. AN **AFFAIR** TO **REMEMBER**
9. CINEMA PARADISO
10. GRAVE OF THE **FIREFLIES**

52. HENCHMEN

```
N W Z B M M X A S L O R G D B
D V J Z O L Q O O D Z G S Z H
H M I K B D P F L E O N A R D
Z U E B V E D I Y I X I K I Z
I P B U O I W I E D B S L G L
E P T G X N R E C U E K B G Q
E M I H A G E N Z K S N P N L
S R J U J V Y A E N E X R M A
M R J O S H U A O M F R K S P
D I X D E J E I L L U M P O U
B I N I C K N A C K L Y T U S
Q R K I L I V M A U F D N R M
A W S R M Y E H S X S C E W M
N R W D T E N M F X N Z O L U
C C I B F Z R H F T W H A T S
```

1.   MR. JOSHUA
2.   MR. IGOE
3.   MINI ME
4.   NICK NACK
5.   JUAN WILD

6.   CLARENCE **BODDICKER**
7.   THE **MINIONS**
8.   **LEONARD**
9.   **KLYTUS**
10. **WEZ**

53. COMING-OF-AGE MOVIES

```
H  I  E  I  L  E  Q  Y  K  E  R  C  W  V  E
S  P  L  O  V  S  V  A  V  J  T  I  H  P  M
I  I  A  I  K  B  W  O  P  F  T  X  X  Q  Y
F  K  H  W  I  T  R  Y  L  H  S  N  J  N  B
E  Q  W  I  G  O  N  V  O  E  Z  Y  R  D  D
L  K  D  E  T  T  U  U  T  J  M  J  W  D  N
B  D  N  D  M  I  T  A  D  K  O  W  V  P  A
M  C  A  Q  M  A  F  U  C  I  W  W  O  Q  T
U  T  D  H  C  F  G  F  K  D  V  Q  K  H  S
R  W  I  A  V  D  X  W  A  S  Y  D  D  L  S
N  M  U  I  M  H  Z  H  B  R  Q  S  V  N  R
G  S  Q  R  Y  D  R  Q  O  F  G  U  O  A  C
E  F  S  I  P  C  A  A  O  N  S  J  U  N  O
L  A  S  T  P  I  C  T  U  R  E  S  H  O  W
K  D  N  A  L  E  R  U  T  N  E  V  D  A  L
```

1. AMERICAN **GRAFFITI**
2. THE **LAST PICTURE SHOW**
3. **RUMBLEFISH**
4. **ADVENTURELAND**
5. REBEL **WITHOUT A CAUSE**
6. **JUNO**
7. **KIDS**
8. **SHOW ME LOVE**
9. **STAND BY ME**
10. THE **SQUID AND THE WHALE**

54. ANIMATED CHARACTERS

```
C A R I M Z L Q C J F D B I N
Y R F A T I M O R G T S J L O
P U U G E Y A M Z J S Z C E S
U T T E J Y A S T H Q B F A P
S I N Y L Z T O M X V O L D M
S X M B H L T H K M M H J D I
I U H E Z O A A G T W W W V S
N Z L N R B N D A I N G V S R
B Q G O F E U V E Q L C N K E
O G A L D P M G R V H Z M F M
O H B A J K N Z D E I T Z R O
T E X B Y W J Z C I J L Q U H
S L S F V T O O L A B X U I B
N S I T A C V B S Q H Y G V X
J A C K S K E L L I N G T O N
```

1. CRUELLA DE VIL
2. ELSA
3. TOTORO
4. BALOO
5. BUZZ LIGHTYEAR
6. HOMER SIMPSON
7. JACK SKELLINGTON
8. PUSS IN BOOTS
9. KANEDA
10. GROMIT

55. KISSES

```
E  J  N  D  K  N  U  K  A  E  J  O  C  G  V
T  O  M  L  U  A  P  Y  L  L  O  H  B  B  T
T  H  Z  C  P  R  A  V  N  E  A  A  Y  Y  T
O  N  C  E  C  I  L  I  A  R  O  B  B  I  E
L  N  X  Z  S  F  P  W  L  O  X  W  B  J  L
R  Y  D  S  A  U  N  E  W  M  B  M  O  V  R
A  B  H  Z  L  P  S  S  R  E  E  H  T  O  A
H  A  Q  T  Y  C  O  P  N  O  N  E  C  Z  C
C  B  Y  V  A  X  R  N  Y  J  P  Q  C  T  S
B  Y  I  R  U  H  I  I  O  U  O  Y  M  J  T
O  Z  R  Q  M  S  F  E  D  L  C  Q  Z  U  T
B  I  I  W  J  Z  Y  L  O  I  M  M  G  I  E
E  B  S  A  A  P  L  H  I  E  W  D  A  T  H
F  S  C  Q  X  L  A  D  Y  T  R  A  M  P  R
F  K  W  T  A  P  E  F  M  Y  G  Q  G  Y  U
```

1. **CHARLES** AND **CARRIE**
2. **ROMEO** AND **JULIET**
3. **LADY** AND THE **TRAMP**
4. **BOB** HARRIS AND **CHARLOTTE**
5. **JOHNNY** AND **BABY**
6. **CECILIA** TALLIS AND **ROBBIE** TURNER
7. **JOHN** PRENTICE AND **JOEY** DRATON
8. **HOLLY** GOLIGHTLY AND **PAUL** VARJAK
9. **RHETT** BUTLER AND **SCARLETT** O'HARA
10. **ENNIS** DEL MAR AND **JACK** TWIST

56. HAMMER HORROR

```
W  Y  D  H  T  J  T  N  C  E  B  F  V  Z  S
G  U  N  E  F  C  X  Q  L  O  L  A  D  O  I
G  K  A  N  V  P  V  B  S  O  M  K  D  M  S
F  S  P  W  A  I  A  Y  W  P  F  V  X  B  T
M  K  S  B  X  N  L  E  I  R  R  X  R  I  E
S  W  U  L  I  C  R  R  C  I  A  C  J  E  R
Z  G  D  M  X  E  E  K  I  Z  N  S  J  S  H
S  W  O  M  W  C  Z  N  O  D  K  A  W  Q  Y
Y  B  T  T  I  P  S  Z  R  F  E  Y  W  S  D
A  L  F  R  Q  O  V  A  M  W  N  S  D  O  E
Q  H  C  X  F  C  C  D  C  Z  S  P  O  N  M
U  U  U  H  Q  U  C  Y  W  Z  T  Q  Y  U  O
S  H  S  J  L  G  Z  N  R  L  E  Z  L  Z  T
R  E  R  A  R  P  N  Y  D  K  I  R  W  R  G
Q  U  A  T  E  R  M  A  S  S  N  B  F  O  U
```

1. THE CURSE OF **FRANKENSTEIN**
2. **VAMPIRE CIRCUS**
3. THE PLAGUE OF THE **ZOMBIES**
4. **QUATERMASS** AND THE PIT
5. THE **NANNY**

6. DR. JEKYLL AND **SISTER HYDE**
7. THE **DEVIL RIDES OUT**
8. THE **ABOMINABLE** SNOWMAN
9. CURSE OF THE **WEREWOLF**
10. HORROR OF **DRACULA**

57. ESSENTIAL DOCUMENTARIES

```
M  I  N  J  O  U  D  C  V  K  R  S  M  Z  N
U  A  O  I  Q  E  J  P  L  L  A  R  M  Z  Y
G  D  N  F  X  G  E  I  F  G  T  E  D  T  T
A  O  A  O  V  Q  M  W  C  S  H  T  I  H  N
T  U  Q  H  N  Y  Y  Q  P  X  E  P  P  I  U
E  I  Z  M  E  W  U  E  F  P  D  U  V  N  O
S  S  S  V  J  C  I  G  Q  N  A  R  G  B  C
O  E  R  N  L  V  I  R  A  W  R  R  J  L  N
F  A  R  I  F  X  N  W  E  W  K  E  T  U  A
H  R  V  M  J  S  O  T  Q  F  S  T  S  E  L
E  N  E  Y  B  R  V  I  T  Q  I  N  T  L  R
A  D  C  A  R  F  F  Q  S  G  D  I  I  I  A
V  W  P  O  W  L  S  I  O  B  E  E  F  N  H
E  E  S  H  Z  F  S  D  B  B  F  S  O  E  N
N  T  H  I  S  I  S  N  O  T  A  F  I  L  M
```

1. **MAN ON WIRE**
2. THE TIMES OF **HARVEY MILK**
3. THE **SORROW AND** THE **PITY**
4. **GATES OF HEAVEN**
5. **THIS IS NOT A FILM**
6. THE **THIN BLUE LINE**
7. THE **INTERRUPTERS**
8. TAXI TO **THE DARK SIDE**
9. **HARLAN COUNTY** U.S.A.
10. **ANVIL!** THE STORY OF ANVIL

58. MOVIES ABOUT MORTALITY

```
A  N  F  H  C  S  K  A  F  L  U  O  V  N  L
Y  B  K  R  T  E  Q  K  A  R  I  I  G  N  A
R  I  O  S  P  A  F  T  I  E  H  G  X  S  E
O  G  A  U  F  I  E  K  B  Z  B  I  E  K  S
T  T  K  C  T  N  I  D  N  N  W  V  Z  H  H
S  W  M  P  N  S  P  J  D  I  E  G  S  V  T
T  O  K  F  W  I  C  H  Q  N  A  Y  C  Z  N
H  V  T  V  L  D  Y  H  P  N  A  K  X  U  E
G  F  V  P  I  E  N  O  M  Z  G  E  E  C  V
I  X  W  L  W  L  U  C  R  I  H  S  F  P  E
A  D  T  I  H  N  J  D  O  L  D  Y  T  I  S
R  B  Z  R  D  Q  W  M  I  O  G  T  O  F  L
T  A  Y  S  E  I  R  R  E  B  W  A  R  T  S
S  T  O  K  Y  O  S  T  O  R  Y  D  V  T  G
E  F  I  L  F  O  G  N  I  N  A  E  M  U  I
```

1. ABOUT SCHMIDT
2. THE SEA INSIDE
3. SEVEN POUNDS
4. WILD **STRAWBERRIES**
5. A MATTER OF **LIFE AND DEATH**
6. THE **STRAIGHT STORY**
7. TOKYO STORY
8. THE **MEANING OF LIFE**
9. THE **SEVENTH SEAL**
10. **IKIRU**

59. WORST VIDEO GAME ADAPTATIONS

```
D  Q  H  N  X  E  Q  F  G  E  M  R  R  R  X
O  U  W  P  O  Q  S  V  F  P  H  E  B  T  A
U  U  X  X  A  I  W  M  O  O  D  S  L  L  B
B  I  N  C  R  G  T  N  E  N  U  I  O  F  A
L  B  L  V  T  H  Y  A  A  O  L  N  O  V  J
E  R  W  W  W  C  E  M  L  J  E  V  D  U  K
D  S  U  P  E  R  M  A  R  I  O  B  R  O  S
R  M  R  Z  P  O  M  A  N  H  H  K  A  J  B
A  X  K  X  C  Y  A  T  X  V  Z  I  Y  F  S
G  D  U  G  O  Y  H  Z  R  P  W  Q  N  T  W
O  X  N  M  B  E  E  Q  V  E  A  Q  E  N  E
N  I  E  H  D  K  W  P  I  W  E  Y  R  O  A
W  N  Q  A  G  N  F  P  Q  L  S  Q  N  Y  P
S  T  R  E  E  T  F  I  G  H  T  E  R  E  K
R  K  T  O  M  B  R  A  I  D  E  R  M  R  A
```

1. WING COMMANDER
2. SUPER MARIO BROS.
3. MORTAL KOMBAT: ANNIHILATION
4. DOUBLE DRAGON
5. MAX PAYNE
6. BLOODRAYNE
7. DOOM
8. STREET FIGHTER
9. ALONE IN THE DARK
10. LARA CROFT: TOMB RAIDER

60. TOUGH GUYS

```
N V X W Q U X X C T H P E N O
R A Y Q R J E S U R R P O P V
E G M A T T H U N T E R D K U
N L G S R F V I O H O I D G R
R I F L I I Y U H O R Y E L O
U A K O P E A N A M Z H B A O
T T I R B J R R A A X C O O Q
K G Q O Y K I C N S Q Y L O S
C N Y I H N H G T D X O I Y S
U A Y C A E Y D L U O K H L Q
R I P N T B P P J N V I P W J
T H O E B V M F A S E M I Z C
C C L X S W B O N O U N I L D
A E Z R K S K V V N E R H W I
M P A U L K E R S E Y L S S L
```

1. REISMAN
2. MATT HUNTER
3. THOMAS DUNSON
4. BRITT
5. MACHETE
6. PHILO BEDDOE
7. MAC "TRUCK" TURNER
8. PAUL KERSEY
9. CHIANG TAI
10. CONAN THE BARBARIAN

61. MACGUFFINS

```
M  Y  U  Y  T  M  R  J  E  S  U  J  L  F  S
A  J  E  K  F  F  Y  E  C  B  L  T  E  T  H
L  G  X  S  S  Y  Z  P  I  J  M  U  E  C  A
T  M  N  T  A  N  O  L  V  F  I  R  L  D  D
E  I  N  I  T  C  A  H  E  X  C  E  K  W  K
S  K  B  B  R  M  F  F  D  E  V  B  V  A  P
E  S  Y  R  Y  E  H  E  S  K  J  E  C  R  H
F  Y  O  V  V  L  N  Y  I  A  M  T  G  E  X
A  C  E  T  H  M  R  O  S  R  K  A  X  R  K
L  H  U  S  F  A  O  H  E  Y  B  K  I  D  Z
C  C  X  A  T  V  M  U  N  H  P  R  R  X  H
O  U  B  I  C  Y  C  L  E  Q  T  S  Z  B  X
N  O  L  I  Q  S  S  O  G  I  B  X  J  U  L
X  I  T  N  A  N  E  V  O  C  F  O  K  R  A
M  T  H  E  H  O  L  Y  G  R  A  I  L  O  O
```

1. 1964 **CHEVY MALIBU**
2. THE **GENESIS DEVICE**
3. THE ONE RING
4. MILITARY SECRETS
5. THE HOLY GRAIL
6. THE **ARK OF** THE **COVENANT**
7. BRIEFCASE
8. THE **MALTESE FALCON**
9. BICYCLE
10. A BOX

62. CAR CHASES

```
R V C W M H A D K D I F G B F
I O A J T H Y B F Q B R O A O
T R A N S P O R T E R U S E O
L O X O I N D Q O U R T E U R
D J L I N S E I R N F F C S P
U X K I H G H P E I I Q O E H
K B O R V N F I V Y X N N I T
I I C J T E D E N G H J D D A
E J R A W E A D K G S V S R E
E K M G N S V N P N P Y V E D
N Z E T C F P X D V Z O H V F
H V I X Z H J H B D O Y I E I
B T O E X R Z J A N I W S N O
Y D E V T R J U C Q P E P N T
D E D A O L E R X I R T A M E
```

1. **TO LIVE AND DIE** IN LA
2. THE **TRANSPORTER**
3. **VANISHING POINT**
4. TOMORROW **NEVER DIES**
5. **FAST FIVE**
6. THE **BOURNE IDENTITY**
7. GONE IN 60 **SECONDS**
8. THE **MATRIX RELOADED**
9. **RONIN**
10. **DEATH PROOF**

63. MUSICALS FOR PEOPLE WHO DON'T LIKE MUSICALS

```
T  S  O  D  Y  I  L  O  V  E  Y  O  U  E  Y
A  Q  I  M  B  A  O  O  C  Q  E  O  K  G  P
B  S  M  R  L  R  N  T  D  C  L  U  Y  U  R
P  O  A  U  U  A  P  P  Y  H  L  A  M  O  Q
T  S  Z  Z  E  K  K  X  N  G  O  U  M  R  O
N  L  K  I  S  J  A  N  Y  G  W  K  J  N  I
Y  D  J  Q  B  Z  O  T  O  E  G  O  R  I  L
C  H  M  I  R  T  N  A  W  C  C  O  L  B
X  I  U  S  O  F  S  D  T  K  Y  P  T  U  B
O  A  O  T  T  F  K  Y  A  K  L  L  E  O  H
J  N  W  H  H  L  O  R  N  T  F  U  L  M  G
H  H  C  P  E  P  T  R  B  D  P  S  N  I  L
L  W  N  E  R  K  R  A  P  H  T  U  O  S  W
C  L  X  M  S  X  P  P  I  Q  G  X  B  X  V
R  O  R  R  O  H  Y  K  C  O  R  M  H  P  Q
```

1. **SOUTH PARK**: BIGGER, LONGER & UNCUT
2. **WILLY WONKA** AND THE CHOCOLATE FACTORY
3. **MOULIN ROUGE**
4. **TOMMY**
5. EVERYONE SAYS **I LOVE YOU**
6. **ONCE**
7. THE **BLUES BROTHERS**
8. THE **ROCKY HORROR** PICTURE SHOW
9. **YELLOW** SUBMARINE
10. THE HAPPINESS OF THE **KATAKURIS**

64. MEMORABLE DEATHS

```
T  O  E  J  T  L  N  C  E  N  T  F  N  B  K
O  H  N  K  Y  N  Q  Y  N  R  I  O  S  U  O
N  S  A  I  L  E  T  G  S  R  S  W  U  T  K
Y  K  K  Z  B  M  T  Q  S  R  W  B  A  C  A
M  X  W  V  T  M  I  T  E  M  N  Q  G  H  R
O  X  U  U  S  D  S  T  R  P  K  A  K  S  D
N  F  Z  F  H  C  S  C  Q  I  B  Z  Q  U  O
T  E  E  M  A  A  R  T  O  B  V  G  E  N  T
A  L  C  N  M  E  X  Q  J  X  Q  V  U  D  S
N  F  N  L  O  N  O  S  W  A  D  K  C  A  J
A  E  L  S  J  E  E  L  I  Q  B  E  N  N  O
R  I  O  H  P  W  X  M  N  Z  T  X  W  C  R
J  T  Z  E  T  K  H  D  W  A  V  B  S  E  C
E  R  Y  P  R  J  U  X  Y  Y  T  K  C  R  C
R  U  S  S  E  L  L  F  R  A  N  K  L  I  N
```

1. KANE
2. JILL MASTERSON
3. BEN
4. **BUTCH** CASSIDY AND THE **SUNDANCE** KID
5. MR. CREOSOTE
6. JACK DAWSON
7. RUSSELL FRANKLIN
8. TONY MONTANA
9. FIRST SCANNER
10. SGT. ELIAS

65. TIME TRAVEL MOVIES

```
S  P  A  B  V  Y  A  Z  S  B  K  R  K  S  A
P  R  I  M  E  R  S  O  Q  O  O  H  T  A  R
D  V  U  M  Z  V  G  I  X  T  P  I  L  T  M
E  E  D  E  A  H  G  Q  A  S  D  H  W  Q  Y
T  A  N  K  T  A  C  N  A  N  H  E  Q  M  O
D  H  R  I  I  I  I  Q  A  N  L  K  P  M  F
N  F  H  Q  H  M  S  B  I  V  S  V  U  Z  D
A  O  Q  R  R  C  E  I  E  P  L  Z  F  R  A
L  C  X  E  R  M  A  M  V  Q  U  T  B  E  R
L  F  T  R  I  N  O  M  V  S  R  G  W  P  K
I  N  V  T  I  N  N  O  E  S  E  U  M  O  N
B  Q  S  Y  K  M  H  W  P  M  T  L  Y  O  E
G  X  A  E  C  W  P  E  M  Q  I  A  S  L  S
A  I  Y  R  U  R  O  O  S  Y  D  T  Y  K  S
E  S  U  O  H  R  E  T  H  G  U  A  L  S  Y
```

1. LES VISITEURS
2. LOOPER
3. TIME BANDITS
4. PRIMER
5. ARMY OF DARKNESS
6. TWELVE MONKEYS
7. SLAUGHTERHOUSE FIVE
8. HOT TUB TIME MACHINE
9. BILL AND TED'S EXCELLENT ADVENTURE
10. THE TERMINATOR

66. SAMURAI MOVIES

```
D  Y  V  S  G  M  J  G  A  K  D  E  G  T  A
I  F  U  J  C  J  V  F  T  S  O  C  D  W  M
W  Y  J  Z  L  Q  I  R  S  E  O  N  R  I  P
N  O  I  L  L  E  B  E  R  V  L  A  S  L  D
Z  M  P  S  H  R  T  G  S  Q  B  E  V  I  E
G  X  O  F  I  B  Q  N  D  P  W  G  X  G  F
A  O  F  O  V  C  I  G  N  M  O  N  Y  H  K
C  Y  Y  R  D  S  N  Z  G  L  N  E  H  T  A
A  L  U  O  S  F  A  Z  N  X  S  V  A  S  G
J  L  H  A  K  T  O  Y  K  Q  Y  D  R  A  Q
J  W  S  F  O  I  R  D  B  Q  D  R  A  M  I
S  S  S  I  N  I  N  E  R  G  A  O  K  U  J
A  M  C  Y  O  J  I  M  B  O  L  W  I  R  V
K  H  W  M  Q  N  S  J  H  G  W  S  R  A  Z
I  H  B  X  U  N  P  M  W  K  C  S  I  I  B
```

1. **HARAKIRI**
2. **ZATOICHI**
3. SAMURAI **REBELLION**
4. THE **SWORD OF DOOM**
5. **LADY SNOWBLOOD:** BLIZZARD FROM THE NETHERWORLD
6. THE **TWILIGHT SAMURAI**
7. **SWORD** OF **VENGEANCE**
8. 13 **ASSASSINS**
9. **YOJIMBO**
10. **GOYOKIN**

67. GANGSTERS

```
Q O N D V C I R N N L E F B M
F B G X F R F H J E H R O R A
J W E R Z D D A O E N J Y A L
M A X B E R C O V I C Z I D I
Q D W E I V B N U U Q I N T K
K K U E I A Y H Z G C A E E E
Q Y D D N V M A D I H M T C L
Y Y S N K A J K R S D B V J D
M C O Q N U P W D V U I O T J
Q N Z A Y K N L X I W B X Y E
O L L E T S O C K N A R F J B
F X R Y V R S T Y P X I W K E
R A S E A C E L T T I L L D N
O V L H T O M P O W E R S Q A
T O M M Y D E V I T O X U A V
```

1. MAX BERCOVICZ
2. DOUGHBOY
3. MALIK EL DJEBENA
4. LEO O'BANNON
5. FRANK COSTELLO
6. HAROLD SHAND
7. TOMMY DEVITO
8. LITTLE CAESAR
9. RAY VERGO
10. TOM POWERS

68. MILITARY MEN

```
B V K Y Q B I O B P N J N C G
C M D M B H X J P I M O W K P
N O G R M N S Q C C T H P C V
H K L W A Q N H Q T Z N S T Z
A P G O T H O A A V T W E V U
R E J J N L C P F N L I M W W
T Z Z T S E E I Y H P N A U D
M D B O E G L W R T F G J B X
A B N V R S U D M U F E M F P
N L I O N E L M A N D R A K E
W T E X L B B J B X V P I Z H
F G E M V I R G I L H I L T S
Y E R O G L I K M A I L L I W
F H C Z O I V C X B V S I A B
M G B D L R D R L B N E W Q Z
```

1. **RICHARD**
2. SGT. **WILLIAM JAMES**
3. GENERAL **GEORGE PATTON**
4. GROUP CAPTAIN **LIONEL MANDRAKE**
5. **COLONEL DAX**
6. GUNNERY SERGEANT **HARTMAN**
7. COLONEL **NICHOLSON**
8. LIEUTENANT COLONEL **WILLIAM KILGORE**
9. CAPTAIN **VIRGIL HILTS**
10. PRIVATE **JOHN WINGER**

69. WOMANIZERS

```
M W B S Q E J C M Z R Y G J K
F A V Z E Y A A W F E D E A V
P O H N T S H B C K V I O C I
N E O A A Y H G C K R A R K R
B P R N R T Q A C T A P G J C
Y F O X R G M V W F G O E E F
O V R T N K S V D F E I R R U
A N H J N I Q U M S V R O I P
Z M I A F E P A C Z A D U C F
Q L R N P U E B S R D I N H X
T F Z K X Y J B L K A B D O P
Y E N U A L E D D N O M Y A R
B L A C K D Y N A M I T E X Z
I J E K A L F I E E L K I N S
B D E Z G J W J T E D L E X P
```

1. MARCUS GRAHAM
2. DAVE GARVER
3. FRANK MACKEY
4. ALFIE ELKINS
5. GEORGE ROUNDY

6. RAYMOND DELAUNEY
7. BLACK DYNAMITE
8. JACK
9. JACK JERICHO
10. CASANOVA

70. TWIST ENDINGS

```
P T N E N Q Z Y D P N E B N U
F L R A W W Q R S T M H E S S
Q N A L K S O Y U A B E S E U
G K H N C W C T G Q R W J U A
Y Z W Z E H J G A G R T T Q L
X B V K O T N N T N I T M I S
A U G Q V I O N D W I F E L U
C L S Z Y H E F C C Z H V O S
R C N R K L J I T I Z Y C B P
Z T C J Y W N D P H B R Q A E
I H V O G V L Z M W E N X I C
O G S J N M B E L D L A O D T
P I E G A N A H P R O M P S S
D F F P B I V J O Q J D Y E M
Y A D S L O O F L I R P A L S
```

1. APRIL FOOL'S DAY
2. CHINATOWN
3. FIGHT CLUB
4. SOYLENT GREEN
5. PLANET OF THE APES
6. THE USUAL SUSPECTS
7. PSYCHO
8. THE ORPHANAGE
9. LES DIABOLIQUES
10. THE CRYING GAME

71. ACTOR-DIRECTOR PARTNERSHIPS

```
M  I  F  U  N  E  K  U  R  O  S  A  W  A  N
B  F  N  P  B  C  D  D  R  K  W  N  A  E  N
B  F  H  I  L  F  A  X  S  F  Z  S  T  Y  A
O  R  I  N  E  D  E  S  E  S  R  O  C  S  E
F  T  B  O  O  W  U  U  P  Q  F  T  P  Y  L
N  O  M  I  A  T  Z  H  R  I  O  M  M  D  S
R  B  R  B  N  O  A  D  W  M  G  K  J  O  S
B  X  X  D  A  I  Z  E  Z  C  E  S  T  W  E
L  M  O  R  W  E  L  K  K  S  H  K  K  B  N
L  Q  A  E  X  A  A  L  O  N  B  N  L  E  N
P  H  I  I  W  J  Y  L  E  D  E  Y  A  R  I
T  B  O  U  W  X  T  N  N  F  G  L  B  G  U
D  Z  H  T  P  T  N  W  E  F  X  P  L  M  G
R  E  D  L  I  W  N  O  M  M  E  L  F  A  L
E  K  I  N  S  K  I  H  E  R  Z  O  G  N  R
```

1. SCORSESE / DE NIRO
2. ALLEN / KEATON
3. GUINNESS / LEAN
4. HARA / OZU
5. MIFUNE / KUROSAWA
6. FORD / WAYNE
7. SYDOW / BERGMAN
8. LEMMON / WILDER
9. MASTROIANNI / FELLINI
10. KINSKI / HERZOG

72. POP SONGS IN MOVIES

```
L  I  W  J  N  A  I  M  E  H  O  B  S  L  H
L  G  E  Q  Y  X  N  E  H  K  T  X  I  U  X
O  O  U  N  D  B  D  Y  M  R  O  J  R  S  S
R  T  Z  K  I  U  R  B  B  A  Q  D  B  D  X
N  Y  D  G  P  G  E  D  L  A  Y  P  A  Q  R
K  O  R  S  E  M  A  M  T  G  B  O  X  G  S
C  U  U  O  B  A  M  M  U  S  R  Y  D  R  G
O  B  T  H  W  F  S  R  I  Y  R  F  M  J  G
R  A  N  Z  V  G  D  F  R  J  O  P  L  E  B
T  B  E  W  R  Y  D  T  R  M  V  I  E  I  B
Z  E  G  N  M  H  N  L  E  F  A  Q  F  L  B
M  F  N  A  L  U  S  T  F  O  R  L  I  F  E
U  U  N  N  O  S  E  Y  E  R  U  O  Y  N  I
M  T  Q  C  Q  W  C  B  J  O  L  P  W  R  S
K  A  W  R  I  W  D  A  D  B  C  I  C  V  Q
```

1. IN DREAMS
2. HURDY GURDY MAN
3. BOHEMIAN RHAPSODY
4. BE MY BABY
5. OLD TIME ROCK N ROLL
6. TAKE ME HOME COUNTRY ROADS
7. LUST FOR LIFE
8. I GOT YOU BABE
9. IN YOUR EYES
10. IMAGINE

73. MOVIES ABOUT FASHION

```
P  B  Z  B  C  T  N  F  V  F  R  O  Y  H  T
O  F  D  L  P  Z  S  P  U  E  Y  T  C  M  A
L  F  I  O  J  Z  B  N  D  H  I  N  O  O  V
L  A  C  B  H  H  N  N  A  C  A  D  N  Z  C
Y  F  I  H  I  Y  A  P  E  B  E  D  I  A  J
M  M  B  G  F  L  L  H  B  M  I  O  T  Y  Q
A  Q  I  A  O  A  T  W  F  U  N  I  N  H  I
G  V  C  O  A  D  A  K  G  K  R  D  E  J  J
O  E  Z  A  N  V  U  Z  C  A  I  G  L  X  Z
O  P  N  A  B  I  T  T  E  R  T  E  A  R  S
F  P  X  G  D  M  Q  W  K  B  B  H  V  E  Z
I  E  G  T  H  P  Z  N  C  V  F  N  E  N  E
S  S  E  P  T  E  M  B  E  R  I  S  S  U  E
P  Q  D  R  D  X  X  Z  M  R  B  U  W  A  G
A  D  A  R  P  S  R  A  E  W  L  I  V  E  D
```

1. **SEX AND THE CITY**
2. THE **BITTER TEARS** OF PETRA VON KANT
3. WHO ARE YOU? **POLLY MAGOO?**
4. **FUNNY FACE**
5. **GIA**
6. THE **SEPTEMBER ISSUE**
7. THE **DEVIL WEARS PRADA**
8. **COCO** BEFORE CHANEL
9. **VALENTINO:** THE LAST EMPEROR
10. **ZOOLANDER**

74. MOVIES DEALING WITH EXISTENTIALISM

```
K H B X L P F X T G L P Y B C
B A L T H A Z A R V S S T U D
A P Y R J L V V U O Y R U J E
H C I V O K L A M L X P A T W
Q J Q U I E T E A R T H E J Y
R N Q A G R D V N N M X B R R
W S D I M G N D S S U M N U N
S E E B A K C U H O Q A A I U
M F Z L S T U I O U L L C L E
T V C Z I A W X W X V A I T U
V T A S T E O F C H E R R Y C
D L R O W E H T F O D N E I Z
I Y Z X E E Q V M N J S M X S
F F R D T G O Q J O J Q A I Q
O R D I N A R Y P E O P L E D
```

1. THE **TRUMAN SHOW**
2. **SOLARIS**
3. THE **QUIET EARTH**
4. **AMERICAN BEAUTY**
5. **TASTE OF CHERRY**
6. UNTIL THE **END OF THE WORLD**
7. **ORDINARY PEOPLE**
8. I HEART **HUCKABEES**
9. AU HASARD **BALTHAZAR**
10. BEING JOHN **MALKOVICH**

75. GREEDY DEVILS

```
A  S  X  S  T  A  F  K  F  L  R  J  V  S  T
A  M  A  R  T  M  U  V  V  G  I  O  Z  H  G
R  I  R  V  Y  W  D  T  E  S  G  R  E  G  F
U  L  O  W  Y  I  C  S  B  B  O  D  I  E  N
E  E  W  R  I  N  R  C  F  K  U  A  Q  C  L
W  R  I  B  V  O  C  P  K  K  B  N  M  J  Y
T  G  T  F  U  B  H  E  E  S  K  B  S  U  K
R  R  B  R  A  X  G  S  W  Q  Y  E  I  B  A
S  O  X  K  I  N  H  J  D  T  P  L  Z  F  P
C  G  J  P  O  A  R  O  O  N  R  F  Z  J  C
R  A  K  D  J  A  L  I  W  C  U  O  Y  X  P
O  N  R  I  R  B  U  Z  O  S  U  R  X  A  G
O  O  W  G  Q  I  C  A  N  I  R  T  U  I  Z
G  E  N  J  U  R  O  T  O  B  E  E  Y  G  H
E  P  L  A  I  N  V  I  E  W  Y  S  L  P  T
```

1. TUCO
2. EBENEZER **SCROOGE**
3. JORDAN BELFORT
4. TRINA
5. THE DUKES
6. SMILER GROGAN
7. DOBBS
8. GENJÛRÔ AND TÔBEE
9. DANIEL **PLAINVIEW**
10. GORDON GEKKO

76. COUPLES

```
J  E  S  S  E  C  E  L  I  N  E  J  T  E  L
K  F  C  T  J  N  A  I  A  L  U  O  T  W  U
M  A  N  H  O  I  C  K  I  Y  E  L  E  E  D
Y  J  R  B  A  N  R  R  H  G  L  E  L  D  Q
A  L  S  V  E  P  Y  R  Q  V  Y  B  R  U  K
C  M  L  B  X  L  K  M  E  G  J  T  A  A  H
E  E  I  A  W  R  L  O  A  G  R  R  C  M  D
S  D  O  R  S  Q  V  A  L  R  M  W  S  D  G
E  Y  V  L  U  Y  Y  Y  E  O  I  O  T  L  D
I  E  B  L  H  T  R  A  C  D  W  A  T  O  P
L  C  D  K  J  C  V  R  L  U  W  S  E  R  D
K  C  Q  B  A  T  V  K  A  F  J  A  H  A  Y
H  A  O  R  T  O  C  V  U  H  P  L  R  H  R
J  J  N  S  C  R  C  N  R  S  I  U  B  D  M
T  B  I  E  E  C  I  L  A  Y  N  O  T  C  H
```

1. JESSE AND CÉLINE
2. TONY AND MARIA
3. RHETT AND SCARLETT
4. ALEC AND LAURA
5. HARRY AND SALLY
6. BELLA AND EDWARD
7. TONY AND ALICE
8. TOULA AND IAN
9. TOM AND GERRI
10. HAROLD AND MAUDE

77. CONTROVERSIAL MOVIES

```
B  I  N  A  I  R  B  F  O  E  F  I  L  I  V
I  I  P  T  S  I  R  H  C  I  T  N  A  M  D
C  V  R  S  E  M  I  D  W  E  V  H  S  G  A
L  T  P  T  R  I  U  M  P  H  L  M  T  A  M
A  K  T  P  H  G  O  D  L  A  P  F  T  O  Y
S  O  E  F  N  O  Q  F  B  Q  Q  B  E  B  O
T  L  W  Y  H  L  F  I  P  I  R  E  M  N  W
T  A  B  P  A  P  N  A  G  C  K  Q  P  E  C
A  S  N  B  W  N  S  S  N  O  S  M  T  L  B
N  R  I  M  A  S  O  G  W  A  W  Q  A  V  K
G  W  M  C  I  A  C  E  W  D  T  L  T  K  M
O  F  Q  O  R  B  M  T  F  F  S  I  I  Y  T
P  F  N  M  E  O  C  G  N  C  Z  I  O  F  M
C  S  X  E  Q  S  X  N  W  S  X  D  N  N  H
A  S  U  T  P  M  O  E  W  Y  I  S  G  T  P
```

1. THE **EXORCIST**
2. THE **BIRTH OF A NATION**
3. **SALO**
4. **TRIUMPH** OF THE WILL
5. **CANNIBAL** HOLOCAUST
6. THE **LAST TEMPTATION** OF CHRIST
7. THE **PASSION** OF THE CHRIST
8. **LIFE OF BRIAN**
9. **LAST TANGO** IN PARIS
10. **ANTICHRIST**

78. BARS IN MOVIES

```
Q  R  T  J  U  U  G  Q  S  B  C  E  R  K  C
Y  E  L  S  I  E  S  O  M  D  F  J  O  N  O
Y  T  V  P  U  O  G  V  L  A  L  R  D  H  Y
K  S  T  R  P  O  H  R  C  D  O  P  D  A  O
R  Y  V  W  X  N  J  S  E  V  R  U  H  X  T
M  O  D  G  C  V  K  E  A  E  G  O  R  A  E
C  E  Q  X  N  C  O  Z  M  J  L  T  O  J  U
L  U  O  H  I  V  H  U  K  L  H  Y  E  M  G
P  L  X  R  V  U  Q  L  B  C  G  C  S  N  L
G  B  A  C  L  U  B  S  U  G  A  R  R  A  Y
S  M  T  H  E  L  A  S  T  R  E  S  O  R  T
R  O  X  H  L  D  B  Y  Z  N  A  O  P  U  A
G  D  H  Q  I  O  C  A  S  D  K  U  X  G  L
S  L  W  Y  E  O  O  N  K  C  Q  H  T  M  I
Z  Q  E  K  T  E  F  P  P  U  R  B  U  L  I
```

1. **KOROVA** MILK BAR
2. **CLUB SUGAR RAY**
3. THE **GOLD ROOM**
4. **COYOTE UGLY**
5. **THE LAST RESORT**
6. **GREELYS**
7. **MOS EISLEY** CANTINA
8. **PLEASURE ISLAND POOL HALL**
9. THE **BLUE OYSTER**
10. **RICK'S CAFE** AMERICAIN

79. DYSTOPIAN FUTURES

```
B Y J R X Y A U F N H W B G N
L N Y E A C D Y D Z E W T A A
A W V R V A U V Y X A M D A M
D E F A H R E N H E I T V B N
E L Q A Z C D H R W K K B O O
R N F B L O R L I G S S P Y I
U P Y O B I A U D M I C V A T
N Y Y M L D P I H L Q W A N I
N V D O X I V S O K A E O D L
E Z J A J E Z P U K C D F H O
R J E Q R D O A I G B U F I M
O U E G M R W R R N B J P S E
Y Z E R T B A G J B B F M D D
C N V E S E K F Z A X G B O F
T V M Q V I H T J P C W S G F
```

1. DIVERGENT
2. MAD MAX
3. BRAZIL
4. IDIOCRACY
5. METROPOLIS
6. FAHRENHEIT 451
7. A BOY AND HIS DOG
8. AKIRA
9. DEMOLITION MAN
10. BLADE RUNNER

80. VAMPIRES

```
O U M E G Y J K P A R K H G C
L S L H A H Y O X A E R U N H
M I R I A M B L A Y L O C K R
N C O U N T D R A C U L A I I
C E K S N H C O S F F O S C S
M A L R Y M B F I Y G O G A T
H A R L E O V A H E G V B V O
K T R M U H H R N U S Z F G P
S J Y T I C G G L K Z P O A H
V N M K I L D A G N Q O S Q E
U R Q Q I N L R Q O W U U Q R
O S U N Z E E A A M I S N X L
S Y Y R B W S C M W X L J Y E
P J H C Q E G D I R D N A D E
K V M U Z B H W U E C E L N K
```

1. EDWARD CULLEN
2. GRAF ORLOK
3. BELA LUGOSI
4. MIRIAM BLAYLOCK
5. **CARMILLA** KARNSTEIN
6. CHRISTOPHER LEE
7. JERRY **DANDRIDGE**
8. ELI
9. COUNT DRACULA
10. MARTIN

81. COMEDY TROUPES AND DOUBLE ACTS

```
P  S  B  P  S  R  V  H  R  W  R  V  O  S  G
V  B  E  W  S  Y  N  M  L  E  G  L  R  R  N
E  G  R  G  Z  F  E  F  D  M  L  G  G  E  O
T  J  G  B  O  J  M  L  T  E  T  Q  R  H  H
F  Q  K  E  Y  O  I  U  T  S  R  B  T  T  C
P  G  G  T  P  W  T  S  W  B  C  U  D  O  D
S  S  T  C  E  N  O  S  J  P  Y  N  I  R  N
B  L  N  N  V  C  O  I  E  P  P  I  P  B  A
S  O  E  S  T  E  M  M  Z  E  G  S  V  X  H
B  G  U  O  U  W  B  G  I  U  R  T  H  R  C
B  I  B  P  X  E  Y  Y  E  S  N  H  I  A  E
W  B  W  H  O  Z  E  S  G  N  V  J  T  M  E
A  Y  L  M  O  N  T  Y  P  Y  T  H  O  N  H
Y  D  R  A  H  D  N  A  L  E  R  U  A  L  C
S  I  W  E  L  D  N  A  N  I  T  R  A  M  H
```

1. THE CHRISTOPHER **GUEST** TROUPE
2. **LAUREL AND HARDY**
3. EDGAR WRIGHT, **SIMON PEGG** AND NICK FROST
4. **CHEECH AND CHONG**
5. RICHARD PRYOR AND **GENE WILDER**
6. **MONTY PYTHON**
7. DEAN **MARTIN AND** JERRY **LEWIS**
8. THE **THREE STOOGES**
9. THE **MARX BROTHERS**
10. **ABBOTT** AND **COSTELLO**

82. BATTLES

```
G  P  I  S  T  D  Q  C  P  C  C  D  C  Q  A
T  H  E  R  M  O  P  Y  L  A  E  E  U  O  I
P  R  K  E  Q  L  L  Y  R  H  E  A  I  T  N
M  A  O  C  D  M  D  Z  A  I  R  T  R  L  O
U  M  B  U  H  S  G  R  C  O  Z  H  A  H  D
R  M  E  V  R  F  M  H  S  U  R  S  S  Z  E
Q  M  S  M  J  K  I  L  D  A  G  T  S  F  E
W  K  T  V  A  M  E  Z  E  M  D  A  I  I  R
A  I  U  D  O  R  C  S  R  H  E  R  E  E  F
X  S  S  N  Z  G  N  P  D  W  E  Y  R  V  C
I  M  J  D  X  U  Q  H  F  R  H  A  S  C  H
S  I  F  X  R  D  M  F  E  R  I  N  O  S  Z
Q  A  M  J  N  K  D  O  U  M  A  F  G  C  X
E  G  D  I  R  B  G  N  I  L  R  I  T  S  L
U  U  O  M  A  H  A  B  E  A  C  H  X  P  N
```

1.	**THERMOPYLAE**	6.	**HELM'S DEEP**
2.	THE BATTLE FOR **ARNHEM**	7.	**FREEDONIA** VS. SYLVANIA
3.	**DEATH STAR** ASSAULT	8.	**OMAHA BEACH** LANDING
4.	THE BATTLE OF THE **ICHIMONJI** CLAN	9.	**ROURKE'S DRIFT**
5.	**STIRLING BRIDGE**	10.	THE CHARGE OF THE **CUIRASSIERS**

83. COPS IN MOVIES

```
H T U N Q D Y J J K Z A U J N
H S B B I T L I G R I V A O O
D Y K K V S M S G P A B E H S
P R E C M M V Q S S S K S N R
M C V L A D B P X K J R U M E
T M N L Y B Y B W Y E T O C D
K F O J H O X H R V N Y L C N
W N I B E R D K N A R F C L U
E Y E L O F L E X A I T J A G
S V K P X D L L Y G N A F N E
S O C U T M P H S E A J A E G
S A T A C H Y E X R P B E J R
H A N K Q U I N L A N O F G A
X E T Y P C Z S H Z L Y P Z M
D E G E O R G E E L L E R B Y
```

1. JIM MALONE
2. FRANK DREBIN
3. POPEYE DOYLE
4. JACQUES CLOUSEAU
5. GEORGE ELLERBY

6. JOHN MCCLANE
7. AXEL FOLEY
8. MARGE GUNDERSON
9. HANK QUINLAN
10. VIRGIL TIBBS

84. MOVIES FEATURING ROAD TRIPS

```
M  R  P  R  W  C  O  Z  D  E  Q  S  N  J  E
B  U  D  R  N  C  I  I  A  U  N  T  E  S  S
R  A  P  E  I  U  N  S  S  Y  S  R  B  M  I
B  V  I  P  D  S  Y  E  V  C  M  A  R  H  U
I  O  Y  B  E  R  C  T  Z  O  M  I  A  B  O
X  A  W  N  I  T  H  I  T  A  V  G  S  E  L
H  P  A  D  F  G  M  O  L  U  H  H  K  V  D
O  J  E  Z  I  N  R  O  J  L  M  T  A  K  N
Q  R  X  N  G  C  S  L  V  M  A  S  U  H  A
P  C  E  B  Y  W  B  D  M  I  D  T  S  P  A
A  N  O  C  Z  F  G  B  D  A  E  O  Y  G  M
O  P  L  K  Y  D  Q  T  K  A  H  R  B  H  L
I  E  Q  W  D  A  C  E  U  Y  R  Y  A  O  E
M  T  S  N  I  A  R  T  S  E  N  A  L  P  H
D  U  M  B  A  N  D  D  U  M  B  E  R  B  T
```

1.	THE **MUPPET MOVIE**	7.	**DUMB AND DUMBER**
2.	THE **STRAIGHT STORY**	8.	**PRISCILLA,** QUEEN OF THE DESERT
3.	**EASY RIDER**		
4.	**PLANES, TRAINS** AND AUTOMOBILES	9.	**NEBRASKA**
5.	**THELMA AND LOUISE**	10.	THE **MOTORCYCLE** DIARIES
6.	IT HAPPENED **ONE NIGHT**		

85. FEMME FATALES

```
S I L L Y H P H M K R L E H J
C F X V N G F L K L L N B C U
K A C L C O A D A S O U N R D
B L T Z X Y N U N T G X S A Y
L L H H X Q R N S Q Z O M M B
X Y P P E A R E A X Y H J Y A
Q T E V H R N Y M D T F G T R
C P Y U W N I Z O B A U J T T
N O N X A J B N R R J R X I O
T T O Z O O N Y E O Z M U K N
U G U Y G B Z Y S P G G B A N
K S N E K C A R B N N Y L X L
J E S S I C A R A B B I T O S
M A N N A S C H M I D T C X N
C H T K E J D M Q A V V Q I O
```

1. **PHYLLIS** DIETRICHSON
2. **LAURA DANNON**
3. **KITTY MARCH**
4. **SUZANNE STONE** MARETTO
5. **JESSICA RABBIT**
6. **CATHERINE** TRAMELL
7. **JUDY BARTON**
8. **LAURA HUNT**
9. **LYNN BRACKEN**
10. **ANNA SCHMIDT**

86. PSYCHOPATHS

```
I  I  H  J  A  K  X  G  R  U  P  B  F  S  A
K  K  K  Z  Z  M  Y  A  L  P  V  R  R  P  Y
E  A  Z  A  S  A  W  G  X  X  N  X  A  D  V
Y  B  K  A  Z  I  C  K  F  Z  S  T  N  O  M
A  K  D  I  P  A  O  H  R  G  R  X  K  N  G
W  C  H  Z  H  H  M  E  A  I  R  F  B  L  N
B  U  N  X  D  A  D  A  C  R  U  Q  O  O  Z
I  U  Z  N  X  Y  R  K  Y  C  I  V  O  G  E
I  R  K  S  R  G  B  A  O  I  Q  A  T  A  I
H  Y  I  N  L  A  N  B  D  K  M  Q  H  N  B
U  Y  H  C  T  O  J  N  C  X  W  A  U  S  G
K  O  O  E  L  C  Y  O  R  U  W  W  S  T  E
J  D  M  F  T  E  Z  C  W  Z  F  Q  V  A  B
G  A  L  L  E  W  O  P  Y  R  R  A  H  A  H
N  A  N  N  I  E  W  I  L  K  E  S  E  Z  D
```

1. ZACHARIAH
2. FRANK BOOTH
3. PATRICK BATEMAN
4. HARRY POWELL
5. ASAMI YAMAZAKI
6. BEGBIE
7. JOHN RYDER
8. ANNIE WILKES
9. KAKIHARA
10. DON LOGAN

87. COMEDY HORROR MOVIES

```
Y  S  Q  N  F  A  S  H  D  R  D  O  N  S  T
U  A  E  E  F  C  H  Q  O  A  D  Q  A  H  X
D  I  S  V  R  Y  H  N  E  O  E  P  M  A  N
F  Y  Y  E  M  X  D  A  G  K  J  Y  U  O
G  X  A  S  N  R  N  G  T  R  T  Y  R  N  D
Q  M  S  R  N  I  A  P  V  E  I  N  E  O  N
E  R  O  T  A  M  I  N  A  E  R  P  T  F  O
Z  T  J  R  E  T  V  R  C  V  O  C  E  T  L
Z  G  B  R  F  N  Q  L  Y  E  U  X  M  H  N
K  R  J  I  W  E  R  E  M  T  Q  D  E  E  I
G  D  I  B  K  L  I  Y  N  W  F  D  C  D  O
E  V  I  L  D  E  A  D  B  R  H  I  U  E  M
S  D  O  O  W  E  H  T  N  I  N  I  B  A  C
H  U  A  U  W  N  U  O  L  P  A  X  T  D  J
Q  J  X  N  U  M  M  V  T  O  P  A  K  C  Z
```

1.	REANIMATOR	6.	SEVERANCE
2.	PIRANHA	7.	SHAUN OF THE DEAD
3.	CEMETERY MAN	8.	SCREAM
4.	BRAINDEAD A.K.A. DEAD OR ALIVE	9.	THE **CABIN IN THE WOODS**
5.	**EVIL DEAD** II	10.	AN AMERICAN WEREWOLF **IN LONDON**

88. DANCING IN THE MOVIES

```
C O Q O Y Q V P E X N R N C H
D A U Y O K D N C C N I I R O
H I P X O N A D O B F C E S L
O R R X W L U T B I H F T R Y
E F H T P L N K S F R U S X G
I Y D R Y P P H X Y I F N H R
H Z I M O D E R N T I M E S A
C A S U X R A P R N U N K X I
I A N J K L U N Z P P X N C L
O W M I H H Z I C L J I A N Q
T A N R L L M Y S I B S R H A
A G P B V V V W R W Y N J F L T
Z R E B M E M D L O G G D C U
P U L P F I C T I O N X D U M
K D R E T R A P A E D N A B O
```

1. ZATOICHI
2. AIRPLANE
3. MODERN TIMES
4. DIRTY DANCING
5. MONTY PYTHON AND THE **HOLY GRAIL**
6. THE **FISHER KING**
7. AUSTIN POWERS IN **GOLDMEMBER**
8. YOUNG **FRANKENSTEIN**
9. PULP FICTION
10. BANDE À PART

89. RED MENACE MOVIES

```
Q  S  D  L  R  O  W  E  H  T  F  O  R  A  W
S  I  E  A  N  O  T  H  E  R  W  O  R  L  D
C  R  L  L  G  C  N  W  O  N  K  N  U  S  C
I  C  E  H  I  C  S  L  Y  S  P  B  B  R  S
E  W  X  C  K  M  J  N  S  Q  T  Q  H  E  R
D  N  B  H  U  O  N  A  Z  T  B  T  B  H  A
G  B  E  Q  O  A  M  O  H  W  R  G  E  C  M
A  W  Z  A  V  R  S  E  I  A  X  C  O  T  S
M  B  C  Y  E  A  B  G  E  L  E  D  A  A  R
R  J  K  T  A  L  Y  D  N  K  L  I  O  N  E
B  R  A  C  O  Y  N  I  Z  I  T  I  W  S  D
R  U  D  B  R  A  I  V  K  B  Y  S  M  Y  A
Q  T  T  K  L  J  R  P  M  B  I  L  G  D  V
O  G  Z  S  C  C  Z  X  W  Z  P  W  F  O  N
G  H  I  H  Y  X  H  B  S  H  D  N  E  B  I
```

1. **THE BLOB**
2. X THE **UNKNOWN**
3. 20 **MILLION MILES** TO EARTH
4. INVASION OF THE **BODY SNATCHERS**
5. THE **QUATERMASS** XPERIMENT
6. THE THING FROM **ANOTHER WORLD**
7. THE **WAR OF THE WORLDS**
8. EARTH VS. THE **FLYING SAUCERS**
9. **INVADERS** FROM **MARS**
10. THIS **ISLAND EARTH**

90. BEST ADAPTATIONS OF A TV SERIES

```
K T G N B L Y S P Q C J I Y D
T U H G U L S O C O Z A J T M
D J E E S G O G W I R C G I F
D A P M F L D B F U D K W N A
N Z K M E U O E M V H A C E I
G A X H C Y G A K E T S Y R D
Y C T B B P S I T A W S Z E O
J N P E O W Q Y T Z N L Y S T
I S B Z A N L V K I P E O G G
O O K L O S D L U E V D H Y R
P X T R A F F I C Y V E C T Y
O U N G C O F I O H A T H U N
O B E A V I S B U T T H E A D
K E R T R A T S Z B I D P Y P
S K A L F X D I K S I X Y X S
```

1. THREE **OUTLAW SAMURAI**
2. **BEAVIS** AND **BUTTHEAD** DO AMERICA
3. **THE FUGITIVE**
4. **JACKASS**: THE MOVIE
5. **COWBOY BEBOP**: THE MOVIE
6. **STAR TREK**
7. THE NAKED GUN
8. **SERENITY**
9. IN THE LOOP
10. **TRAFFIC**

91. FRENCH NEW WAVE FILMS

```
N  N  J  D  P  I  F  I  C  R  Y  Z  B  U  Y
I  V  W  Z  A  P  S  J  A  R  V  C  R  M  J
H  H  S  R  M  B  B  K  M  D  T  L  E  B  F
T  U  N  L  E  L  N  W  A  K  Z  P  A  R  U
I  S  Z  X  M  H  L  E  S  A  I  W  T  E  B
W  M  J  H  J  W  C  W  I  E  X  Y  H  L  U
E  M  O  N  A  M  O  U  R  R  V  U  L  L  B
R  T  Z  I  Z  L  Y  R  O  E  A  C  E  A  B
I  H  T  N  B  B  O  J  A  B  Q  M  S  S  H
F  R  C  L  T  T  V  N  A  B  E  T  S  T  J
E  E  X  A  L  X  N  A  W  H  J  L  B  V  B
H  X  L  E  M  I  J  D  N  A  S  E  L  U  J
T  Y  F  E  V  I  L  O  T  E  F  I  L  Y  M
V  O  H  J  F  D  O  A  H  S  V  F  O  W  O
U  A  D  T  Q  G  N  C  C  Y  U  S  R  K  E
```

1. **BREATHLESS**	6.	THE 400 **BLOWS**
2. **PIERROT LE FOU**	7.	HIROSHIMA **MON AMOUR**
3. **MY LIFE TO LIVE**	8.	THE **UMBRELLAS** OF CHERBOURG
4. LAST YEAR AT **MARIENBAD**	9.	**JULES AND JIM**
5. **THE FIRE WITHIN**	10.	**LE BOUCHER**

92. SLASHER MOVIES

```
A  X  N  L  M  B  B  L  M  T  J  C  T  W  I
E  S  L  E  K  Y  C  I  H  H  P  V  H  A  M
N  R  T  I  E  Q  B  E  U  X  Z  Q  E  S  S
D  V  A  R  I  W  B  L  V  L  V  B  P  N  L
I  R  Q  Y  A  U  O  W  O  Y  O  A  R  I  E
L  N  I  J  R  N  R  L  L  O  Q  F  O  A  E
B  I  Q  N  H  H  G  I  L  X  D  X  W  H  P
M  O  I  H  Z  F  D  E  K  A  G  Y  L  C  A
R  N  X  I  R  V  K  F  R  O  H  P  E  S  W
G  R  Y  I  P  N  P  Z  F  C  E  G  R  A  A
V  X  D  B  K  K  T  F  Y  H  A  Q  F  X  Y
P  A  R  T  T  S  I  R  U  O  T  L  S  E  C
Y  D  F  T  K  J  Q  V  G  G  B  S  L  T  A
B  L  A  C  K  C  H  R  I  S  T  M  A  S  M
B  C  H  K  K  C  T  H  W  F  N  L  L  S  P
```

1. WHEN **A STRANGER CALLS**
2. **SLEEPAWAY CAMP**
3. **THE BURNING**
4. **TOURIST TRAP**
5. **HALLOWEEN**
6. THE **TEXAS CHAINSAW** MASSACRE
7. **BLACK CHRISTMAS**
8. **MY BLOODY** VALENTINE
9. **THE PROWLER**
10. **FRIDAY** THE 13TH

93. WOMEN IN A MAN'S WORLD

```
H  V  M  H  B  P  J  S  S  E  S  Y  J  A  G
A  I  G  A  P  A  W  B  O  D  E  B  D  R  N
F  E  L  W  Y  S  M  Z  K  L  I  I  D  V  I
G  N  Z  D  B  A  K  Z  P  J  R  A  K  F  L
V  N  A  E  Y  H  L  I  W  E  Q  F  E  J  R
O  A  P  U  U  J  R  A  M  H  J  V  U  Q  A
W  M  Y  R  S  N  O  S  M  B  T  C  E  W  T
F  L  H  N  E  I  S  H  H  B  M  K  L  C  S
L  J  U  L  B  E  C  J  N  B  E  H  F  F  E
W  I  L  V  C  X  N  A  O  S  S  R  K  Y  C
O  E  I  N  F  N  J  E  A  G  O  C  T  B  I
I  T  I  D  U  G  P  S  R  T  A  N  Z  R  R
A  R  E  A  M  L  R  P  B  P  K  O  H  W  A
P  A  T  P  E  M  B  E  R  T  O  N  P  X  L
N  O  S  R  E  D  N  U  G  E  G  R  A  M  C
```

1.	CLARICE STARLING	6.	ELLEN RIPLEY
2.	PRINCESS MERIDA	7.	MARGE GUNDERSON
3.	PAI (PAIKEA APIRANA)	8.	VIENNA
4.	HILDY JOHNSON	9.	NAUSICAA
5.	MAYA LAMBERT	10.	PAT PEMBERTON

94. CAMEOS

```
B C C R P Y A M G F X B N O O
I Y H V T Q Z R R W O R A U K
L F E U U V W E P R M U M A E
L Z W S C M R K S L X C K E F
M Y C M U K H O V B R E C C T
U E D N V B N H Q Y B W A R H
R Z E G E W Y O Y U B I J A A
R C T A E Z X R R O P L H M O
A M Y L M B E F A R B L G L Y
Y R L P H M D C Z G I I U E O
N E E T S G N I R P S S H C H
S B N U O I L I X U D F H R K
M A R S H A L L M C L U H A N
A R T A N I S K N A R F X M T
H S L H V F S X P L T N S C J
```

1. BRUCE WILLIS
2. ORSON WELLES
3. FRANK SINATRA
4. GARY BUSEY
5. HUGH JACKMAN
6. MARSHALL MCLUHAN
7. CHUCK NORRIS
8. BILL MURRAY
9. BRUCE SPRINGSTEEN
10. MARCEL MARCEAU

95. ASSASSINS

```
R  S  H  T  D  G  C  N  S  R  H  D  W  P  J
O  O  O  B  L  H  A  N  N  A  Z  R  M  E  A
B  L  U  S  T  O  P  D  C  X  Q  X  F  A  L
K  D  O  S  U  S  T  H  J  F  B  C  N  G  G
B  N  G  C  P  T  Y  A  P  V  O  T  N  G  Y
P  C  A  Y  M  D  B  F  S  S  O  O  W  X  C
B  P  M  L  K  O  Z  N  T  N  J  X  W  F  I
M  E  I  A  B  G  W  E  C  H  X  K  V  C  L
A  T  I  K  I  N  L  H  A  W  K  I  N  S  Z
V  S  T  V  M  L  I  M  K  A  J  A  F  I  X
C  B  T  P  O  G  I  T  P  C  U  W  C  L  U
R  A  O  Y  U  K  L  W  R  Q  H  R  E  E  A
B  U  C  R  B  P  V  J  I  A  G  J  F  E  N  V
N  Z  H  E  I  O  Z  F  C  H  M  D  K  C  V
O  A  U  P  M  G  L  F  O  C  W  X  V  E  E
```

1. GHOST DOG
2. MARTIN BLANK
3. NIKITA
4. HANNA
5. JEF COSTELLO
6. ANTON CHIGURH
7. LONE WOLF A.K.A. OGAMI ITTO
8. HAWKINS
9. SILENCE
10. AH JONG

96. SPACESHIPS

```
G R F D L O G F O T R A E H D
A E G R O F Y E L L A V I D I
R X T J J X W Q R R T Z L E S
E S I R P R E T N E S S U T C
T A U W V B W M O U K E O F O
M A G I W A I M S H R R R K V
S I F L R Q L I T S A E S P E
X H L Z E I Z Y R O D N T G R
J Z M L H T S O O O D I J A Y
T Z W R E L H K M N Z T C N O
K J C N O N V J O Q B Y Z Z N
A U P M P A N B W O K T L Y E
V Y W A C Y P I T U W A A R Y
Z R E C U A S S U T A A L K M
Q G H W Y R B M D M Z B A F A
```

1. THE **DARK STAR**
2. THE **MILLENNIUM** FALCON
3. **U.S.S. ENTERPRISE**
4. **NOSTROMO**
5. **EAGLE** 5

6. THE **HEART OF GOLD**
7. **KLAATUS SAUCER**
8. **SERENITY**
9. THE **VALLEY FORGE**
10. **DISCOVERY ONE**

97. SO BAD THEY'RE GOOD

```
L  J  K  O  L  V  Y  B  T  J  T  K  R  Z  Q
T  I  L  Q  E  O  F  A  B  B  I  S  D  S  W
E  L  B  L  M  V  L  T  B  P  L  E  U  I  O
C  C  R  W  D  T  A  T  V  P  L  A  Z  J  L
R  F  G  H  N  D  S  L  V  T  N  W  U  H  T
O  O  Q  S  A  B  H  E  A  I  G  Q  M  H  O
F  K  F  Q  C  K  G  F  U  F  J  Q  E  O  D
A  J  K  B  A  Y  O  I  I  U  J  U  E  Y  X
G  K  K  J  M  R  R  E  T  T  N  W  U  K  R
E  T  M  K  C  B  D  L  P  I  R  F  A  H  O
M  Q  A  E  L  N  O  D  V  U  H  O  E  Y  U
U  T  I  M  Q  Z  N  E  W  X  X  B  L  K  J
A  W  E  M  O  O  R  E  H  T  R  Z  A  L  B
Q  O  N  C  N  S  H  O  W  G  I  R  L  S  Q
A  T  P  Y  E  U  Y  Y  C  Q  D  Z  I  F  N
```

1. GYMKATA
2. FLASH GORDON
3. MAC AND ME
4. MASTERS OF THE UNIVERSE
5. MEGAFORCE

6. BATTLEFIELD EARTH
7. THE ROOM
8. DELTA FORCE 2
9. SHOWGIRLS
10. TROLL 2

98. SUPERHERO MOVIES

```
X C D T S L A H S C H S L E S
J J U R U R N C Y K P P R N E
X Z X B P L E U L P Z I T Q L
N M N B E I N G C B O D E W B
X V I E R Q P X N N Q E B N I
U D L D M B Q O U E N R A C D
L W A O A X L T R Q V M E F E
C M D R N V F I A Z N A R A R
F Y L E K L G X O O T N F M C
U P W B D K O Z R L X J W U N
L W D A L A N I M O S B B P I
W W L X G I L I K R X C C R F
B Z N A M T A B G E M L I X Z
T Z P L R C W W U H M U L Q K
W U O W W O R C E H T Z K Y F
```

1. BLADE
2. SPIDER-MAN
3. IRON MAN
4. **AVENGERS** ASSEMBLE
5. THE **DARK KNIGHT**
6. SUPERMAN
7. THE **INCREDIBLES**
8. X-MEN
9. BATMAN
10. THE CROW

99. MOST STYLISHLY DRESSED CHARACTERS

```
S  A  Q  B  W  X  X  I  N  G  B  I  D  S  Y
C  H  N  M  O  I  R  E  F  I  M  Q  I  E  Z
P  C  R  N  Z  T  H  N  T  D  N  Q  W  H  I
J  X  R  T  E  Z  S  N  A  E  S  E  T  G  R
R  H  O  F  I  K  D  E  E  T  F  Z  N  U  E
O  V  U  L  H  A  C  L  I  Q  V  R  S  H  S
Y  S  U  N  C  G  I  M  Y  R  O  E  W  D  E
A  S  X  J  W  E  U  W  R  V  P  B  O  R  N
J  F  A  E  L  G  E  J  I  E  S  N  D  A  I
L  P  B  E  E  M  Z  I  P  G  G  L  N  W  R
K  P  R  W  N  T  H  Q  R  H  N  N  H  O  E
A  O  J  U  L  I  A  N  K  A  Y  E  I  H  V
L  Y  R  Z  O  M  U  W  J  M  M  U  G  G  E
R  E  N  O  C  L  A  F  E  G  R  O  E  G  S
D  I  C  K  I  E  G  R  E  E  N  L  E  A  F
```

1.	GINGER MCKENNA	6.	GEORGE FALCONER
2.	SEVERINE SERIZY	7.	PRIEST
3.	LORELEI LEE	8.	HOWARD HUGHES
4.	DICKIE GREENLEAF	9.	SU LI-ZHEN
5.	MARIE ANTOINETTE	10.	JULIAN KAYE

100. GREAT COMEDY MOVIES YOU MAY NOT HAVE SEEN

```
G  E  Y  J  S  F  W  V  H  F  B  U  W  I  O
R  T  O  X  Z  Y  A  L  S  L  K  A  M  L  Z
E  E  C  F  S  U  N  E  D  D  E  N  U  R  O
A  F  H  M  F  R  R  W  L  I  U  C  W  W  N
T  E  L  A  E  I  O  H  S  W  K  Y  P  C  S
E  D  I  E  E  Z  C  I  P  Y  E  D  D  K  M
S  R  U  X  T  F  O  E  M  U  B  N  X  B  A
T  U  H  M  Q  E  D  A  S  B  K  Q  A  T  L
D  O  X  I  G  P  N  V  O  P  P  B  J  T  L
A  J  U  R  K  I  N  D  H  E  A  R  T  S  C
D  H  U  M  L  A  Z  E  G  Y  E  C  R  V  H
J  O  E  H  K  C  D  Q  J  M  A  Q  E  H  A
B  W  I  T  H  N  A  I  L  A  N  D  I  X  N
Y  Z  A  R  C  E  B  T  S  U  M  S  D  O  G
P  L  L  I  F  K  S  J  U  G  A  W  W  C  E
```

1. THE DISCREET CHARM OF THE **BOURGEOISIE**
2. **KIND HEARTS** AND CORONETS
3. **OFFICE SPACE**
4. WORLD'S **GREATEST DAD**
5. **O LUCKY MAN**
6. THE **GODS MUST BE CRAZY**
7. **A NEW LEAF**
8. **JOUR DE FETE**
9. **WITHNAIL AND I**
10. **SMALL CHANGE** A.K.A. POCKET MONEY

MOVIES PUZZLE SOLUTIONS

CROSSWORD SOLUTIONS

1. ANTIHEROES

ACROSS
2. WITH NO NAME
4. THE BANDIT
8. LUKE JACKSON
9. SNAKE

DOWN
1. JOHNNY
3. FERRIS BUELLER
4. TRAVIS BICKLE
5. DRIVER
6. OH DAE-SU
7. CROKER

2. MANIC PIXIE DREAM GIRLS

ACROSS
3. SUGAR KANE
8. CATHERINE
9. CLEMENTINE
10. MADISON

DOWN
1. SUSAN VANCE
2. SAM
4. GOLIGHTLY
5. ANNIE HALL
6. TONI SIMMONS
7. COLBURN

3. SPORTING MOMENTS

ACROSS
2. UNLIKELY
3. IF YOU BUILD IT
5. DISTANCE
10. INCHES SPEECH

DOWN
1. EXPLODING
4. THE LONG GAME
6. CROSSING
7. TEAM EVIL
8. LARUSSO
9. ABRAHAMS

4. QUESTS

ACROSS
3. WAY HOME
6. TREASURE
9. GOLDEN FLEECE
10. THE ROOM

DOWN
1. MORDOR
2. PIRATE BOOTY
4. PAMELA ANDERSON
5. JUPITER
7. EL DORADO
8. COVENANT

5. CARS

ACROSS
6. BATMOBILE
8. CADILLAC
10. CHALLENGER

DOWN
1. HERBIE
2. DODGE CHARGER
3. MACH FIVE
4. PONTIAC
5. LINCOLN
7. BLUESMOBILE
9. DELOREAN

6. HAUNTED HOUSES

ACROSS
4. CONJURING
5. ORPHANAGE
6. THE OTHERS
7. HAUNTING
8. POLTERGEIST
9. GHOSTS

DOWN
1. THE GRUDGE
2. GULL COTTAGE
3. INNOCENTS
7. HELL HOUSE

7. HIGH SCHOOL MOVIES

ACROSS
1. HEATHERS
3. ELECTION
4. BREAKFAST CLUB
7. CLUELESS
9. RUSHMORE
10. MEAN GIRLS

DOWN
2. AMERICAN PIE
5. BLACKBOARD
6. TEN THINGS
8. GREASE

8. MONSTERS

ACROSS
5. GRABOIDS
7. GIANT TROLLS
10. CRAWLING EYE

DOWN
1. GREMLINS
2. THE KRAKEN
3. GODZILLA
4. KONG
6. BRUNDLEFLY
8. THE MONSTER
9. CLOVER

9. FAMILIES

ACROSS
4. TENENBAUMS
5. SIMPSONS
7. LIFE IS SWEET
9. HOOVERS
10. GRISWOLDS

DOWN
1. CORLEONES
2. ADDAMS
3. BREWSTERS
6. SAWYERS
8. BANKS

10. AVENGERS

ACROSS
3. MATTIE ROSS
5. CHEN ZHEN
6. THE BRIDE
8. JENNIFER HILLS
9. COFFY
10. GEUM JA LEE

DOWN
1. CHARLES RANE
2. KERSEY
4. MAXIMUS
7. BRUCE WAYNE

11. HEISTS

ACROSS
1. RIFIFI
3. INSIDE MAN
8. CASH ON DEMAND
10. LAVENDAR HILL

DOWN
2. ITALIAN JOB
4. SNATCH
5. DOG DAY
6. OCEAN'S ELEVEN
7. RUN LOLA RUN
9. THE KILLING

12. PERFORMANCES AGAINST TYPE

ACROSS
4. HENRY FONDA
5. ROBIN
6. HYE JA KIM
8. ALBERT
10. CHARLIZE THERON

DOWN
1. DEBORAH KERR
2. ANISTON
3. PATRICK SWAYZE
7. LANSBURY
9. DENZEL

13. FILM NOIR
ACROSS
2. BIG SLEEP
3. ASPHALT JUNGLE
6. DOUBLE INDEMNITY
9. BIG CLOCK
10. LAURA
DOWN
1. THIEVES HIGHWAY
4. BLOOD SIMPLE
5. GILDA
7. ODD MAN OUT
8. POSTMAN

14. DOCUMENTARIES ABOUT CINEMA
ACROSS
1. VISIONS
5. APOCALYPSE
8. CELLULOID
10. MOVIE CAMERA
DOWN
2. STORY FILM
3. MY BEST FIEND
4. SCORSESE
6. A.K.
7. PERVERT'S GUIDE
9. LA MANCHA

15. ANDROIDS
ACROSS
6. GUNSLINGER
8. DATA
9. IRON GIANT
DOWN
1. ROBBY THE ROBOT
2. KUSANAGI
3. WALL-E
4. JOHNNY FIVE
5. GIGOLO JOE
7. MARIA
10. THREEPIO

16. SIDEKICKS
ACROSS
4. SAMWISE GAMGEE
6. CAL NAUGHTON
7. GARTH ALGAR
9. SHORT ROUND
10. MITCH
DOWN
1. DR. WATSON
2. DUDE
3. WANG CHI
5. PEDRO SANCHEZ
8. RENFIELD

17. PARTIES
ACROSS
5. RED DEATH
6. WIDE SHUT
7. ANIMAL HOUSE
9. THIS IS THE END
10. SOCIETY
DOWN
1. WEIRD SCIENCE
2. PARTY
3. DOLCE VITA
4. BOOGIE NIGHTS
8. OLD SCHOOL

18. TOUGH GIRLS
ACROSS
1. XIAO MEI
5. ALICE
9. THE BRIDE
10. RED SONJA
DOWN
2. MAGGIE FITZGERALD
3. CHINA O'BRIEN
4. MAY DAY
6. SARAH CONNOR
7. NEYTIRI
8. SELENE

19. SEQUELS
ACROSS
4. WEEKS
7. DAWN OF THE DEAD
8. MAD MAX
9. SUPREMACY
10. TOY STORY
DOWN
1. MANON DES SOURCES
2. INFERNAL AFFAIRS
3. BRIDE OF
5. CHINA
6. HELLBOY

20. FICTIONAL PLACES
ACROSS
2. TOONTOWN
5. HOGSMEADE
7. NARNIA
8. NEXUS
9. SEAHAVEN
10. PANEM
DOWN
1. HUNDRED ACRE WOOD
3. SHANGRI LA
4. NEVERLAND
6. WONDERLAND

21. MISGUIDED BELIEVERS
ACROSS
6. ABIN COOPER
8. HARRY POWELL
9. SISTER JEAN
10. SUMMERISLE
DOWN
1. MOLA RAM
2. FARNSWORTH
3. SIMON
4. CARDINAL ROARK
5. FREDDIE QUELL
7. BARRY

22. HEROES
ACROSS
2. BROKOVICH
4. ATTICUS FINCH
8. JEFFERSON
9. SHOSANNA
10. JOHN CHANCE
DOWN
1. ROBIN HOOD
3. INDIANA JONES
5. SPARTACUS
6. REE DOLLY
7. WILL KANE

23. BUDDY MOVIES
ACROSS
5. SUNDANCE KID
8. WHEELS ON MEALS
9. MIDNIGHT RUN
10. STIR CRAZY
DOWN
1. UP IN SMOKE
2. MIDNIGHT
3. LETHAL WEAPON
4. DEFIANT ONES
6. DUMB DUMBER
7. HEAVENLY CREATURES

24. MEDICAL DOCTORS
ACROSS
1. MALCOLM SAYER
3. YURI ZHIVAGO
6. VAN HELSING
7. BLOCK
9. MILLAR
10. STEPHEN MATURIN
DOWN
2. CHRISTIAN SZELL
4. NICHOLAS GARRIGAN
5. MONTGOMERY
8. HAWKEYE

25. UNDERRATED MASTERPIECES

ACROSS

1. LONE STAR
5. DREAMS
8. NOSFERATU
9. LADY VENGEANCE
10. THE GAME

DOWN

2. TRANSFORMERS
3. EYES WIDE SHUT
4. NIGHT FEVER
6. NAKED LUNCH
7. CABLE GUY

26. 1980s ACTION MOVIES

ACROSS

2. RUNNING MAN
4. RAMBO
5. DELTA FORCE
6. ROAD HOUSE
8. DIE HARD
9. BLOODSPORT

DOWN

1. ALIENS
2. ROBOCOP
3. LETHAL WEAPON
7. PREDATOR

27. INSPIRATIONAL MOVIES

ACROSS

3. GRAPES OF WRATH
6. MOCKINGBIRD
9. PIANIST
10. SCHOOL ROCK

DOWN

1. SHAWSHANK
2. DEAD POETS
4. WONDERFUL LIFE
5. BILLY ELLIOT
7. BEAUTIFUL
8. AMELIE

28. AMBIGUOUS ENDINGS

ACROSS

2. INCEPTION
4. CAST AWAY
7. FIVE EASY PIECES
8. SHANE
10. COMEDY

DOWN

1. PANS LABYRINTH
3. TAKE SHELTER
5. ANATOMY
6. THE THING
9. LOCK STOCK

29. FEMALE VILLAINS

ACROSS

2. CAPTAIN LEWIS
4. LADY TREMAINE
6. BABY JANE
9. HARRINGTON
10. RATCHED

DOWN

1. REGINA GEORGE
3. PARKER
5. MAGGIE WHITE
7. CHANDLER
8. DANVERS

30. BIOPICS

ACROSS

2. TOPSY TURVY
6. ELEPHANT
7. LA VIE EN ROSE
8. LINCOLN
10. MALCOLM X

DOWN

1. SOCIAL NETWORK
3. SCHINDLER'S
4. PERSEPOLIS
5. YANKEE DOODLE
9. PARTY

31. FAMILY MOVIES

ACROSS

2. SPIRITED AWAY
5. E.T.
6. WIZARD OF OZ
7. WILLY WONKA
8. WRONG TROUSERS
9. TOY STORY
10. JUNGLE BOOK

DOWN

1. WILD THINGS ARE
3. PRINCESS BRIDE
4. TOTORO

32. ANTI-ESTABLISHMENT MOVIES

ACROSS

2. IF
7. CUCKOO'S NEST
8. CONFIGURATION
9. EASY RIDER
10. NETWORK

DOWN

1. PUNISHMENT
3. REDS
4. FOOTLOOSE
5. PUTNEY SWOPE
6. LONG DISTANCE

33. VILLAINS

ACROSS

5. CHILD CATCHER
6. SILVA
8. JANINE CODY
9. SCAR
10. HENRY POTTER

DOWN

1. NOAH CROSS
2. SZELL
3. KHAN
4. EDWIN EPPS
7. HANS LANDA

34. SCENE-STEALING PERFORMANCES

ACROSS

2. DICAPRIO
3. HEATH LEDGER
6. PETER SELLERS
10. PETERSON

DOWN

1. VIOLA DAVIS
4. RUTHERFORD
5. ALEC BALDWIN
7. EUGENE LEVY
8. RALPH BROWN
9. JUDI DENCH

35. WAR MOVIES

ACROSS

2. SOLDIER ORANGE
4. CULLODEN
6. TORA
8. HEAVEN EARTH
9. CROSS OF IRON
10. ENEMY GATES

DOWN

1. DOWNFALL
3. IWO JIMA
5. COME AND SEE
7. DAS BOOT

36. PRIVATE INVESTIGATORS

ACROSS

2. NICK CHARLES
5. MIKE HAMMER
6. FLETCH
8. PHILLIP MARLOWE
9. JAKE GITTES
10. EDDIE VALIANT

DOWN

1. SAM SPADE
3. HARRY ANGEL
4. JEFF BAILEY
7. JOHN SHAFT

37. MAD SCIENTISTS

ACROSS

3. STRANGELOVE
8. HERBERT WEST
9. ZARKOV
10. FRANK N. FURTER

DOWN

1. INVENTOR
2. CATHETER
4. EMMETT BROWN
5. HFUHRUHURR
6. MOREAU
7. PRETORIUS

38. MARTIAL ARTS

ACROSS

4. LONE WOLF MCQUADE
7. HERO
8. REDBELT
9. KILL BILL
10. POLICE STORY

DOWN

1. CROUCHING TIGER
2. JUDO STORY
3. KUNG FU HUSTLE
5. DRUNKEN MASTER
6. MR. VAMPIRE

39. MOVIES ABOUT CELEBRITY

ACROSS

5. KING OF COMEDY
6. CELEBRITY
9. ALMOST FAMOUS
10. BYE BYE BIRDIE

DOWN

1. BLING RING
2. LA DOLCE VITA
3. SUNSET
4. TO DIE FOR
7. I'M STILL HERE
8. YOUNG THINGS

40. PRISON MOVIES

ACROSS

7. HUNGER
8. A PROPHET
9. GRANDE ILLUSION
10. RESCUE DAWN

DOWN

1. MIDNIGHT EXPRESS
2. CHICKEN RUN
3. STALAG
4. SCORPION
5. ALCATRAZ
6. SHAWSHANK

41. SHOOT-OUTS

ACROSS

3. HOT FUZZ
4. HEAT
7. DESPERADO
8. BUGSY MALONE
10. THE MATRIX

DOWN

1. SHOOT 'EM UP
2. UNTOUCHABLES
5. WILD BUNCH
6. HARD BOILED
9. SHOOTIST

42. CONCERT MOVIES

ACROSS

1. LAST WALTZ
3. HEART OF GOLD
4. MAKING SENSE
7. GIMME SHELTER
9. BANGLADESH
10. WHITE STRIPES

DOWN

2. ZIGGY STARDUST
5. HEIMA
6. MONTEREY POP
8. THE SAME

43. PERFORMANCES BY CHILDREN

ACROSS

3. OLIVER TWIST
6. CLAUDIA
8. IRIS
9. DEVEREAUX
10. PHILLIPE

DOWN

1. MATHILDA
2. ANTOINE DOINEL
4. COLE SEAR
5. DAVID ZELLABY
7. OLIVE HOOVER

44. SPIES AND SECRET AGENTS

ACROSS

3. JAMES BOND
5. JASON BOURNE
6. ALEX LEAMAS
8. JANE SMITH
9. GERD WIESLER
10. OSBOURNE COX

DOWN

1. HARRY PALMER
2. GEORGE SMILEY
4. DEVLIN
7. MRS. ISELIN

45. MOVIES ABOUT MOVIES

ACROSS

2. GUIDO
3. SULLIVANS
5. STARDUST MEMORIES
7. BOULEVARD
9. COCK AND BULL
10. THE PLAYER

DOWN

1. SINGIN' IN THE RAIN
4. ED WOOD
6. THE ARTIST
8. MULHOLLAND

46. VISUAL EFFECTS

ACROSS

5. BRACHIOSAURUS
6. PSEUDOPOD
8. GRAVITY

DOWN

1. PARIS
2. POD RACE
3. TERMINATOR
4. HOLLOW MAN
6. PEARL HARBOR
7. LIGHT CYCLE
8. GOLLUM

47. ALIENATION

ACROSS

3. GHOST WORLD
4. LONELY PLACE
5. STEPPENWOLF
6. TAXI DRIVER
7. ERASERHEAD
8. PASSENGER

DOWN

1. PRIVATE IDAHO
2. THE WALL
4. LA STRADA
6. TRANSLATION

48. COOLEST CHARACTERS

ACROSS

3. JACKIE BROWN
5. SLIM BROWNING
7. TYLER DURDEN
8. MICHEL POICCARD
9. TONY STARK
10. PETER VENKMAN

DOWN

1. WILLIAMS
2. JEF COSTELLO
4. BLONDE
6. MARK HUNTER

49. CONTEMPORARY BLACK-AND-WHITE MOVIES

ACROSS

3. WHITE RIBBON
5. FRANCES HA
9. THE ARTIST
10. DOWN BY LAW

DOWN

1. LA HAINE
2. WHO WASN'T THERE
4. SCHINDLER'S LIST
6. ED WOOD
7. ASTRONAUT
8. PI

50. WEIRD WESTERNS

ACROSS

2. BLACK TIGER
7. WESTERN DJANGO
9. ZACHARIAH
10. TINY TOWN

DOWN

1. FACES OF DR. LAO
3. EL TOPO
4. VALLEY OF GWANGI
5. STRAIGHT TO HELL
6. GREASERS
8. DEAD MAN

51. MOVIES THAT'LL MAKE YOU CRY

ACROSS

1. BUTTERFLY
4. MY LEFT FOOT
6. BAMBI
7. TITANIC
8. LOVE STORY
10. OLD YELLER

DOWN

2. LIFE IS BEAUTIFUL
3. AFFAIR TO REMEMBER
5. CINEMA PARADISO
9. FIREFLIES

52. HENCHMEN

ACROSS

2. MR. JOSHUA
3. MR. IGOE
6. MINI ME
8. NICK NACK
9. JUAN WILD

DOWN

1. CLARENCE BODDICKER
4. MINIONS
5. LEONARD
7. KLYTUS
10. WEZ

53. COMING OF AGE

ACROSS

2. AMERICAN GRAFFITI
5. PICTURE SHOW
7. RUMBLE FISH
10. ADVENTURELAND

DOWN

1. WITHOUT A CAUSE
3. JUNO
4. KIDS
6. SHOW ME LOVE
8. STAND BY ME
9. WHALE

54. ANIMATED CHARACTERS

ACROSS

6. CRUELLA DE VIL
7. ELSA
9. TOTORO
10. BALOO

DOWN

1. BUZZ LIGHTYEAR
2. HOMER SIMPSON
3. JACK SKELLINGTON
4. PUSS IN BOOTS
5. KANEDA
8. GROMIT

55. KISSES

ACROSS

1. CHARLES / CARRIE
5. ROMEO / JULIET
8. LADY / TRAMP
9. BOB / CHARLOTTE

DOWN

1. CECILIA / ROBBIE
2. JOHN / JOEY
3. HOLLY / PAUL
4. RHETT / SCARLETT
6. ENNIS / JACK
7. JOHNNY / BABY

56. HAMMER HORROR

ACROSS

2. FRANKENSTEIN
3. VAMPIRE CIRCUS
5. ZOMBIES
6. QUATERMASS
9. SISTER HYDE
10. NANNY

DOWN

1. DEVIL RIDES OUT
4. ABOMINABLE SNOWMAN
7. WEREWOLF
8. DRACULA

57. ESSENTIAL DOCUMENTARIES

ACROSS

1. MAN ON WIRE
4. HARVEY MILK
5. SORROW PITY
7. GATES OF HEAVEN
8. NOT A FILM
10. THIN BLUE LINE

DOWN

2. INTERRUPTERS
3. DARK SIDE
6. HARLAN COUNTY
9. ANVIL

58. MOVIES ABOUT MORTALITY

ACROSS

3. ABOUT SCHMIDT
6. SEA INSIDE
8. SEVEN POUNDS
9. WILD
10. LIFE AND DEATH

DOWN

1. STRAIGHT STORY
2. TOKYO
4. MEANING OF LIFE
5. SEVENTH SEAL
7. IKIRU

59. WORST VIDEO GAME ADAPTATIONS

ACROSS

2. COMMANDER
5. SUPER MARIO
8. ANNIHILATION
9. DOUBLE DRAGON

DOWN

1. MAX PAYNE
3. BLOODRAYNE
4. DOOM
5. STREET FIGHTER
6. IN THE DARK
7. TOMB RAIDER

60. TOUGH GUYS

ACROSS

4. REISMAN
7. MATT HUNTER
10. THOMAS DUNSON

DOWN

1. BRITT
2. MACHETE
3. PHILO BEDDOE
5. MAC "TRUCK" TURNER
6. PAUL KERSEY
8. CHIANG TAI
9. CONAN

61. MACGUFFINS

ACROSS

2. CHEVY MALIBU
8. GENESIS DEVICE
10. ONE RING

DOWN

1. MILITARY SECRETS
3. HOLY GRAIL
4. ARK OF THE COVENANT
5. BRIEFCASE
6. MALTESE FALCON
7. BICYCLE
9. BOX

62. CAR CHASES

ACROSS

2. TO LIVE AND DIE
5. TRANSPORTER
7. VANISHING POINT
8. NEVER DIES
9. FAST FIVE
10. IDENTITY

DOWN

1. SECONDS
3. MATRIX RELOADED
4. RONIN
6. DEATH PROOF

63. MUSICALS FOR PEOPLE WHO DON'T LIKE MUSICALS

ACROSS

2. SOUTH PARK
6. WILLY WONKA
7. MOULIN ROUGE
8. TOMMY
9. I LOVE YOU
10. ONCE

DOWN

1. BLUES BROTHERS
3. ROCKY HORROR
4. YELLOW SUBMARINE
5. KATAKURIS

64. MEMORABLE DEATHS

ACROSS

6. KANE
7. JILL MASTERSON
9. BEN

DOWN

1. BUTCH AND SUNDANCE
2. MR. CREOSOTE
3. JACK DAWSON
4. RUSSELL FRANKLIN
5. TONY MONTANA
8. SCANNER
10. ELIAS

65. TIME TRAVEL MOVIES

ACROSS

4. LES VISITEURS
8. LOOPER
9. TIME BANDITS
10. PRIMER

DOWN

1. DARKNESS
2. TWELVE MONKEYS
3. FIVE
5. TIME MACHINE
6. BILL AND TED
7. TERMINATOR

66. SAMURAI MOVIES

ACROSS

2. HARAKIRI
4. ZATOICHI
7. REBELLION
10. SWORD OF DOOM

DOWN

1. LADY SNOWBLOOD
3. TWILIGHT
5. VENGEANCE
6. ASSASSINS
8. YOJIMBO
9. GOYOKIN

67. GANGSTERS

ACROSS

4. MAX BERCOVICZ
6. DOUGHBOY
7. MALIK EL DJEBENA
9. LEO O'BANNON
10. FRANK COSTELLO

DOWN

1. HAROLD SHAND
2. TOMMY DEVITO
3. LITTLE CAESAR
5. RAY VERGO
8. TOM POWERS

68. MILITARY MEN

ACROSS

4. RICHARD
7. WILLIAM JAMES
10. GEORGE PATTON

DOWN

1. MANDRAKE
2. COLONEL DAX
3. HARTMAN
5. NICHOLSON
6. KILGORE
8. VIRGIL HILTS
9. JOHN WINGER

69. WOMANIZERS

ACROSS

3. MARCUS GRAHAM
6. DAVE GARVER
7. FRANK MACKEY
8. ALFIE
10. GEORGE ROUNDY

DOWN

1. DELAUNEY
2. DYNAMITE
4. JACK
5. JACK JERICHO
9. CASANOVA

70. TWIST ENDINGS

ACROSS

3. APRIL FOOL'S DAY
5. CHINATOWN
7. FIGHT CLUB
9. SOYLENT GREEN
10. APES

DOWN

1. USUAL SUSPECTS
2. PSYCHO
4. ORPHANAGE
6. DIABOLIQUES
8. CRYING GAME

71. ACTOR–DIRECTOR PARTNERSHIPS

ACROSS

4. SCORSESE
6. ALLEN / KEATON
8. GUINNESS / LEAN
9. HARA / OZU
10. MIFUNE / KUROSAWA

DOWN

1. FORD / WAYNE
2. BERGMAN
3. LEMMON / WILDER
5. FELLINI
7. KINSKI / HERZOG

72. POP SONGS IN MOVIES

ACROSS

3. IN DREAMS
4. HURDY GURDY
6. BOHEMIAN
8. BE MY BABY
9. OLD TIME

DOWN

1. TAKE ME HOME
2. LUST FOR LIFE
3. I GOT YOU BABE
5. IN YOUR EYES
7. IMAGINE

73. MOVIES ABOUT FASHION
ACROSS
2. SEX AND THE CITY
4. BITTER TEARS
8. POLLY MAGOO
9. FUNNY FACE
10. GIA
DOWN
1. SEPTEMBER
3. DEVIL WEARS PRADA
5. COCO
6. VALENTINO
7. ZOOLANDER

74. MOVIES DEALING WITH EXISTENTIALISM
ACROSS
2. TRUMAN SHOW
3. SOLARIS
5. QUIET EARTH
9. AMERICAN BEAUTY
10. TASTE OF CHERRY
DOWN
1. END OF THE WORLD
4. ORDINARY PEOPLE
6. HUCKABEES
7. BALTHAZAR
8. MALKOVICH

75. GREEDY DEVILS
ACROSS
4. TUCO
5. GORDON GEKKO
6. PLAINVIEW
7. SMILER GROGAN
9. GENJURO / TOBEE
DOWN
1. SCROOGE
2. THE DUKES
3. JORDAN BELFORT
8. DOBBS
10. TRINA

76. COUPLES
ACROSS
2. JESSE/ CELINE
3. TONY / MARIA
4. RHETT / SCARLETT
8. ALEC / LAURA
9. HARRY / SALLY
10. BELLA / EDWARD
DOWN
1. TONY / ALICE
5. TOULA / IAN
6. TOM / GERRI
7. HAROLD / MAUDE

77. CONTROVERSIAL MOVIES
ACROSS
3. EXORCIST
7. BIRTH OF A NATION
9. SALO
10. TRIUMPH
DOWN
1. CANNIBAL
2. LAST TEMPTATION
4. PASSION
5. LIFE OF BRIAN
6. LAST TANGO
8. ANTICHRIST

78. BARS IN MOVIES
ACROSS
3. KOROVA
4. CLUB SUGAR RAY
6. GOLD ROOM
8. COYOTE UGLY
9. THE LAST RESORT
10. GREELYS
DOWN
1. MOS EISLEY
2. POOL HALL
5. BLUE OYSTER
7. RICKS CAFÉ

79. DYSTOPIAN FUTURES
ACROSS
2. DIVERGENT
3. MAD MAX
4. BRAZIL
5. IDIOCRACY
7. METROPOLIS
8. FAHRENHEIT
9. A BOY AND HIS DOG
DOWN
1. AKIRA
2. DEMOLITION MAN
6. BLADE RUNNER

80. VAMPIRES
ACROSS
4. EDWARD CULLEN
7. GRAF ORLOK
8. BELA LUGOSI
9. MIRIAM BLAYLOCK
DOWN
1. CARMILLA
2. CHRISTOPHER LEE
3. JERRY DANDRIDGE
5. ELI
6. DRACULA
10. MARTIN

81. COMEDY TROUPES AND DOUBLE ACTS
ACROSS
4. GUEST
7. LAUREL AND HARDY
9. SIMON PEGG
10. CHEECH / CHONG
DOWN
1. GENE WILDER
2. MONTY PYTHON
3. DEAN MARTIN
5. THREE STOOGES
6. MARX
8. ABBOT / COSTELLO

82. BATTLES
ACROSS
3. THERMOPYLAE
7. ARNHEM
9. DEATH STAR
10. ICHIMONJI
DOWN
1. STIRLING
2. HELM'S DEEP
4. FREEDONIA
5. OMAHA BEACH
6. ROURKE'S DRIFT
8. CUIRASSIERS

83. COPS IN MOVIES
ACROSS
2. JIM MALONE
4. FRANK DREBIN
5. POPEYE DOYLE
8. CLOUSEAU
9. GEORGE ELLERBY
10. JOHN MCCLANE
DOWN
1. ALEX FOLEY
3. MARGE GUNDERSON
6. HANK QUINLAN
7. VIRGIL TIBBS

84. ROAD TRIPS
ACROSS
6. MUPPET MOVIE
8. STRAIGHT
9. EASY RIDER
10. PLANES TRAINS
DOWN
1. THELMA / LOUISE
2. ONE NIGHT
3. DUMB / DUMBER
4. PRISCILLA
5. NEBRASKA
7. MOTORCYCLE

85. FEMME FATALES
ACROSS
2. PHYLLIS
4. LAURA DANNON
5. KITTY MARCH
7. SUZANNE STONE
8. JESSICA RABBIT
9. CATHERINE
10. JUDY BARTON
DOWN
1. LAURA HUNT
3. LYNN BRACKEN
6. ANNA SCHMIDT

86. PSYCHOPATHS
ACROSS
1. ZACHARIAH
3. FRANK BOOTH
7. PATRICK BATEMAN
10. HARRY POWELL
DOWN
2. ASAMI YAMAZAKI
4. BEGBIE
5. JOHN RYDER
6. ANNIE WILKES
8. KAKIHARA
9. DON LOGAN

87. COMEDY HORROR MOVIES
ACROSS
5. REANIMATOR
6. PIRANHA
7. CEMETERY MAN
9. BRAINDEAD
10. EVIL DEAD
DOWN
1. SEVERANCE
2. SHAUN OF THE DEAD
3. SCREAM
4. CABIN IN THE WOODS
8. IN LONDON

88. DANCING IN THE MOVIES
ACROSS
3. ZATOICHI
8. AIRPLANE
9. MODERN TIMES
10. DIRTY DANCING
DOWN
1. HOLY GRAIL
2. FISHER KING
4. GOLDMEMBER
5. YOUNG
6. PULP FICTION
7. BANDE A PART

89. RED MENACE MOVIES
ACROSS
3. THE BLOB
4. UNKNOWN
5. MILLION MILES
8. BODY SNATCHERS
9. QUATERMASS
10. ANOTHER WORLD
DOWN
1. WAR WORLDS
2. FLYING SAUCERS
6. MARS
7. ISLAND EARTH

90. BEST ADAPTATION OF A TV SERIES
ACROSS
2. OUTLAW SAMURAI
7. BEAVIS BUTTHEAD
10. FUGITIVE
DOWN
1. JACKASS
3. COWBOY
4. STAR TREK
5. NAKED GUN
6. SERENITY
8. IN THE LOOP
9. TRAFFIC

91. FRENCH NEW WAVE FILMS
ACROSS
2. BREATHLESS
4. PIERROT LE FOU
8. MY LIFE TO LIVE
10. MARIENBAD
DOWN
1. THE FIRE WITHIN
3. BLOWS
5. MON AMOUR
6. UMBRELLAS
7. JULES AND JIM
9. LE BOUCHER

92. SLASHER MOVIES
ACROSS
2. STRANGER CALLS
5. SLEEPAWAY CAMP
7. BURNING
10. TOURIST TRAP
DOWN
1. HALLOWEEN
3. TEXAS CHAIN SAW
4. BLACK CHRISTMAS
6. MY BLOODY
8. PROWLER
9. FRIDAY

93. WOMEN IN A MAN'S WORLD
ACROSS
6. CLARICE
8. PRINCESS MERIDA
9. PAI
10. HILDY JOHNSON
DOWN
1. MAYA LAMBERT
2. ELLEN RIPLEY
3. MARGE
4. VIENNA
5. NAUSICAA
7. PAT PEMBERTON

94. CAMEOS
ACROSS
3. BRUCE WILLIS
4. ORSON WELLES
6. SINATRA
8. GARY BUSEY
9. HUGH JACKMAN
10. MCLUHAN
DOWN
1. CHUCK NORRIS
2. BILL MURRAY
5. SPRINGSTEEN
7. MARCEAU

95. ASSASSINS
ACROSS
1. GHOST DOG
4. MARTIN BLANK
5. NIKITA
7. HANNA
9. JEF COSTELLO
10. ANTON CHIGURH
DOWN
2. OGAMI ITTO
3. HAWKINS
6. SILENCE
8. AH JONG

96. SPACESHIPS
ACROSS
1. DARK STAR
4. MILLENNIUM FALCON
6. ENTERPRISE
7. NOSTROMO
8. EAGLE
9. HEART OF GOLD
10. KLAATUS SAUCER
DOWN
2. SERENITY
3. VALLEY FORGE
5. DISCOVERY ONE

97. SO BAD THEY'RE GOOD

ACROSS
1. GYMKATA
5. FLASH GORDON
6. MAC AND ME
7. UNIVERSE
9. MEGAFORCE
10. BATTLEFIELD

DOWN
2. THE ROOM
3. DELTA FORCE
4. SHOWGIRLS
8. TROLL

98. SUPERHERO MOVIES

ACROSS
4. BLADE
6. SPIDER-MAN
8. IRON MAN
10. AVENGERS

DOWN
1. DARK KNIGHT
2. SUPERMAN
3. INCREDIBLES
5. X-MEN
7. BATMAN
9. THE CROW

99. MOST STYLISHLY DRESSED CHARACTERS

ACROSS
1. GINGER MCKENNA
6. SEVERINE
9. LORELEI LEE
10. DICKIE

DOWN
2. ANTOINETTE
3. GEORGE FALCONER
4. PRIEST
5. HOWARD HUGHES
7. SU LIZHEN
8. JULIAN KAYE

100. GREAT COMEDY MOVIES YOU MAY NOT HAVE SEEN

ACROSS
3. BOURGEOISIE
4. KIND HEARTS
5. OFFICE SPACE
6. GREATEST DAD
8. O LUCKY MAN
9. MUST BE CRAZY
10. A NEW LEAF

DOWN
1. JOUR DE FETE
2. WITHNAIL AND I
7. SMALL CHANGE

101. FAUX DOCUMENTARIES

ACROSS
1. GUFFMAN
3. FORGOTTEN SILVER
5. THREADS
9. MAN BITES DOG
10. WAR GAME

DOWN
2. F FOR FAKE
4. THIS IS SPINAL TAP
6. GIFT SHOP
7. LOCH NESS
8. ZELIG

102. THIEVES, PICKPOCKETS, AND BURGLARS

ACROSS
1. BILBO BAGGINS
4. FRANK
6. JACK FOLEY
9. JOHN ROBIE
10. BOB MONTAGNÉ

DOWN
2. SELINA KYLE
3. PROFESSOR MARCUS
5. THE PHANTOM
7. ARTFUL DODGER
8. MICHEL

103. REMAKES BETTER THAN ORIGINALS

ACROSS
3. HEAT
4. A STAR IS BORN
7. TRUE GRIT
9. BODY SNATCHERS

DOWN
1. BEN HUR
2. OCEAN'S ELEVEN
3. HIS GIRL FRIDAY
5. THE FLY
6. KNEW TOO MUCH
8. TRUE LIES

104. FISTFIGHTS

ACROSS
5. FIGHT CLUB
7. MACREEDY
10. SEAN THORNTON

DOWN
1. WONG FEIHUNG
2. BORAT AZAMAT
3. COLT
4. PHILO BEDDOE
6. HAPPY GILMORE
8. RED GRANT
9. NADA

105. EXPLOITATION MOVIES

ACROSS
5. LAST HOUSE
6. GUILLOTINE
8. DEEP THROAT
9. ILSA
10. FOXY BROWN

DOWN
1. FACES OF DEATH
2. SHAFT
3. ONE EYE
4. HANZO THE RAZOR
7. DEATH RACE

106. MADE FOR TV MOVIES

ACROSS
4. FATAL VISION
5. THE DAY AFTER
6. BRIAN'S SONG
8. WHISTLE
9. DUEL
10. WOMAN IN BLACK

DOWN
1. NIGHT STALKER
2. AN EARLY FROST
3. BULLETIN
7. OF THE DARK

107. MOVIES FEATURING PETS

ACROSS
4. FLIPPER
6. RATATOUILLE
9. TARZAN
10. FREE WILLY

DOWN
1. GREMLINS
2. A FISH CALLED WANDA
3. HARRY POTTER
5. THE THIN MAN
7. THE ARTIST
8. BORN FREE

108. STRANGEST MOVIES

ACROSS
5. HOLY MOUNTAIN
9. MEET THE FEEBLES

DOWN
1. PAPRIKA
2. PHANTOM OF LIBERTY
3. LOST HIGHWAY
4. FORBIDDEN ZONE
6. PITFALL
7. THE IDIOTS
8. VISITOR Q
10. TETSUO

WORD SEARCH SOLUTIONS

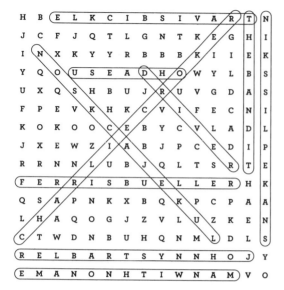

1. ANTIHEROES

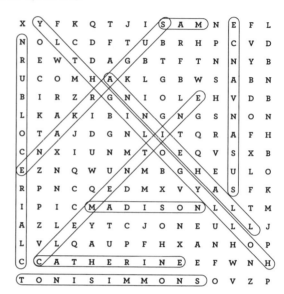

2. MANIC PIXIE DREAM GIRLS

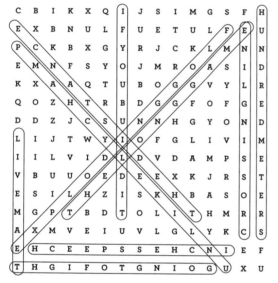

3. SPORTING MOMENTS

4. QUESTS

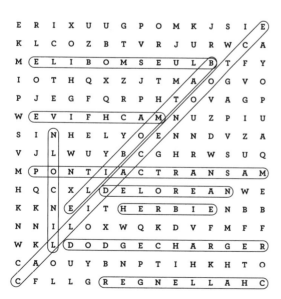

5. CARS

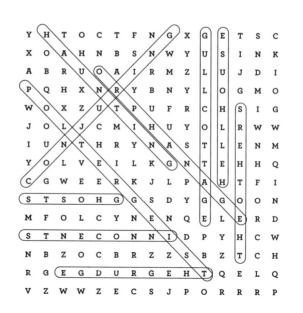

6. HAUNTED HOUSES

```
E T A B E F P E G O K U P O Q
P H C B B Y A A H G E H R U K
N E K A R K E H T Z V J C H P
T M C Z Z I I G O D Z I L L A
A O K H Y X C N N I J P I T A
H N P Y X Q N B G I J R Z T E
S S C O O Z T S L K L P J S R
D T V A O T N D J S O W Q U I
I E E N H I S I M N R N A Z T
O R U Z L P I Q V J K B G R R
B X O M H F X E R R E V O L C
A C E Y L F E L D N U R B X G
R T A F H X Y J B F G N C F
G I A N T T R O L L S D W R L
L S O Z P N N Q I X G Q H C H
```

```
B I B B X F E S V D D C E N T
F R I H W T R O O X R Y A C L N
F T E A Z E W I J C A H I L T
A V D A H V W H R C O C R U H
J G E T K A V U M F B D M E I
Y F A I A S W A L K D S L N S
J E O W P H A C V X C L C E G
H N F T M N S S N P A V F S H
C W L O M Y A I T G L S V S I
X L R Y P C Y C R C B D L G I
C E W F K O G E I B L O C R H
S L R I G N A E M R Z U W B M
P F T F Z S D Z D I E F B M T
Q M D B E Z Y I F K P M Z O E
E L E C T I O N F J W M A T Q
```

```
L G S T X Y G P W B S Q M P B
E E L A J M U E G H U A A A G
W R L E D I R B E H T U T S Z
R L I E M J U K L T L M D T I
N E H Z N E H C I K A E I R T
S W R O N A O E E N C A W W E
H I E Y Z F R R L X K A O K B
Q C F O F O S S J N S L I R G
B E I Y S E Y I E C P M A U M
B K N S Y E R O E L B I G L B
X W N A Z O C C X S R D Y S U
Z X E C T V N C X O Y A A V P
H G J V C W M J X Y K H H E
O H K C D I O W I F O M N C K
S U M I C E D S U M I X A M C
```

```
L I F E I S S W E E T R I E H
G Y K S L T O S G X O J O T O
E R B B Y N E E R C S R E V
M B I M A I X N S V K M R E
Y K W S E W N E E W N A F V
N K P H W T N U Y N A D R S
P Q T W A O R J Y M B D A O
E J K G E P L B Z F R A Q X
M V F L N I B D A M E V U U
M O R F O B F U S G W V Z M
A O V S T O O S N O S P M I S
C I Y G F G R K N N T Q O G
P K K E A Y G W P W E R R O
D G U J C S R B J M I R Y O K
A X L D S R E Y W A S F P N A
```

```
J T R O B I N W I L L I A M S
E O P I K C B M O H D D P X A
N W A O T Q A L E Z N E D A N
N E T U F O L V Y O V T L X G
I Q R P X A B Q F Y S V Y N E
F E O C H B W R V X J O G D L
E R K J U N T P L H Y N M I A
A I S V E M B E L S Y R L N A
N S W H K G R R K A P Q I M N
I U A E W A O B Q T C P D V S
T Y Z R R E K H A R O B E D U
O K E Q P Z S J N U Q B K C R
N O R E H T E Z I L R A H C Y
```

```
T H E I T A L I A N J O B T F
D O G D A Y A F T E R N O O N
E N T V J E R N T N U M M C C
E N A H X U P W Q Q N S L E H
E A V M E L Q M X K L X L A U
H M Y I E K T X C C O H I N S
H E I Z R D I D V X L I H S Z
Z D D C O X N L D I A V R E G
A I J I H U D O L Q R O E L N
M S V R Q T J P H I U H D E U
V N O N H C T A N S N G V G G
R I F I F I M E J U A G E E S
N Q L T F V R X K H P C V N D
Z N A M R B A H F B U X A R D
R O Y Y I D K U J P E Z L I Z
```

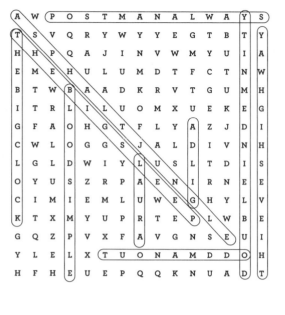

13. FILM NOIR

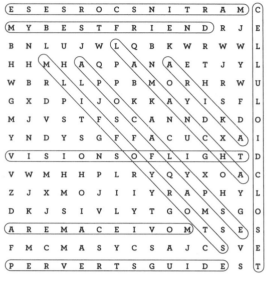

14. DOCUMENTARIES ABOUT CINEMA

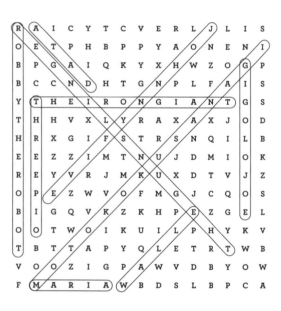

15. ANDROIDS

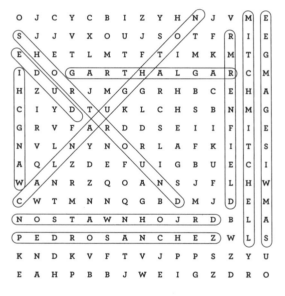

16. SIDEKICKS

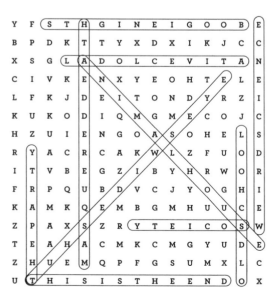

17. PARTIES

18. TOUGH GIRLS

19. SEQUELS

```
T S B J Q O C M T D B W S G M
S W O E O H Y T X A E M R E V
O K U M I X O O U E F L I Z J
J Q R G C A B Y K D R Z A R S
H W N N S M L S X E A C F F R
S J S I Y A E O D T K O A E
L M U F T M H H R Z F E A L I T
S C P E L P O Y C O N A A N C
T Z R B B O H V I N S D A N C H
E F E Q Y E Y U G W T I R H
X Q M Q Z K Z M A E A E I V
Q Y A U X S M B I D I C F H
S E C R U O S S E D N O N A M
E N Y W A E V N M O Q Z I V X
```

20. FICTIONAL PLACES

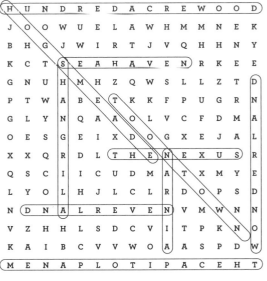

```
H U N D R E D A C R E W O O D
J O O W U E L A W H M M M N E K
B H G J W I R T J V Q H H N Y
K C T S E A H A V E N R K E E
G N U H M H Z Q W S L L Z T D
P T W A B E T K K F P U G R N N
G L Y N Q A A O L V C F D N A
O E S G E I X D O G X E J A L
X X Q R D L T H E N E X U S R
Q S C I I C U D M A T X M Y E
L Y O L H J L C L R D O P S D
N D N A L R E V E N V M W N N
V Z H H L S D C V I T P K N O
K A I B C V V W O A A S P D W
M E N A P L O T I P A C E H T
```

21. MISGUIDED BELIEVERS

```
L L E U Q E I D D E R F F N A
N G Y B S B N Z C B R A A B M
H A R R Y P O W E L L R I A A
X A E E X U J H U M F N M R L
I X X J O S J R N R C S I R Y
D A K Z R L Z S K O H W G Y M
U K Y I L E L B O N F O P Y M
M F T F K L T P L J N R I N
F R U Z N I E S Z T H T R Y F
I P A R W R M S I N K H U Y T
E L S I R E M M U S D R O L R
C A R D I N A L R O A R K V C
G N S O S P A O K A N L F M K
N A M Y L O H E H T N O M I S
E K H N O I E C W P H G W V N
```

22. HEROES

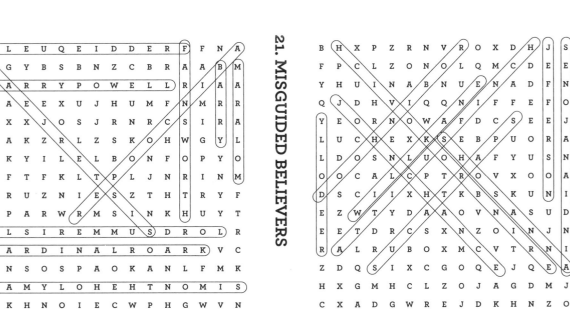

```
B H X P Z R N V R O X D H J S
F P C L Z O N O L Q M C D E E
Y H U I N A B N U E N A D F N
Q J D H V I Q Q N I F F E J O
Y E O R N O W A F D C S E E J
L U C H E X K S E B P U O R A
L D O S N L U O H A F Y U S N
O O C A L C P T R O V X A K A
E Z W T Y D A A O V N A S U D
E E T D R C S X N Z O I N J N
R A L R U B O X M C V T R N I
Z D Q S I X C G O Q E J Q E A
H X G M H C L Z O J A G D M J
C X A D G W R E J D K H N Z O
```

23. BUDDY MOVIES

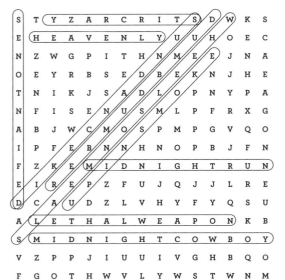

```
S T Y Z A R C R I T S D W K S
E H E A V E N L Y U U H O E C
N Z W G P I T H N M E E J N A
O E Y R B S E D B E K N J H E
T N I K J S A D L O P N Y P A
N F I S E N U S M L P F R X G
A B J W C M O S P M P G V Q O
I P F E B N H N O P B J F N X
F Z K E M I D N I G H T R U N
E I R E P Z F U J Q J J L R E
D C A U D Z L V H Y F G C S U
A L E T H A L W E A P O N K B
S M I D N I G H T C O W B O Y
V Z P P J I U U I V G H B Q O
F G O T H W V L Y W S T W N M
```

24. MEDICAL DOCTORS

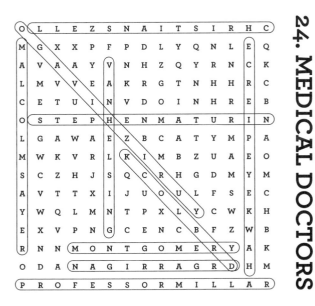

```
O L L E Z S N A I T S I R H C
M G X X P F P D L Y Q N L E Q
A V A A Y V N H Z Q Y R N C K
L M V V E A K R G T N H R C
C E T U I N V D O I N H R E B
O S T E P H E N M A T U R I N
L G A W A E Z B C A T Y M P A
M W K V R L K I M B Z U A E O
S C Z H J S Q C R H G D M Y M
A V T T X I J U O U L F S E C
Y W Q L M N T P X L Y C W K H
E X Y R N N C E N C B F Z W R
R N N M O N T G O M E R Y A K
O D A N A G I R R A G R D H
P R O F E S S O R M I L L A R
```

25. UNDERRATED MASTERPIECES

26. 1980s ACTION MOVIES

27. INSPIRATIONAL MOVIES

28. AMBIGUOUS ENDINGS

29. FEMALE VILLAINS

30. BIOPICS

26. 1980s ACTION MOVIES

```
Z J P O J L Y U I D A E E U C
E U N U F D U R E P S N J B W
N K F E H G K L X U A B T C R
F O G S V Z T V O M C R D N F
R L P B W A Y H L D V T W K V
A U F A F M D I E H A R D U B
M M N O E A L I E N S O M L N
B O R R N O W U C I K G B O K V
E T E T V N F A S E D C W E E
K T O Y A X G W H S G O G P K
M L F A V D Q M P T M P R V B
A L D I J Z E O A G E Z V B K
O U X U O F R R W N P L M L O
W Y O B K T H G P H G I R V K
```

25. UNDERRATED MASTERPIECES

```
L W S Q S N O D X F Y Y H C S
A X X R A Q F E R A N J Z A G
D Y Z I E K D S U E D M R B E
Y N C I F M G J O Y A A F L E
V P M X N A R S U I U M O E Q
E Z M Q S C P O T U B Y S G G
N U Z B T L R H F E H R Y U K
G H T Z A O A B Y S C F F Y H
E R E V E F T H G I N R R W S
A Y A X T H S P A T O A W E A
N M I X E A E M I K I T R Q A
C R T G R Y N O S F E R A T U
B A F R S O J R W J U Y Y R
O M H C N U L D E K A N F F O M
E Y E S W I D E S H U T Z D M
```

28. AMBIGUOUS ENDINGS

```
D K C N S Z P R Q Z O D T K S
E S M V D O S G N Y G M U I M
T H T T T M K D N D Y S H N O
I A L B D R P T H L Q U T G K
N K L P K J P H Y G Q N N I
S E C E I P Y S A E E V I F N
I D Z E S V L W J G Z U R C G
X N X K P H A R B N U Y Y B A
Z H I I K T E W P I H F B R
I T P S S I I L Z H H W A E L
V B U A M A V O T T J H L S
Y N C G O R I X N E Y C N C
U Y J S S T T C S H R C N L
R E D R U M Y M O T A N A C S
Y Z B Y O A U G P I U U G F
```

27. INSPIRATIONAL MOVIES

```
E L S W R V S Q E D E N H M D
F I A T S I N A I P E H T E R
I F O Y C S I O R P N H A K I
L E U S H U F N B M D D R Q B
L I Y V O L I C Q N P M W A G
U S X W O W C X V O T B F X N
F B S J L J W E E U U K O I I
R E N B O E S T U M N X S G C
E A Q D F I S U S A Q T E T O
D U L Y R L M K H J Q D P U M
N T T Q O E C S Y Q M E A D W
O I L H C M W R A W R M R X A
W F D V K A F X D K N N G C X
R U M C H K S P L O C C K S I
U L W S T O I L L E Y L L I B
```

29. FEMALE VILLAINS

```
G S F D N I F H I R O T L Q R
Y R W O O Q P G N X Y A Z J E
M E L R S M N K Y X D B O J R
Z V V E D R U H W Y F E V H R
O N P E U D R P T S A J Y Y P
Q A F N H R S R L F Y H J X P
Y D W L E A C K P Y J W E H I
F S S D E N M R H O V S T A L
I R J W A K A R T F C H B L I
S M U I J I T L I A E Z F M R
C M N S Y K C X R N E G E S R
E Q Y P G D H W G E D G H G P
M A R G A R E T W H I T E P T
Q Q E A B X D Y J G Q W O T A
E G R O E G A N I G E R T N K
```

30. BIOPICS

```
B E Q Y U R Y O D T X B Z O V
J Y L D A K L M J M R E H U Q
E A I E O N A K L G L U N Q L
L F N E P X K O R S M G P A P
P H C R F C E I G N B U V I A
O Y O X N L A L E B X I V Z Q
E U L E A H O N T E D E U Z Z
P Q N M K P D U T E O T W I Y
Y D O R E O P J N M T O F W M
T O P S Y T U R V Y A A D I F
R Z R R B Q O F U F M N S L F
A E S E T S Z S K U D V U Z E
P M A F E H L S S S F N B X F E
K R O W T E N L A I C O S A V
S C H I N D L E R S L I S T Y
```

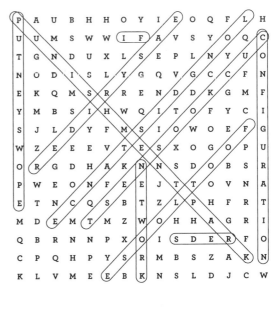

32. ANTI-ESTABLISHMENT MOVIES

31. FAMILY MOVIES

34. SCENE-STEALING PERFORMANCES

33. VILLAINS

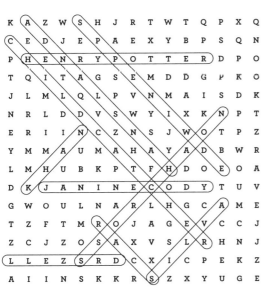

36. PRIVATE INVESTIGATORS

35. WAR MOVIES

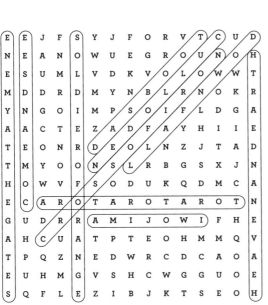

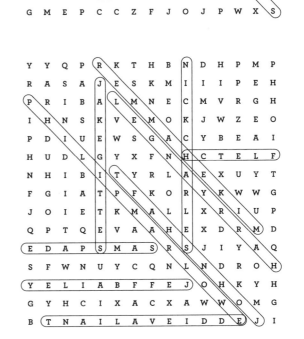

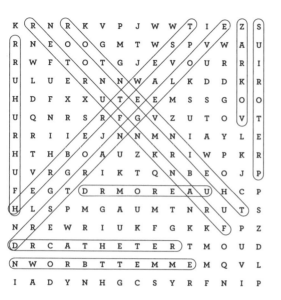

37. MAD SCIENTISTS

```
K R N R K V P J W W T I E Z S
R N E O O G M T W S P V W A U R
U W F T O T G J E V O U R K O I
H L U E R N N W A L K D D S G O
U D F X X U T E E M S S S O V T
R Q N R S R F G V Z U T O O J E
H R I I E J N N M N I A Y L E R
U T H B O A U Z K R I W P K P
F V R G R I K T Q N B E O J S
H E G T D R M O R E A U H C S
N L S P M G A U M T N R U T
R E W R I U K F G K K F P Z
D R C A T H E T E R T M O U D
N W O R B T T E M M E M Q V L
I A D Y N H G C S Y R F N I P
```

38. MARTIAL ARTS MOVIES

```
L M O W C N S V W J P Y M T R
U O H I B S W T U O R P A I E
F O N Q T F Q D T O L F J X G
V P Z E D L O C T L K W X F I
K U J L W S E S I M O T Z I T
E L O W T O E B K C G V O N
Y F E O Z C L V D H D K F T H
O C R T I L A F K E X W V M I
V Y U L I M N V O R E H C
V Z O K P R L Q Y C P B B L U
B P C I X K V C Z B Q B E M O
S X R A R T J A X B F U D Q R
Z E Y A H F J R U L F E A E R
T R E T S A M N E K N U R D C
K U N G F U H U S T L E D F E
```

39. MOVIES ABOUT CELEBRITY

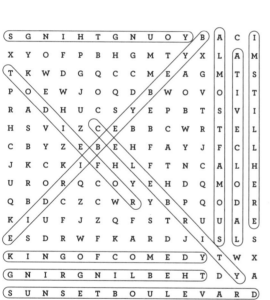

```
S G N I H T G N U O Y B A C I
X Y O F P B H G M T Y X L A M
T K W D G C C M E A G M T S
P O E W J O Q D B W O V O I T
R A D H U C S Y E P B T C L I
H S V I Z C E B B B C W R A L
C B Y Z E B E H F A Y J F L H
J K C K I F H L F T N C A O E
U R O R Q C O Y E H D Q M D R
Q B D C Z C W R Y B P Q O A E
K I U F J Z Q F S T R U U
E S D R W F K A R D J I S L
K I N G O F C O M E D Y T W X
G N I R G N I L B E H T D Y A
S U N S E T B O U L E V A R D
```

40. PRISON MOVIES

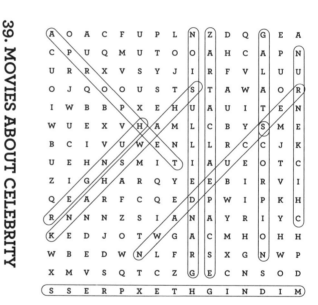

```
A O A C F U P L N Z D Q G E A
C P U Q M U T O O A H C A P N
U R R X V S Y J I R F V L U R
O J Q O O U S T A W A O R E
I W B B P X E H U I T E N E K
W U E X H A M L C B Y S M C
B C I V U W E N L R C J K I
U E H N S M I T I A U E O H
Z I G H A R Q Y E E B I R V
Q E A R F C Q E D P W I P K I
R N N N Z S I A N A R R I H
K E D J O T W G A C M H O H
W B E D N L F R S X G N W P
X M V S Q T C Z G E C N S O D
S S E R P X E T H G I N D I M
```

41. SHOOT-OUTS

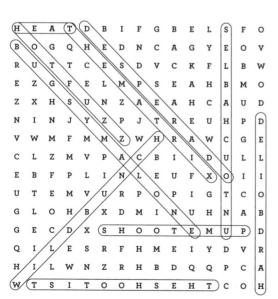

```
H E A T D B I F G B E L S F O
B O G Q H E D N C A G Y E O V
R U T T C E S D V C K F L B W
E Z G F E L M P S E A H B M O
Z X H S U N Z A E A H C A U D
N I N J Y Z P J T R E U H P E
V W M F Z W H R A W C L D I
C L Z M V P A C B I D U L I O
E B E P L I N L E U F X O I I
U T E M V U R P O P I G T C O
G L O H B X D M I N U H N A B
G E C D X S H O O T E M U P R
Q I L E S R F H M E I Y D V R
H I L W N Z R H D D Q Q P C A H
W T S I T O O H S E H T C O H
```

42. CONCERT MOVIES

```
K H S E D A L G N A B T K E E
D L O G F O T R A E H N W M
K H R X N M S R B E K H W A A
A L D E O G X Y L D I P F S S
J X X E W X L A N T A G F E E
W G I M M E S H E L T E R H S
Z P G U F T P S E U D O F N T
Z V R W T T C O I F O A I S
Q B G A G R I R T H M O F K N
W T L D I G S B M R X A A I A
V T O P O P Y E R E T N O M M
Z B E J N T B M W D P W B E
T S U D R A T S Y G G I Z O R
P D O F Q U H M K R J K Z T T
N O R T H E R N L I G H T S S X
```

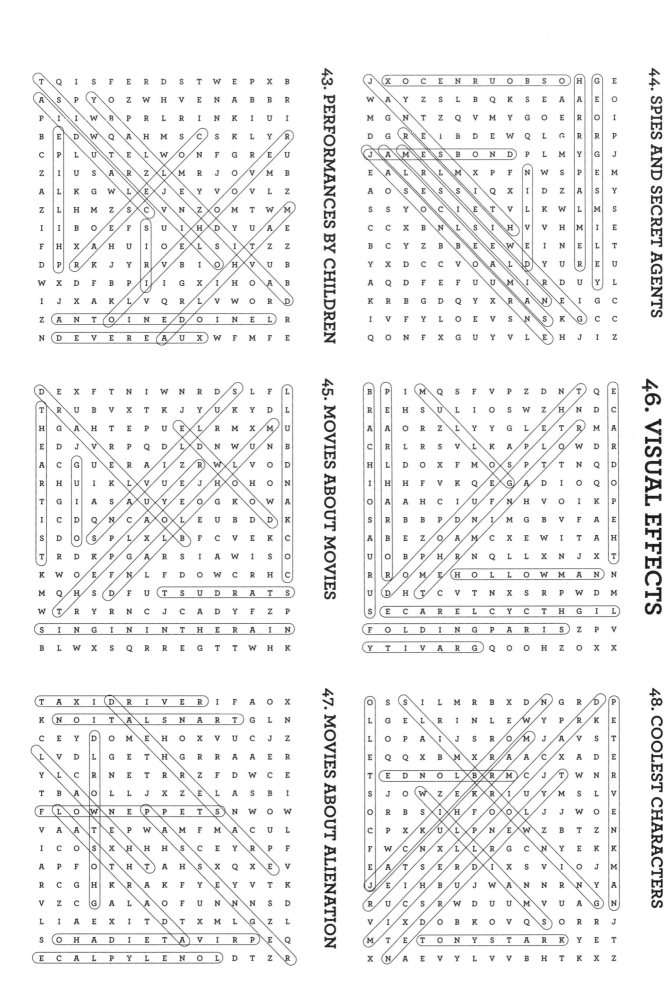

43. PERFORMANCES BY CHILDREN

44. SPIES AND SECRET AGENTS

45. MOVIES ABOUT MOVIES

46. VISUAL EFFECTS

47. MOVIES ABOUT ALIENATION

48. COOLEST CHARACTERS

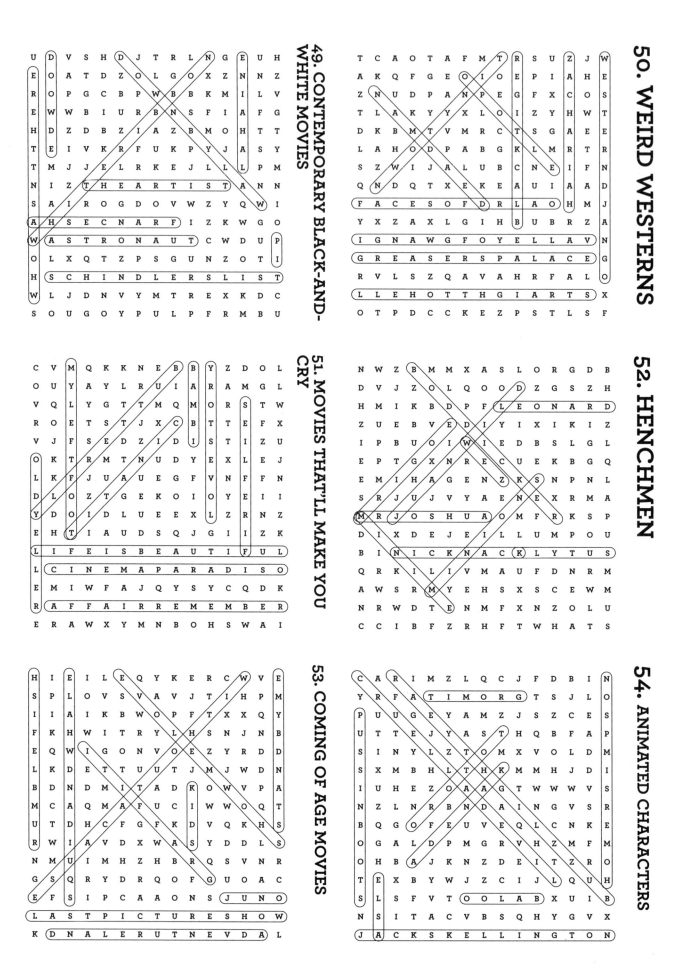

50. WEIRD WESTERNS

49. CONTEMPORARY BLACK-AND-WHITE MOVIES

52. HENCHMEN

51. MOVIES THAT'LL MAKE YOU CRY

54. ANIMATED CHARACTERS

53. COMING OF AGE MOVIES

55. MOVIE KISSES

```
E J N D K N U K A E J O C G V
T O L U A P Y L L O H B B T
T H Z C P R A V N E A A Y Y T
O N C E C I L I A R O B B I
R Y D S A U N E W M B M O V R
A B H Z L P S S R E E H T O A
H A Q T Y C O P N O N E C Z C
C B V A X R N Y J P Q C T S
B Y I R U H I I O U O Y M J T
O Z R Q M S F E D L C Q Z U T
B I I W J Z Y L O I M M G I E
E B S A A P L H I E W D A T H
F S C Q X L A D Y T R A M P R
F K W T A P E F M Y G Q G Y U
```

56. HAMMER HORROR

```
W Y D H T J T N C E B F V Z S
G U N E F C X Q L O L A D O I
G K A N V P V B S O M K D M S
F S P W A I A Y W P F V X B T
M K S B X N L E I R R X R I E
S W U L I C R C I A C J E S R
Z G D M X E E K I Z N S J S H
S W O M W C Z N O D K A W Q Y
Y B T T I P S Z R F E Y W S D
A L F R Q O V A M W N S D O E
Q H C X F C C D C Z S P O N M
U U U H Q U C Y W Z T Q U U O
S H S J L G Z N R L E Z L Z T
R E R A R P N Y D K I R W R G
Q U A T E R M A S S N B F O U
```

57. ESSENTIAL DOCUMENTARIES

```
M I N J O U D C V K R S M Z N
U A O I Q E J P L L A R M Z Y
G D N F X G E I F G T E D T T
A O A O V Q M W C S H T I H N
T U Q N Y Y Q P X E P P I U O
E I Z M E W U E F P D U V N C
S S V J C I G Q N A R G B L A
O E R N L V I R A W R J L R L
F A R I F X N W E W K E T U A
H R V M J S O T Q F S T S E R
E N E Y B R V I T Q I N T L A
A D C A R F F Q S G D I I I H
V W P O W L S I O B E E F N H
E E S H Z F S D B B F S O E N
N T H I S I S N O T A F I L M
```

58. MOVIES ABOUT MORTALITY

```
A N F H C S K A F L U O V N L
Y B K R T E Q K A R I I G N A
R I O S P A F T I E H G X S E
O G A U F I E K B Z B I E K S
T K C T N I D N N W V Z H H T
S W M P N S P J D I E G S V N
H V T V L D Y H P N A K K U E
O F V P I E N O M Z G E E C V
I X W L W L U C R I H S F P E
A D T I H N J D O L D Y T I S
R B Z R D W M I O G T O F L
T A Y S E I R R E B W A R T S
S T O K Y O S T O R Y D V T G
E F I L F O G N I N A E M U I
```

59. WORST VIDEO GAME ADAPTATIONS

```
D Q H N X E Q F G E M R R R X
O U W P O Q S V F P H E B T A
U U X X A I W M O O D S L L B
B I N C R G T N E N U I O F A
L B L V T H Y A A O L N O V J
E R W W W C E M L J E V D U K
D S U P E R M A R I O B R O S
R M R Z P O M A N H H K A J A
A X K X C Y A T X V Z I Y F S
G D U G O Y H Z R P W Q N T W
O X N M B E E Q V E A Q E N E
N I E H D K W P I W E Y R O A
W N Q A G N F P Q L S Q N Y P
S T R E E T F I G H T E R E K
R K T O M B R A I D E R M R A
```

60. TOUGH GUYS

```
N V X W Q U X X C T H P E N O
R A Y Q R J E S U R R P O P V
E G M A T T H U N T E R D K U
N L G S R F V I O H O I D G R
I F L I I Y U H O R Y E L O O
U A K O P E A N A M Z H B A O
T T I R B J R R A A X C O O Q
C G Q O Y K I C N S S Y L L S
U N Y I H N H G T D X O I Y S
R A Y C A E Y D L U O K H L Q
I P N T B P P J N V I P W J H
T H O E B V M F A S E M I Z C
C L X S W B O N O U N I L D
A E Z R K S W B O N U N E R H W I
M P A U L K E R S E Y L S S L
```

62. CAR CHASES

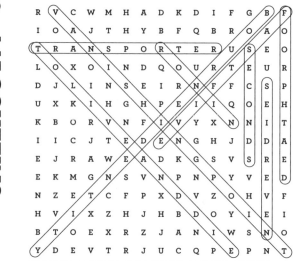

61. MACGUFFINS

64. MEMORABLE DEATHS

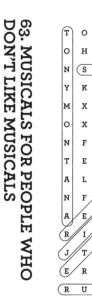

63. MUSICALS FOR PEOPLE WHO DON'T LIKE MUSICALS

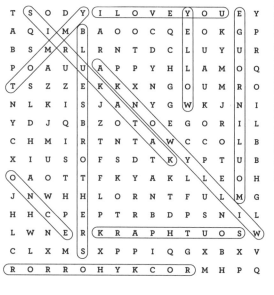

66. SAMURAI MOVIES

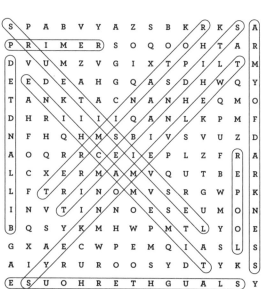

65. TIME TRAVEL MOVIES

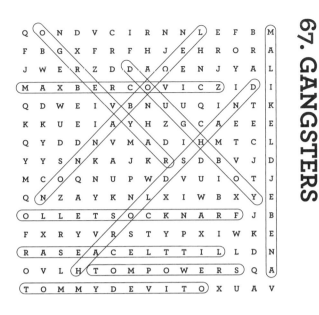

67. GANGSTERS

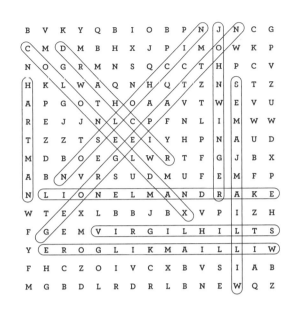

68. MILITARY MEN

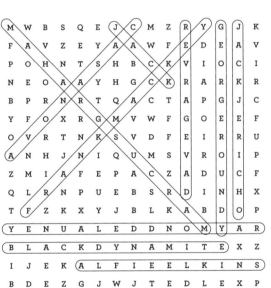

69. WOMANIZERS

70. TWIST ENDINGS

71. ACTOR-DIRECTOR PARTNERSHIPS

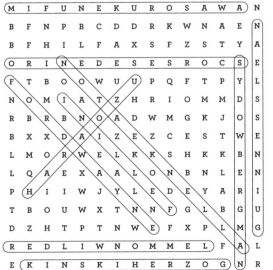

72. POP SONGS IN MOVIES

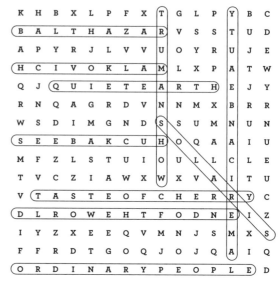

```
K H B X L P F X T G L P Y B C
B A L T H A Z A R V S T U D E
A P Y R J L V V U O Y R U J E
H C I V O K L A M L X P A T W
Q J Q U I E T E A R T H E J J
R N Q A G R D V N M X B R R N
W S D I M G N D S S U M N U N
S E E B A K C U H O Q A A I U
M F Z L S T U I O U L L C L E
T V C Z I A W X W X V A I T U
V T A S T E O F C H E R R Y C
D L R O W E H T F O D N E I Z
I Y Z X E E Q V M N J S M X S
F F R D T G O Q J O J Q A I Q
O R D I N A R Y P E O P L E D
```

```
P B Z B C T N F V F R O Y H T
O F D L P Z S P U E Y T C M A
L F I O J Z B D H I N O N Z C
L A C B H H N N A C A D N J A
Y F I H I Y A P E B E D I A J
M M B G F L L M B M I O T Y Q
A Q I A O A T W F U N I N H I
G A V C O A D A K G K R D E J J
O E Z A N V U Z C A I G L X Z
O P N A B I T T E R T E A R S
F P X G D M Q W K B B H V E Z
I E G T H P Z N C V F N E N E
S S E P T E M B E R I S S U E
P Q D R D X X Z M R B U W A G
A D A R P S R A E W L I V E D
```

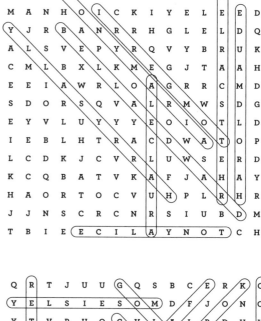

```
J E S S E C E L I N E J T E L
K F C T J N A I A L U O T W U
M A N H O I C K I Y E L E E D
Y J R B A N R R H G L E D U A
A L S V E P Y R Q V Y B R U H
C M L B X L K M E G J T A C D
E E I A W R L O A G R R C M D
S D O R S Q V A L R M W S D O
E Y V L U Y Y Y E O I O T L O
I E B L H T R A C D W A T P E
L C D K J C V R L U W S E R D
K C Q B A T V K A F J A H A H
H A O R T O C V U H P L R R D
J J N S C R C N R S I U B D M
T B I E E C I L A Y N O T C H
```

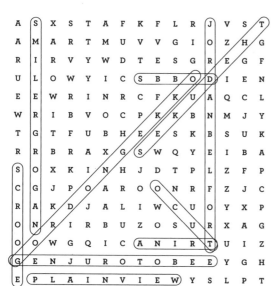

```
A S X S T A F K F L R J V S T
A M A R T M U V V G I O Z H G
R I R V Y W D T E S G R E G F
U L O W Y I C S B B O D I E N
E E W R I N O V C P K K B N Y
W R I B V O C P K K B N J J Y
T G T F U B H E E S B S U K
T R B R A X G S W Q Y E I B A
S O X K I N H J D T P L Z F P
C G J P O A R O O N R F Z J C
R A K D J A L I W C U O Y X P
O N R I R B U Z O S U R X A G
O O W G Q I C A N I R T U I Z
G E N J U R O T O B E E Y G H
E P L A I N V I E W Y S L P T
```

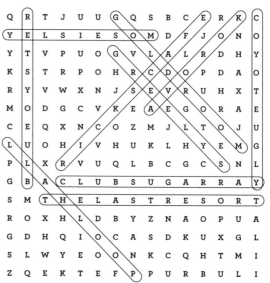

```
Q R T J U U G Q S B C E R K C
Y E L S I E S O M D F J O N O
Y T V P U O G V L A L R D H Y
K S T R P O H R C D O P D A O
R Y V W X N J S E V R U H X T
M O D G C V K E A E G O R A E
C E Q A C N C O Z M J L T O U
L U O H I V H U K L H Y E M G
P L X R V U Q L B C G C S N L
G B A C L U B S U G A R R A Y
S M T H E L A S T R E S O R T
R O X H L D B Y Z N A O P U A
G D H Q I O C A S D K U X G L
S L W Y E O O N K C Q H T M I
Z Q E K T E F P P U R B U L I
```

```
B I N A I R B F O E F I L I V
I I P T S I R H C I T N A M D
C V R S E M I D W E V H S G A
L T P T R I U M P H L M T A M
A K T P H G O D L A P F T O Y
S O E F N O Q F B Q Q B E B O
T L W Y H L F I P I R E M N W
A A B P A P N A G C E P L T B
N S N B W N S S N O S M T L B
G R I M A S O G W A W A V K S
W M C I A C E D B L T K E M A
A Q O R B M T F T S I I Y T C
P F N M E O C G N C Z I O F M
C S X E Q S X N W S X D N N H
A S U T P M O E W Y I S G T P
```

80. VAMPIRES

```
O U M E G Y J K P A R K H G C
L S L H A H Y O X A E R U N H
M I R I A M B L A Y L O C K R
N C O U N T D R A C U L A I I
C E K S N H C O S F F O S C S
M A L R Y M B F I Y G O G A T
H A R L E O V A H E G V B V O
K T R M U H H R N U S Z F G P
S J Y T I C G G L K Z P O A H
V N M K I L D A G N Q O S H E
U R Q Q I N L R Q O W U U Q R
O S U N Z E E A A M I S N X L
S Y Y R B W S C M W X L J Y E
P J H C Q E G D I R D N A D D
K V M U Z B H W U E C E L N K
```

79. DYSTOPIAN FUTURES

```
B Y J R X Y A U F N H W B G N
L N Y E A C D Y D Z E W T A A
A W V R V A U V Y X A M D A M
D E F A H R E N H E I T V B N
E L Q A Z C D H R W K K B O O
R N F B L O R L I G S S P Y I
U P Y O B I A U D M I C V A T
N Y Y M L D P I H L Q W A N I
N V D O X I V S O K A E O D L
E Z J A J E Z P U K C D F H O
R J E Q R D O A I G B U F I M
O U E G M R W R R N B J P S E
Y Z E R T B A G J B B F M D F
C N V E S E K F Z A X G B O F
T V M Q V I H T J P C W S G F
```

82. BATTLES

```
G P I S T D Q C P C C D C Q A
T H E R M O P Y L A E E U O I
P R K E Q L L Y R H E A I T N
M A O C D M D Z A I R R H A O
U M B U H S G R C O Z H S L D
R M E V R F M H S U R S S E E
Q M S M J K I L D A G T S F R
W K T V A M E Z E M D A I I F
A I U D O R C S R H E R E E V
X S S N Z G N P D W E Y R V C
I M J D X U Q H F R H A S C H
S I F X R D M F E R I N O S Z
Q A M J N K D O U M A F G C X
E G D I R B G N I L R I T S L
U U O M A H A B E A C H X P N
```

81. COMEDY TROUPES AND DOUBLE ACTS

```
S S E P T G W O T R R W C G G
R E X E V G H W E O V F J N O
E Q R G V B S E D M E U M H H
H Q L E O J P L P K K Q V N N
T S R R M O I A X N T O T S S
O Q N X E W T W A K O M N O D
R M G T E V R S R R V M Z L N
B S X N A K U G E L F I I R A
X Q E V G M U W Y E E E Z S H
R G B Q V E Z K L V R W B M C
A S J U S L Y Z W S E H C R E
M O N T Y P Y T H O N W T E H
Y D R A H D N A L E R U A L C
S I W E L D N A N I T R A M C
A B B O T T C O S T E L L O N
```

84. ROAD TRIPS

```
M R P R W C O Z D E Q S N J E
B U D R N C I I A U N T R S S
R A P E I U N S S Y S R B M I
B V I P D S Y E V C M A H U O
I O Y B E R C T Z O M I A U L
X A W N I T H I T A V A R H D
H P A D F G M O L U H O I N A
O J E Z I N R O J L M T S U M
Q R X N G C S L V M A S U H A
P C E B Y W B D M I D T T A O
A N O C Z F G B D A E O Y R A
I E Q W D A C E U Y R Y A O H
M T S N I A R T S E N A L P H
D U M B A N D D U M B E R B
```

83. COPS IN MOVIES

```
H T U N Q D Y J J K Z A U J N
H S B B I T L I G R I V A O O
D Y K K V S M S G P A B E H R
P R E C M M V Q S S S K N M S
M C V L A D B P X K J R U O E
T M N L Y B Y W Y E T O L C N
K F O J H O X H R V N Y O C U
W N I B E R D K N A R F C L G
E Y E L O F L E X A I T J A E
S V K P X D L L Y G N A F N E
S O C U T M P H S E A J A N E
S A T A C H Y E X R P B E J M
H A N K Q U I N L A N O F G M
X E T Y P C Z S H Z L Y P Z
D E G E O R G E E L L E R B Y
```

85. FEMME FATALES

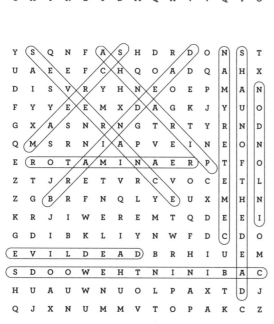

86. PSYCHOPATHS

87. COMEDY HORROR MOVIES

88. DANCING IN THE MOVIES

89. RED MENACE MOVIES

90. BEST ADAPTATIONS OF TV MOVIES

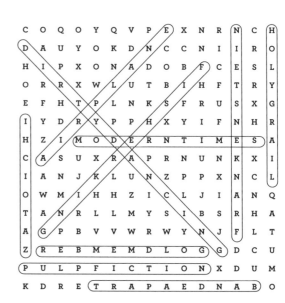

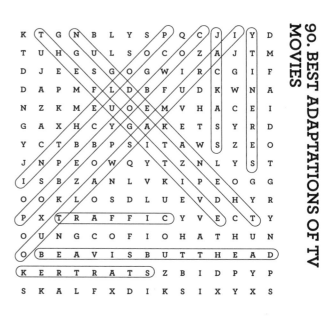

91. FRENCH NEW WAVE FILMS

```
N N J D P I F I C R Y Z B U Y
I V W Z A P S J A R V C R M J
H H S R M B S K M D T L E B F
T U N L E L N W A K Z P A R U
I S Z X M H L E S A I W T E E
W M J H J W C W I E X Y H L U
E M O N A M O U R R V U L L B
R T Z I Z L Y R O E A C E A B
I H T N B B O J A B Q M S S H
F R C L T T V N A B E T S T J
E E X A L X N A W H J L B V B
H X L E M I J D N A S E L U J
T Y F E V I L O T E F I L Y M
V O H J F D O A H S V F O W O
U A D T Q G N C C Y U S R K E
```

92. SLASHER MOVIES

```
A X N L M B B L M T J C T W I
E S L E K Y C I H P V H E A M
N R T I E Q B E U X Z Q E N S
D V A R I W B L V L V B P R L
I R Q Y A U O W O Y O A R I E
L N I J R N R L L O Q F O W E
B I Q N H H G I L X D X W L P
M O I H Z F D E K A G Y I H A
R N X I R V K F R O H P E S W
G R Y I P N P Z F C E G R A A
V X D B K K T F Y H A Q F X Y
P A R T T S I R U O T L S E C
Y D F T K J Q V G G B S L T A
B L A C K C H R I S T M A S M
B C H K K C T H W F N L L S P
```

93. WOMEN IN A MAN'S WORLD

```
H V M H B P J S S E S Y J A G
A I G A P A W B O D E B D R N
F E L W Y S M Z K L I I D V I
G N Z D B A K Z P J R A K F L
V N A E Y H L I W E Q F E J R
O A P U U J R A M H J V U Q A
W M Y R S N O S M B T C E W T
F L H N E I S H H B M K L C S
L J U L B E C J N B E H F F E
W I L V C X N A O S S R K Y C
O E I N F N J E A G O C T B I
I T I D U G P S R T A N Z R R
A R E A M L R P B P K O H W A
P A T P E M B E R T O N P X L
N O S R E D N U G E G R A M
```

94. CAMEOS

```
B C C R P Y A M G F X B N O O
I Y H V T Q Z R R W O R A U K
L F E U U V E P R M U C A E F
M Y C M U K H O V B R E C T H
U E D N V B N H Q Y B W A H A
R Z E G E W Y O Y U B I J R O
R C T A E Z X R O P L A M L Y
A M Y L M B E F A R B L G I I
Y R L P H M D C Z G I I U E H
N E E T S G N I R P S S S C H
S B N U O I L I X U D F H R K
M A R S H A L L M C L U H A N
A R T A N I S K N A R F X M T
H S L H V F S X P L T N S C J
```

95. ASSASSINS

```
R S H T D G C N S R H D W P J
O O O B L H A N N A Z R M E A
B L U S T O P D C X Q X F A L
K D O S U S T H J F B C N G G
B N G C P T Y A P V O T N G Y
P C A Y M D B F S O O W X C C
B P M L K O Z T N J X W F I I
M E I A B G W E C H X K V C L
A T I K I N L H A W K I N S Z
V S T V M L I M K A J A F I X
C B T P O G I T P C U W C L U
R A O Y U K L W R Q H R E E A
B U C R B P V J I A G J F N V
N Z H E I O Z F C H M D K C V
O A U P M G L F O C W X V E E
```

96. SPACESHIPS

```
G R F D L O G F O T R A E H D
A E G R O F Y E L L A V I D I
R X T J J X W Q R R T Z L E S
E S I R P R E T N E S S U T C
T A U W B W M O U K E O R K O
M A G I W A I M S H R R R K V
S I F L R Q L I T S R O E S E
X H L Z E I Z Y R O D I J A R
J Z M L H T S O O O D I J A N
T Z W R E L H K M N Z T C N L
K J C N O N V J Q O B B Y Z Z
A U P M P A N B W O K T L Y A
V Y W A C Y P I T U W A A R Y
Z R E C U A S S U T A A L K M
Q G H W Y R B M D M Z B A F A
```

```
L J K O L V V Y B T J T K R Z Q
T I L Q E O F A B B I S D S W
E L B L M V L T B P L E U I O
C C R W D T A T V P L A Z J L
R F G H N D S L V T N W U H T
O O Q S A B H E A I G Q M H O
F K F Q C K G F U F J Q E O D
A J K B A Y O I I U J U E Y X
G K K J M R R E T N W U K R
E T M K C B D L P I R F A H O
M Q A E L N O D V U H O E Y U
U T I M Q Z N E W X X B L K J
A W E M O O R E H T R Z A L B
Q O N C N S H O W G I R L S Q
A T P Y E U Y Y C Q D Z I F N
```

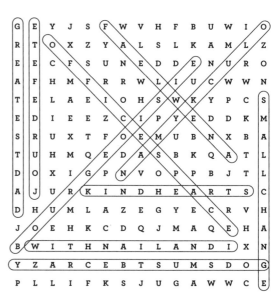

```
S A Q B W X X I N G B I D S Y
C H N M O I R E F I M Q I E H Z
P C R N Z T H N T D N Q W H I R
J X R T E Z S N A E S E T G U E
R H O F I K D E E T F Z N U H S
O V U L H A C L I Q V R S N E
Y S U N C G I M Y R O E W O D N
A S X J W E U W R V P B O R R I
J F A E L G E J I E S N D A R
L P B E E M Z I P G G L N W V E
K P R W N T H Q R H N N H O R V
A O J U L I A N K A Y E I H G E
L Y R Z O M U W J M M U G G S
R E N O C L A F E G R O E G
D I C K I E G R E E N L E A F
```